The Beauty of the **Human Soul**

OSHO

Extemporaneous talks given by Osho in
Rajneeshpuram, Oregon, USA

AUTHENTIC LIVING

The Beauty of the **Human Soul**

PROVOCATIONS INTO CONSCIOUSNESS

OSHO

This book is a selection of talks (Chapters 11-14, 16, 17, 20, 23, 26, 29) from an original series previously published as *From Personality to Individuality* by Osho, given to a live audience. All of Osho's talks have been published in full as books, and are also available as original audio recordings. Audio recordings and the complete text archive can be found via the online OSHO Library at www.osho.com/library

OSHO MEDIA INTERNATIONAL
New York • Zurich • Mumbai
an imprint of
OSHO INTERNATIONAL
www.osho.com/oshointernational

Distributed by Publishers Group Worldwide
www.pgw.com

Library of Congress Catalog-In-Publication Data is available

Printed in India by Manipal Technologies Limited, Karnataka

Print edition: ISBN 978-0-918963-13-0
eBook edition: ISBN 978-0-88050-196-5

Contents

About the Authentic Living Series

The "Authentic Living" Series is a collection of books based on Osho's responses to questions from his international audience at meditation events.

About this process of asking questions, Osho says:

How do you ask a question which can be meaningful – not simply intellectually but existentially? Not just for verbal knowledge, but for authentic living? There are a few things which have to be remembered:

Whatever you ask, never ask a ready-made question, never ask a stereotyped question. Ask something that is immediately concerned with you, something that is meaningful to you, that carries some transforming message for you. Ask that question upon which your life depends.

Don't ask bookish questions, don't ask borrowed questions. And don't carry any question over from the past because that will be your memory, not you. If you ask a borrowed question, you can never come to an authentic answer. Even if an answer is given, it will not be caught by you and you will not be caught by it. A borrowed question is meaningless. Ask something that you want to ask. When I say "you," I mean the you that you are this very moment, that is here and now, that is immediate. When you ask something that is immediate, that is here and now, it becomes existential. It is not concerned with memory but with your being.

Don't ask anything that once answered will not change you in any way. For example, someone can ask whether there is a God: "Does God exist?" Ask such a question only if the answer will change you – so that if there is a God then you will be one type of person, and if there is no God you will be a different person. But if it will not cause any change in you to know whether God is or is not, then the question is meaningless. It is just curiosity, not inquiry.

So remember, ask whatever you are really concerned about. Only then will the answer be meaningful for you.

Preface

When you are true and authentic, living your life on your own, in your own light, with no blueprints given by others to you – by the parents, by the priests, by the politicians... When you are moving every day into the unknown with no idea of what is going to happen, with great creativity, sensitivity, awareness, but with no fixed ideology; when you are exploring newer pastures, new peaks of being, then certainly you are no longer a part of the crowd.

The crowd hates individuals for the simple reason that they are so different. It hates them because they are rebels. It hates them because they cannot be enslaved easily; in fact, it is impossible to enslave them. It hates them for their intelligence, it hates them for their joy, it hates them for their creativity. It wants to destroy them.

That's why people are afraid of life: life has many dangers. The path of life is full of hazards. One never knows what is going to happen the next moment; everything is possible. You cannot live with expectations because life has no obligation to fulfill your desires. You can live with an open heart, but you cannot live with expectations. The more expectations you have, the more frustrated you will be.

You can go astray. In death, nobody can go astray; in life you can go astray. In life you can commit errors, mistakes. In fact, if you really want to live you will have to commit many errors and many mistakes. Remember, never be afraid of committing errors and mistakes; otherwise you will be paralyzed because of the fear. Go on committing mistakes and errors. Remember only one thing: don't commit the same mistake again. Once is enough. Invent new mistakes, discover new errors. Don't go on falling in the same ditch, find new ditches. By committing mistakes, by going astray, you grow. That's the only way to grow.

Life is dangerous; death is very cozy, very comfortable. Lying down in your grave, what danger is there? There is no problem, no anxiety. You can't go bankrupt, your wife cannot leave you, you cannot die anymore. You are so safe in death. Life is not safe, anything is possible. Life is full of accidents.

Osho
Beyond Psychology

CHAPTER 1

God: The Phantom Fuehrer

Osho,
Alan Watts once described the universe by saying, "It is as if God is playing a game." If there is no God, who is playing and what is the game?

Alan Watts was a nice guy but the statement he made was stolen from Hindu mythology. That's what he was doing his whole life, but in the West it appeared as if he was giving original insights.

Basically he was trained as a Christian priest and, like every Christian priest, acquired certain knowledge about all the religions so that he could prove Christianity to be the best, the highest, the truest religion. But Alan Watts, seeing the Hindu religion, could not say that the Christian religion was the highest religion that had happened on earth. That's why I say he was a nice guy. He was an honest man.

He renounced his priesthood and remained almost a beggar his whole life. But he was tremendously impressed by Eastern religions – emphatically with the Hindu idea of God playing a game. In Hinduism it is called *leela*. That is one of the contributions of Hinduism to world thought. All other religions believe that God is creating the world; it is a serious affair. Only Hinduism makes it non-serious. Hinduism says it is just a play, a game of hide-and-seek. It is God who is hiding, it is God who is seeking; it is God in men, it is God in women. To Hinduism, existence is made of the stuff called God, and it is not a creation – because creation has implications which Christianity, Judaism, and Mohammedanism are incapable of answering.

First: why in the first place should God create? What is his need? One creates something because of a certain need. You create a house because you need a shelter. You create because there is a certain desire to be fulfilled. Is God full of desires? Then what is the difference between man and God? Is God in need? If even God is in need then there is no possibility of a state where *you* will be free of need: need is going to follow you like a shadow wherever you go, and you can never be free from it. Unless you are free from need, desire, wanting, you are a slave, and you will remain a slave. A God who has a certain need to create is a slave.

The implications are very significant. Was it compulsory for him to create, or optional? If it was compulsory, then God is not all-powerful. Somebody above him orders him to create, and there is no option, he has to do it. Or if you say it was optional, then the question arises why he chose to create rather than not to create? There must be some reason for choosing to.

What reason can God have to choose creation? Then that reason becomes more important than God himself. If even God has to follow rationality, then why should you have to bother about God? You should think about being reasonable, following *reason*, which even God cannot throw away.

Why did God create at a certain moment, at a certain time? What was he doing before that? For eternity he was unemployed. What was that fellow doing all that time? Sleeping? In a coma? Drunk, or what? And suddenly one day he starts creating. There is no reason that Christian theology, Mohammedan religion, or Judaism can supply as to why, at a certain moment, there was this urge to create. In fact the urge to create is something biological, sexual. Sexual energy is your creative energy.

Women have not been great painters and poets and sculptors for the simple reason that their desire to create is immensely fulfilled by bringing up children. To give birth to a child, alive, radiant – what else can be compared to it? You create a painting; howsoever beautiful, it is a dead thing after all. You can create music, you can create song. But what are they compared to a beautiful child?

Just look into the eyes of a child and all your paintings are nothing. The child smiles and all your songs fall flat on the ground. The child tries to walk: all your science, all your art, are nothing compared to the joy when the child feels "I can walk." And when the child speaks for the first time, have you seen the ecstasy?

The mother watches from the first moments in her womb when the child starts moving. An experienced mother, one who has given birth to one or two children, can tell whether the child is a boy or a girl, because the girl remains quiet and the boy starts kicking very early: he is in a hurry to get out. The girl remains silent. And that difference continues in childhood, in youth, in old age.

A woman has a certain stability, a centeredness, a grounding, which a man has not. He is always on the move. Even on holidays he can't sit silently. He will start fixing a clock which is working perfectly well. He will take it apart. There is nothing wrong with the clock – something is wrong with the man! He can't sit still. He will open the bonnet of his car, start doing something, and create a mess. And he will be more tired after the holiday than he ever is after he comes from the office, because for the whole day he cannot just sit still.

I have heard...

A woman hired a nurse to look after her children – she had almost a dozen. She said to the nurse, "Today I will be coming home a little late. The children will create trouble for you but there is no other way, I have to go. Somebody has died, and they are close relatives. I may be back late, so forgive me and be patient. And somehow make all of them go to sleep."

When the woman returned in the middle of the night, she asked, "Have all the children gone to sleep?" The nurse said, "All of them have gone to sleep; just one was creating so much trouble I had to beat him."

The wife asked, "Which one?" – and the nurse showed her.

She said, "My God! It is my husband!"

"But," the nurse said, "he was the most troublesome. The whole day he was doing this and doing that. I somehow kept hold of the others, but this one was too big in the first place. But then I thought that if he won't understand any other language, I will start slapping him. I threw him forcibly onto the bed, but he would sit back up again and try to escape."

Man *is* restless.

A mother can feel very early whether it is a boy or a girl she is carrying in her womb. She feels so contented in giving birth to a child, in helping the child to grow; and that's why she does not need any other kind of creativity. Her creative urge is fulfilled.

But man is in trouble: he cannot give birth to a child, he cannot have the child in his womb. He has to find a substitute, otherwise he will always feel inferior to the woman. Deep down he feels that he is inferior. Because of that feeling of inferiority man tries to create paintings, statues, dramas, he writes poetry, novels, explores the whole scientific world of creativity.

This is all nothing but an effort of man to say to woman, "I am a creator. You are just an instrument in the hands of biology – the child is not your creation. Any woman can do that, but not every man can become Picasso, or Nijinsky, or Nietzsche, or Dostoevsky. *This* is creativity."

This is how man compensates and covers up his inferiority. He has followed this way for thousands of years and by and by has convinced himself, and the woman too, that he is superior to her. He has not allowed the woman the same freedom to create things because he knows perfectly well that woman can be as creative as he is. A woman can create like Picasso and Dostoevsky and Bernard Shaw and Russell; there is no problem in it. All that she will have to do is drop the idea of being a mother, because it is difficult to be a mother *and* to be a Bertrand Russell. There is a conflict of interest. It is difficult to be a woman, a mother, and at the same time be a Picasso, because Picasso's paintings demand – just like a woman – his whole being. His paintings monopolize him. Now, the woman cannot allow that monopoly.

In fact when the first child is born, a rift starts happening between the husband and wife for the simple reason that the woman is now monopolized by the child; the father is secondary. From now onward he cannot be primary, he cannot have priority. Obviously nature is in support of the child because he has a future, and the father is going to die sooner rather than later.

Nature is always with the new, with the growing. Nature is always with the sunrise, never with the sunset. And this is perfectly logical. What is the point of being with the sunset?

Why does God have to create? Perhaps God is not he but she; then God is a woman, and this whole universe is her womb. But then you are bringing God down to the same level of biology as man, as animals, as anybody else.

Or, God is a man but feels somehow inferior to some woman about whom we know nothing. With which woman is he feeling competitive? There must be a woman in his life, and he feels incompetent, inferior. By creating this whole universe he wants to prove to the woman, "Look, *this* is creation." But then God is no longer God: he is just as human, as animal as we are. "Creation" is indefensible.

And what kind of creation has he made? If he is serious – and creation has to be serious – then this life with so much misery, so much suffering, which finally ends in death and darkness, has no meaning at all. If he wanted to create, there was no need to create such a miserable existence, full of anguish, suffering, agony: an existence which is more a curse than a blessing.

Dostoevsky's greatest work, *The Brothers Karamazov* is perhaps the greatest novel in the whole world, in any language. One of the Karamazovs – there are three brothers – one of them says, "If I meet God, all that I want is to return my ticket and for him to tell me where the exit is. Everywhere I see the entrance, but where is the exit? Who is he, that without asking me, produced me, created me? On what authority? I was not even asked whether I wanted to be created; I was not given any alternative."

This is totalitarian, absolutely dictatorial. God seems to be some magnified Adolf Hitler or Joseph Stalin. You were not asked and yet you have to suffer. You were not asked, and you have been given instincts for which you will suffer here and perhaps hereafter. The same theologians, the same priests, go on telling you to destroy your instinctive life completely. God gives instincts to you: *he* is responsible. If anybody has to suffer in hell, only he alone; nobody else is responsible for anything.

A murderer comes with the instinct to murder. A rapist comes with the instinct to rape. Who is responsible for all this? Yet these religions go on telling you that *you* are responsible. God is the creator and you are responsible? You were not even asked what instincts you want. If you had chosen to be a rapist, a murderer, then of course it would be your responsibility and you would have to suffer the consequences. But you simply come with an inbuilt program, so whoever programs you, only he and nobody else is responsible.

Alan Watts understood very clearly that he could not answer this question, which has been raised in the East again and again. Hinduism has found an answer; at least it *appears* to be an answer. Certainly it is better than the idea of creation, but it has its own problems – which Alan Watts was not aware of because he was not well trained in the Eastern roots of religion. It appealed to him – the idea of *leela*, play, seemed to be far better. Life is nothing serious; it is just a game, a play, a drama.

In a drama you may become a thief; that does not mean that you *have* become a thief – you just play the role. In a drama you may become an incarnation of God, Rama, Krishna; that does not mean that you *have* become an incarnation of God, but on the stage before the audience it is accepted without any question. Questioning it would be absolutely foolish: everybody knows that everybody is playing a role.

Hinduism says that this whole existence is just a drama and God is just playing a game. The word *leela*, playfulness, takes away seriousness and its implications. But it brings new implications: why can't God sit silently? – because the people who teach that God is playing a game also teach, "Sit silently in meditation." Why can't he sit silently in meditation and stop all this nonsense?

But Alan Watts could not ask that question. It may not have occurred to him, but it can occur to me: what is the point of all this nonsense? All Hindu sages are teaching: sit silently, unmoving, without any thought, utterly silent, only then will you taste what religion is. It seems God has never tasted religion – he is continuously playing.

At least in creation there was one thing; in six days he was finished. On the seventh day, Sunday, he rested, and we don't know what happened after that. But the Hindu God has to be constantly playing. Now, there is a time to play and there is a time to study – or so each child is being told – and there is a time to sleep.

But this mad Hindu God has no time to sleep, no time to study, no time for anything else: just playing and playing and playing.

He seems to be obsessed. What a big play! – infinite, eternal. And why should he go on playing? Is he not tired? And the same game...

In my village I had a friend whose father used to go to the "movie-talkie" every day. The same film used to be shown for at least six or seven days; it didn't matter, he had to go every day. I asked him, "It seems a little strange that you go to see the same film for seven days."

He said, "Who bothers to watch the film? I sleep! Once in a while in the seven days I see the complete film. Sometimes I see the beginning part, sometimes the middle, sometimes the end. And if someday I am feeling good, then I connect all the parts and see the whole film."

"But," I said, "You can do it in one day."

He said, "I don't want to do it one day. What will I do the remaining six days?" Because in that small place the movie house was the only entertainment: where else to go? I could understand the difficulty of the old man.

But what is God's difficulty? Why does the same game go on and on? And is he still entertained? He must be an idiot. If this is entertainment, even an idiot will start feeling bored: the same type of people continue to be born, the same love affairs, the same children, again and again – and the wheel goes on moving. The same spokes come up and go down; again they come up and again they go down. It is the same wheel, the same spokes.

I am not worried about the wheel, I am worried about the man who goes on moving it – for what purpose? Of course you cannot ask Hindus about the purpose as you can the Christians – not with the same emphasis, because it is a play. But I still ask: play is okay, if he plays once in a while it is understandable, but this continuous play, this repetitive play...? It seems that we are in the hands of a mad God.

Then these same Hindu sages go on saying that you will suffer the consequences of your acts. Strange: God is playful and yet we are going to suffer for our acts – which are God's play! If he wants me to play the role of a thief, okay, but why should I suffer the consequences? The same people on the other hand say, "It is God's playfulness." Great! Accepted – but what about people? They should be completely freed from any consequences: it is God's play. You play cards: you get defeated, or you become victorious – you win, or you lose – but do you think something happens to the king and the queen and the joker of the cards? Whoever wins or whoever loses does not matter to them at all; they are just playing cards. We are just kings, queens, and jokers – mostly jokers. Why should we suffer?

In Hinduism there cannot be these two things together. That was my constant conflict with Hindu sages, *shankaracharyas*, Hindu pundits: if existence is out of playfulness then it is too much to say that we should be thrown into hellfire. If it is somebody else's play and he is never thrown into hellfire, why should we be? The two concepts put together are absolutely opposed to each other. There is no way to make them complementary. I have tried my best – they cannot be made complementary.

If it is God's play, all the consequences are his: we are just puppets in his hand. Then the law of karma is simply crap. With a playful God, what is the meaning of worship? – you can't be serious; if God himself is playful, you have to be playful.

Ramakrishna was right…

Rani Rasmani was a low caste woman of Kolkata but she was a queen, so she made a beautiful temple of Dakshineshwar on the banks of the Ganges; one of the most beautiful shrines. She had enough money and enough of everything, but no brahmin was ready to worship in her temple because the temple had been made by an untouchable. So the temple had also become untouchable, and the god in the temple had become untouchable – and these brahmins are the people who say that it is all playfulness! Even God becomes untouchable because the temple statue has been purchased by the money of an untouchable.

Rani Rasmani never entered the temple, knowing perfectly well that if she entered then there would be no possibility of finding a brahmin priest. She never touched anything of the temple. She used to come just to the boundary and bow down from there. And it was *her* temple – she had poured millions of rupees into it. But no brahmin was ready to enter.

Ramakrishna was a poor, uneducated brahmin. His name at that time was Gadadhar. "Ramakrishna" was later on, when disciples gathered and started feeling that he had some kind of synthesis of

Ram and Krishna in his being. Hence they started calling him Ramakrishna. But his name then was Gadadhar. He was educated only up to the second grade of Bengali – where was he going to find a job? His father died and he had to take care of his mother and his family. He was in such difficulty that he accepted the offer to become the priest in the temple of Dakshineshwar.

All the brahmins said, "Once you become the priest of Rani Rasmani, you are boycotted; you are no longer a brahmin."

He said, "I don't care, it does not matter – I will be worshipping God. Who has purchased the statue, who has made the temple, is not my concern."

He became the priest, but soon complaints started coming about him. Rani Rasmani was very puzzled. What could she do? If she threw him out it would be difficult to find another brahmin. After waiting for a few years, this one courageous young man had come; but now so many complaints came. They were strange complaints about things which could not be accepted, in no way allowed: when Ramakrishna brought food to God, first he would eat some himself in front of God. He would taste the sweet and then offer it to God. Now that was absolutely unheard of.

In the West it would not make much difference. I see people every day placing their roses on the bonnet of the car as only Westerners can – first they smell it; in the East this is impossible. What they are doing is absolutely out of love and respect, there is no question about it. They smell the rose, they kiss it, and then they put it on the car.

That's what Ramakrishna was doing in India. But in India, once you have smelled a flower you cannot offer it to God. Kissing a flower and offering it to God! But he was doing worse still: he was eating the food. He would eat half of the sweet and half he would offer to God.

Rasmani had to call Ramakrishna and ask him, "Don't you know a simple thing? – that first you have to offer the food to God? You spoil all the food and then you offer it to God. We would not even offer it to a guest, and you are offering it to God?"

Ramakrishna said, "My mother used to do it. She never gave me anything without tasting it first, 'Because,' she said, 'if it is not the right taste I will not give it to you.' If my mother did it for me, I think it is perfectly right for me to first taste whether it is worth offering to

God or not. Sometimes it is not worth offering – sometimes too much sugar, sometimes too little sugar; sometimes the taste is just weird.

"Do you want me to give all these things to God? I cannot do that. I can resign from the post, but I cannot do such an inhuman act as offering things which I have not tasted. Perhaps something may be poisonous – the food comes from the market – who knows? I have to be absolutely certain that nothing wrong goes to God."

Rasmani was a woman of great understanding. She said, "I understand. I am a woman and I can feel your mother's mind and I can feel you. Continue. It is my temple and anyway, no other brahmin is ready to be a priest. Your argument is valid. It is my temple, you are my priest. Your salary is doubled from today."

But then there was another problem. Some days he would not open the doors of the temple but keep it locked. The whole day there was no worship; nobody else could enter – it was locked. Other times the worship would continue the whole day. He would dance – people would come and go, but from morning to evening he would be dancing and singing, dancing and singing. And on some days he would simply lock the temple.

Rasmani asked Ramakrishna, "This is now new trouble. What are you doing? Worship has to be done every day; but you need not do it the *whole* day. Are you trying to do it wholesale, that in a day you have done three or four days so far? There is no need."

He said, "No, that is not the point. Sometimes I get angry at God. Then I say, 'Okay, I will see you tomorrow. Remain locked up!' So I keep him locked up. Within three or four days he comes to his senses; then of course I go and I say, 'How are you? Understood the point? Now behave.'"

Rasmani said, "You punish God?"

He said, "Of course, if he does not behave rightly. For example, I am praying for hours and there is no answer from his side; I will not tolerate such a thing. If I have been praying for hours, the whole day, and he just remains standing there dead, I will teach him a lesson: for three or four days, no food, no worship, and he remains locked up. Then he comes to his senses. When on the fifth day I open the doors, he is immediately smiling and welcoming, and within just a few minutes he is ready to answer me."

Rasmani said, "Now, it is very difficult with you, but you are exactly the right person, because if God is playing with the whole world, you have every right to play with him. Go back to the temple: your salary is doubled again."

Slowly, slowly Ramakrishna's fame started spreading, that he was a strange priest, and nobody could stop him because the temple belonged to Rasmani; it was private property and brahmins could not even enter to see what was happening there. They were dying of curiosity! That man's salary went on increasing; it was now four times what it had been. He had started with twenty rupees per month; now it was eighty rupees per month.

In those days one rupee was seven hundred times more valuable than the rupee is today. Eighty rupees was enough for the whole year: clothes, good food, a good house – everything comfortable. Eighty rupees for the whole year, and he was getting eighty rupees per month! There was great jealousy among brahmins, because even in the best temples they were getting two rupees, five rupees at the most. And Ramakrishna was doing such strange things.

Finally they sent a non-brahmin representative to Rasmani to say, "This man should be thrown out – he is not serious enough."

But Rasmani said, "The whole Hindu philosophy is that existence is playfulness. Why should he be serious? I am also not serious. That's why the more complaints come to me, the more I go on increasing his salary. That has stopped the complaints and now nobody comes to complain because they know complaints mean his salary will be doubled again.

"I had to stop the complaints somehow, and I have; now nobody is complaining. I inquire myself; I go round the temple and I inquire of people, 'Do you have any complaints against Ramakrishna?' They say, 'No, he is the right person' – and they know you can't find a more wrong person than Ramakrishna as a priest!

"He knows nothing of Sanskrit; he talks in Bengali – and who has heard that God knows Bengali? To God he insists: 'You have to reply in Bengali because I don't understand any other language.'"

Now, this was absolutely playful. But Hindus on the one hand go on saying it is God's play, and on the other hand they are very serious people. Each small thing will be counted, either for or against you. On the one hand God is playful, but Hindus don't allow *man* to be playful. With whom is God playing? If he is playing he will need another party also to be playful; or is he playing football alone, taking both sides? Then he must have made millions of goals, and there is no problem because he is alone on the field. But then it seems stupid. No, to me there is no God.

I cut the problem from the very root so there is no question of creation and no question of playfulness.

Alan Watts has simply borrowed the idea of *leela* from Hinduism. He shocked Christians, but to me it is nothing; it is just another kind of theology. To him it was new and very revealing, but to me nothing is very revealing. I know all the theologies. They may give different explanations but basically the same questions are relevant to all explanations. If you ask why God created the world, you can ask why does he need to play? Can't he relax? Just create a hot bath and relax? Just for his play, so many people are suffering. Are Adolf Hitler's gas chambers God's playfulness? – must be, because Hindus say, "Without his will not even a leaf can move." So how can Adolf Hitler put millions of Jews in gas chambers without his support? Perhaps it is his playfulness. But now playfulness becomes more serious than creation.

Millions of Soviets simply disappeared in the past sixty years. You cannot even inquire where they have gone because Stalin never believed in wasting time with people who were suspected of being against Communism. Just a suspicion was enough, and the man disappeared. In the middle of the night the cops came; the man disappeared and was never heard of again.

Stalin never believed in putting people in prison, because if you put people in prison, sooner or later you will have to release them. And how many people can you put in prison? How many prisons will you have to create? Economically it is meaningless because you have to feed those people, you have to clothe those people, you have to take care of their medical needs. For what? And if some day you release them they are now more confirmed enemies than ever. It would have been better not to catch them. Perhaps at that time it was only a suspicion – the man was not really against Communism, but now he certainly would be. So Stalin simply believed in cutting off their heads, in finishing the person immediately, disposing of him. It was a shortcut, economical, and no trouble for the future.

This is God's play? The Hindus themselves have been dying of starvation, famine, floods, earthquakes – all these things happen in

India; I think no other country can compete. Every year something or other; the country goes down and down. This is God's play – an earthquake?

In Bhopal a gas plant exploded. Is this God's play? Three thousand people died immediately, and it was not an easy death. I have just seen a film on it – it was terrible. Those people were just like fish thrown onto hot sand. They could not rest: the gas was making them turn their bodies, churning something inside them. They died the most terrible death you can conceive, and one hundred thousand people are still waiting to die in the hospitals.

Is this God's play? No. If this is play then what can crime be? What can sin be? I reject God completely because God is simply a problem which idiots have invented thinking that he will solve all your problems. God has become the only problem which cannot be solved. Whatsoever you do with him, he remains a question mark – unnecessarily.

I simply want to cut the very root: there is no God. There is no creation. There is no play going on. Existence is enough unto itself; it does not need any outside agency. It has its own energy, it has its own intelligence, it has its own life. Existence needs no hypothetical God. And God doesn't help anything. Remember one fundamental principle of all sane thinking: don't bring in a hypothesis which doesn't help to solve anything. On the contrary, because of the hypothesis a thousand other problems start arising. A hypothesis is brought in to solve problems, not to increase them.

God is the most useless hypothesis ever propounded by man. Because of him so much trouble, so many crusades, so much butchering, so many people slaughtered, so many women raped – in the name of God. Please just flush him down the toilet. Forget about God.

Existence is enough unto itself. That's what I teach. Then we cannot throw the responsibility on anybody's head: there is no God, then the whole responsibility falls on us. That is my hidden desire.

Why am I throwing God down the toilet? Because I want man to understand that he is responsible. Because man has the highest consciousness in the whole of existence, you should accept the greatest responsibility. Stars, trees, animals, birds are far below you; you cannot throw the responsibility on them.

To be conscious means you are mature enough now to accept all responsibility for yourself and for the existence that surrounds you.

Then the explosion in the gas factory in Bhopal is *our* responsibility. It was some stupid people there who were not careful enough; it was carelessness. I would not like these people to be punished in hell – no, there is no hell – they should be punished here and now so such an accident does not happen again. There are thousands of similar factories around the world: if it can happen in one factory it can happen in any factory. This was only a poisonous gas; now there are nuclear plants: just one man's carelessness and the world can be finished.

You have created things which are so dangerous, but you have not created a comparable consciousness which can be careful about these things. If you create nuclear weapons... I am not against them because nuclear weapons can prove creative, immensely creative. Anything that can be destructive can always be creative – it all depends on you. The sword in your hand can kill somebody and can also save somebody. The sword is neutral; it is up to you how you use it.

I am not against atomic, nuclear, and other weapons. Though they are tremendously dangerous in the hands of man as he is today, still I say we cannot go back: we cannot dispose of nuclear weapons. That is impossible, because movement backward is impossible; we can only go forward. Then what has to be done? All over the world great concern is being shown by politicians, the intelligentsia, and other humanitarian people that there should be some stop put to it: no more piling up of weapons. Nobody can stop it, it is impossible, and what they are saying is not the right solution. I don't agree with it.

I say: increase man's awareness to the same height as he has increased his dangerous powers, and there is no problem. Don't put a sword in a child's hand – that's true – but let the child learn with a wooden sword. Let him mature, let him become more aware. I am not in favor of disposing of the sword. It cannot be done in the very nature of things.

In the whole history of man is there any precedent where we have gone back a single step on anything? It is against the law of existence to go backward. So don't just hit your head against a wall, do something else: increase man's consciousness, his awareness.

A prince was sent to a Zen master to learn swordsmanship. It is a strange phenomenon, but in Japan it has become a reality that a master of consciousness, a master who teaches meditation, also teaches swordsmanship. To me it is very significant. That is what is needed.

The prince went to the master and he said, "My father has sent me. He is old and he is not going to live much longer – maybe one or two years at the most. He has sent me to you with the urgent message to prepare me before he dies. He would like to see me with your recommendation saying that I am ready, because if I am not ready then he cannot die peacefully.

"In every other way I am ready: I have learned archery, swordsmanship and all kinds of things that are needed in war; I am a master in every dimension. I went back from the university to my father to say that I had all the medals and trophies and certificates; I was ready. He said, 'No, you are not ready yet, because the basic thing is missing. All that you have brought is good, maybe it will be of use some day, but first go to this master to learn meditation, and to combine your warrior's training with meditation. Unless meditation is supporting the warrior in you, you are just an ordinary warrior, and dangerous: I cannot put the kingdom in your hands. I will have to find somebody else. Go fast, and learn fast.'"

The prince said, "I am ready. Whatsoever you say I will do, but be quick."

The master said, "That is the first requirement, that time is not binding. I cannot say how much time it will take – one year, two years, ten years, fifty years – nothing can be said about it. It all depends on you, on how quickly you learn. I will try my best because I am old and I am also in a hurry. I was not going to accept another disciple, but if the king sends you – he is my old friend, we were under the same master learning meditation – I cannot refuse you. Your training starts now."

The prince asked, "What do I have to do?"

The old master said, "You have not to do anything except just ordinary things: cleaning, cooking, drawing the water from the well, cutting wood. But remember one thing: I can hit you any time from behind, so remain alert. Do anything, but remain alert."

The prince said, "What kind of training is this? – but my father has sent me to you so it must be right." He was continually being hit. The old man was really a greatly skilled man. He would walk without any noise; you could not hear the sound of his feet, and suddenly from nowhere he would jump out and hit you hard!

Within fifteen days the prince's whole body was aching. It was difficult to sleep on one side because there it was hurting, and it was difficult to sleep on the other side because it was hurting, but he was happy too because now he had started hearing his master's footsteps. Awareness had grown.

Before he was not so conscious, so those footsteps were making a certain noise but it was so small, so subtle, that it was not in his grasp. Now his awareness, in such conditions, was bound to grow. He had to be alert, continuously alert: while doing anything he knew that the master would be coming. He would be chopping wood, but no other thought would be there other than about the old man: from where would he appear and how would the prince defend himself?

The old man would try to hit him and the prince would just catch his bamboo staff. Within three months the old man could not hit the prince a single time in the whole day. The prince was very happy; he thought, "This is a great day!" And his body was no longer hurting: in three months of continual beating his body had become like steel. Now he understood that he had gained a certain strength that was never in him before.

Now when his hand held a sword, it was not a human hand but one made of steel. He was happy about his body, the way it had become stronger under his master's hits. He was happy that he had become so alert that even when the old man was far away in another room he was able to detect it. He would shout from his room, "Don't try anything – I am alert!"

The master used to come in from his room. One day the prince listened out for noises from the other room for twenty-four hours; and the master could not beat him a single time. The master called the prince to him. The prince was very happy, the old man was also very happy; he said, "Now the second part starts. Up to now I have been hitting you with bamboo – from tomorrow it will be a real sword."

The prince thought, "A real sword! The bamboo was one thing – I managed somehow and remained patient – but now a real sword! If I miss even once I am finished. And if this old fellow can hit me with the bamboo so hard that he has made my whole body like steel, what will he do with a real sword?"

The old man took out his sword and he said, "This is my sword, so look at it. Watch it! This is now going to be after you continually."

The prince's awareness arose like a pillar of light. He could feel it, because danger was there and now it was not a joke: it was a question of life and death.

So the old man started trying to hit him but could not succeed for three months; not even a single time did he hit him. The prince's awareness was going higher every day: he could save himself immediately. The prince was doing all kinds of work; from the back the master would try to hit. With closed eyes he would be sitting in meditation; the master would go to hit him and he would jump aside and save himself.

The master called him, and said, "I am happy. The second part of training is over." The prince said, "I am tremendously grateful and happy. I never thought that there was such a possibility inside me to be so alert. Not even a small breeze can pass by me without me knowing it. Not even a single thought can move within me without me knowing it. I am happy that there is still something to learn.

"At first I was very hesitant, reluctant, unwilling: I was here just because my father had sent me. But now it is me, and I don't think of my father and the kingdom or anything else. All I think of is to bring my consciousness to its highest peak, because the joys that I have known I was not even aware of, I could not have even dreamed about them. So start the third step."

The master said, "The third step is, while you are sleeping I will hit you with the real sword."

The young man said, "That is perfectly right – I am ready. I was afraid even of the bamboo; now I am not afraid of your real sword, not even in my sleep. Lately I have been watching myself sleeping. Turning, I know I am turning. When sleep comes to my body I know that sleep is descending... Descending... Descending... That it has taken over my whole body. But I am just like a flame inside, not asleep."

The master started trying to hit the prince, but the moment he entered his room the prince would wake up. He tried for three months but he could not strike him even once. Then the master gave the prince his sword and said, "Your father will understand, because he knows this is the sword my master had given to me. Now you are capable of having a sword because you also have a higher quality of consciousness. Now the need for the sword is left far behind."

This is what has to be done; the responsibility is man's. God has been a very dangerous hypothesis: it took all responsibility from you. God was responsible for everything, and you were not responsible for anything at all. He created everything, he will dissolve everything. He sends his son to save you. You are just a puppet: you can be created, you can be saved. And what a humiliating way he created you – with mud!

I think it must have happened here, in the Big Muddy Ranch; otherwise from where could he find so much mud? And why is it called the Big Muddy Ranch? – he must have created man just here. He created you from mud. Couldn't he be a little more respectful? He could have created you from something precious, from gold, from platinum. If he could create from mud he could create from gold, but he is an old Jew, miserly: from mud!

That is the meaning of *humus* – humidity mixed with mud: *humus*. From *humus* come the words *human*, *humanity*. *Adam* also means mud, earth – that is Hebrew. You are just playthings in God's hands. Whether he creates you seriously or non-seriously it doesn't matter: one thing is certain, that he is the sole proprietor of the whole drama. Where is your responsibility? There is no possibility of your responsibility if there is a God.

If humanity has become irresponsible it is because of God, not in spite of him. It is because of him and because of all that the religions have been teaching you: that God created the world, and that God is compassionate and kind. All rubbish. He is not there at all. And what kindness? What compassion? He is a creation of the cunning priesthood because without him they cannot exploit. That is an absolutely necessary hypothesis for exploiting man.

Drop the idea of God and suddenly you will feel a freedom, a spaciousness, an expansion and a great responsibility. There is just nobody above you. You are the highest peak of creation, of existence, of life. There is nobody above you. A sense of great responsibility arises in you. To me that is what makes you religious.

You start feeling responsible for all the animals, the birds. How can you be violent to them? How can you go on eating meat? Impossible. You are the highest in consciousness, and this is what you are doing to poor animals? You cannot afford to do it. With responsibility, your humanity becomes awake. For the first time you can raise your head and you can stand straight. Freedom and responsibility come together, and when the joy of freedom and the joy of responsibility meet, it is so great that I have called that moment, the moment of ecstasy. Then you are so blessed that you can bless the whole existence.

Your very being is a blessing, a continual blessing to everyone far and near, man or animal. You cannot misbehave even with a rock. You will be respectful without any regard to whom it concerns. Your respectfulness will simply be there, unaddressed. You will be grateful just because so much freedom, so much responsibility, so much joy, and so much ecstasy, are born to you. How can you avoid feeling gratitude?

People ask me what will be the place of worship, of devotion in my religion because they think worship and devotion are impossible without a God. I want to say to you that they are impossible *with* a God. The whole idea of God is so ugly that I cannot be devoted to such an idiotic hypothesis. I cannot worship God, I don't see any reason to worship him.

To me, devotion is the refined quality of love. It has nothing to do with to whom. It is not a question of to whom it is addressed: Jehovah, God, Jesus, Buddha. It is not a question of it being addressed. It is a quality in your heart. You feel full of reverence for everything that is. You feel a great love for all that is. It is not a question of whether the person is worthy of it or not, because love is not a business. It is not a question of whether the other is worthy or not, the question is whether your heart is overflowing with love or not. If it is overflowing it will reach to those who are worthy, it will reach to those who are unworthy. It will not discriminate at all.

The cloud is full, and it showers. Do you think it showers on good people's forms only, and avoids bad people's forms? – that it showers only on good Christians, good Hindus, good Jews, and simply does not shower on the form of an atheist? It simply showers because it is so full. Devotion is overflowing love.

Ordinary love is addressed to somebody. That is the raw quality of love, not yet refined. It needs an object, and it is in a very small quantity – that's why lovers are so jealous. There is a reason behind it which they may not know. They may think jealousy is not good, and of course it is not good; but they don't know *why* it is not good. They think jealousy is not good – and that is not true. To have such a small quantity of love energy is not good; out of that, as a by-product, comes jealousy.

The woman is afraid her lover may love some other woman too. And he has such a small quantity of love, how can she afford for him to go to some other woman? If he goes to some other woman then she remains starved, because she knows him and how much love he has. It is not even enough for herself, so how is she able to have a project of Share-a-Home? – no.

The man is so afraid that even if his wife is just laughing with the neighbor, it is enough to make him boil within, because he knows how little laughter she has: if she is wasting it with the neighbor, then what about him? She is happy with the neighbors – laughing, smiling, gossiping – and when the husband comes home, she is lying down, she has a headache. Strangely enough, as the husband enters the compound, immediately the wife starts having a headache. Just a moment before she was laughing with the neighbor, but her husband – the very word gives her a headache. "So he is back again; the same rotten old fellow."

But the real problem is because both have such a small quantity of love and both are aware of it. You know that if love is given to somebody else then your share is lost. It is like share-a-home, but you don't have any home anymore – somebody else is sharing it.

Devotion is love overflowing. Even when there is nobody, it is overflowing – to things, to tables, to chairs, to walls. It is just overflowing, it is not a question of to whom. This you have to understand, it is a fundamental law of my religion: as awareness grows, simultaneously love grows. They cannot remain separate, they move together.

If you can grow in love, you will grow in awareness; if you grow in awareness, you will grow in love.

It is easier to grow in awareness because there are very definite, scientific ways to grow in awareness. With love it is difficult, because it is a very slippery thing, it slips out of your hand. Awareness you can hold tight. But don't be worried: if you are growing in awareness, simultaneously your love will always keep on the same level as your awareness. This is my experience.

I never say a single thing which is not my experience. I have never seen a single inch of difference between awareness and love in me. Just let your awareness go higher, and love immediately moves to the same level. They always keep the same level.

When awareness is at its peak, love overflows; that overflowing love is devotion. And when love and awareness are there, are you just going to sit and not do anything? Perhaps once in a while there will be a man like me who will simply sit and do nothing; but most probably everybody is going to do something. That something will come out of awareness and love. I call that act, worship.

Whatever you do – cook food, clean a floor, chop wood – whatever you do, your awareness and your love is showering. It is worship. No mantra is needed, no prayer is needed, no God is needed. In my religion there is a place for devotion, there is a place for worship. But there is no place for God at all.

I am keeping everything that is essential and discarding everything that is nonessential. The priesthood was interested in the nonessential because that nonessential could be used for exploitation. The essential cannot be used for exploitation; the essential will destroy the priesthood immediately. If your awareness grows and your love becomes devotion, one thing is certain: you will not be a Jew, you will not be a Hindu, you will not be a Mohammedan. Your awareness cannot allow such stupidities. Your love, your devotion, will not allow you to go to a temple, to a mosque, to a *gurudwara*, to a synagogue, to a church, because it is simply idiotic.

There is no point in going anywhere. Wherever you are, your devotion is flowing. Wherever a religious man sits, there is the temple, there is the church, there is the synagogue.

A small, beautiful story...

The founder of Sikhism, Nanak, was one of those beautiful people for whom I have immense love. He was a simple man. He had just one disciple, and that too because he loved to sing: all his teachings were delivered in singing, spontaneous singing – not like a poet composing – and his disciple would play on a simple instrument just to give music to what the master was saying.

Nanak traveled – he is the only Indian teacher who traveled outside of India. Mahavira and Buddha never went outside their state, Bihar, not even all over India. Shankara went all over India but not beyond India's boundaries. Nanak is the only exception; he went to Arabia. He reached Mecca, where the sacred shrine of the Mohammedans is, the black stone, Kaaba.

The stone is rare. Scientifically, it is a very big stone, perhaps fallen from some star or planet; it is not of the earth. Almost every day, twenty-four hours a day, thousands of stones fall. In the night when you see one and you say, "A star is falling," it is not a star; it is just a stone that was floating in the vacuum around the earth and suddenly comes into the gravitational area of the earth. Then the earth pulls it down. Thousands of stones fall every day, sometimes very big stones.

This stone in Kaaba is perhaps the biggest that has fallen. It is not of the earth – that much has been scientifically determined. That is, it is a meteorite. And how are meteorites created? They are created when a star dies or a planet dies and falls into fragments. For millions of years those fragments may go on and on moving in the vacuum till they come to a gravity field; then they are just pulled downward. The pull is so tremendous that the falling stone and the field of the air struggle against each other so the stone burns up. It is the forced entry the stone makes in the air that makes it burn.

You see those "stars" falling; those are not stars, stars are very big – if a star falls onto the earth, the earth is finished! Our sun is a star. It is sixty thousand times bigger than this earth; and it is a very mediocre star – there are stars millions of times bigger than our sun. Our earth is a very small place.

Nanak reached Kaaba. Mohammedans could not believe it because they could see that he was a great teacher, but when night came he slept with his feet toward the Kaaba. That is very disrespectful. The keepers came and said to him, "You being a great teacher, this behavior seems to be very unlikely. You come from India where people know how to be respectful, and yet you are keeping your feet toward our sacred stone? You are hurting our feelings. To us this stone represents God, to us this stone *is* God; so please turn your feet in the opposite direction."

Nanak said, "I knew you would come, hence my feet are toward the Kaaba. Now you want me to turn them in the opposite direction?" They said yes. Nanak said, "You can do that – but remember, *your* God may be just confined to this stone, *my* God is not so confined. Wherever you move my feet he is there."

The story – which must be just a story – is that they moved his feet, but wherever they moved his feet the Kaaba moved. This must be a story because stones, even if they have fallen from the sky, are after all stones. And man hasn't that much sensitivity: you can't expect from a stone that it will move. But the story is beautiful. It simply says that wherever you are, if you are full of awareness and devotion the temple is there, the shrine is there. In fact your overflowing love creates a shrine around you. You move with it wherever you go.

Bodhidharma was asked, "If you are thrown into hell, will you resist?"

He laughed and said, "For what? – because wherever Bodhidharma is, is the lotus paradise. I will be immensely happy because my entry into heaven or into hell is exactly the same. I am Bodhidharma. If I enter into hell, hell will be immediately transformed into a heaven. I would prefer to go to hell, because otherwise who will transform it?"

My religion has devotion as part of awareness. The meaning of devotion is of love, not toward a God, but toward all that is.

My religion has worship; but then worship is not a certain chanting of mantras, prayers, Ave Marias. Worship is your creativeness with a heart full of love and a being overflowing with awareness. Then whatsoever you do is worship. Or if you happen to be a man like me, lazy, then not doing is your worship. I have never felt for a single moment that I am not a worshipper.

My worship is just not to do anything: just to sit silently, doing nothing, and the grass grows by itself – real grass!

CHAPTER 2

Death: The Ultimate Orgasm

Osho,
In other religions death is almost never spoken of and when it is mentioned the tones are grave and fearful. In your religion, death is talked about freely and happily. Is this significant?

It is certainly one of the most significant things. It determines whether a religion is authentic or pseudo. The pseudo-religion knows nothing about death. In fact it knows nothing about life either, hence the fear, the fear of both. It is not possible to be afraid only of death because death is not separate from life, death is part of life. It is not the termination of life, it is an incident *in* life; life continues. Death happens many times, millions of times; it is a mere incident. But the pseudo-religions are afraid of both. The pseudo-religions are afraid of living too.

You should understand that first; only then can you understand why they are afraid of death. They are all in favor of renouncing life. They are all based on an anti-life attitude: something is wrong in life, life is born out of the original sin, it is not right that you are living. Adam and Eve were punished because they wanted to live, they wanted to know, they wanted to understand, explore, inquire –

this is their original sin. You are the inheritors of Adam and Eve. You are born in sin.

Religions cannot support your living. They cannot teach you the art of how to live, and live intensely and totally. They can teach you only how to escape from life, how to avoid knowing the truth. You can relate it to the story of the original sin: the original sin was that Adam and Eve wanted to know what life was all about. They wanted to taste eternal life. Why just go on living a momentary, temporal existence which can be terminated any time by anything – a small accident, and you are finished. Is there something more, or is this all? This was their original sin. So what will be the original virtue? You can infer it very easily. The original virtue will be to renounce life. Adam and Eve were trying to know eternal life; they wanted to become eternal, like gods.

The pseudo-religions say you should renounce life totally, so you go against Adam and Eve – you have to go against them if you want to enter the Garden of Eden again – and renounce inquiry, doubt, skepticism, because these are the ways of knowing. This story is very symbolic. It gives you the whole key to all religions. What Adam and Eve have done, the religions have been trying to undo so that you are again accepted by God, welcomed back into heaven. Religions are afraid of life, are afraid of knowing – life and knowing are not separate. It is because of this story they appeared to be separate, because in a story they have to be separate: a tree of eternal life, a tree of knowledge. But in fact, living *is* knowing. Knowing *is* living.

There is no other way to know, except to live it. And there is no other way to live, unless you are aware of what you are living. Knowing and living are inseparable. The knower becomes enlightened, but he also becomes afire with life.

The pseudo-religions teach you to be afraid of life too – you have forgotten it in your question – they are not only afraid of death. They don't talk about death; it is thought unmannerly to talk about death. It is not good etiquette if you are sitting at a dinner table and you start talking about death. What to say about a dinner table! Even at the grave when people are gathered together to pay their last homage they don't talk about death.

It was one of my pastimes in my childhood to follow every funeral procession. My parents were continually worried: "You don't know the man who has died, you have no relationship, no friendship with him. Why should you bother and waste your time?" – because the Indian funeral takes three, four or five hours: first going out of the city, the procession walking, taking the dead body, and then burning the body on the funeral pyre. And you know Indians, they can't do anything efficiently: the funeral pyre won't catch fire; it will just live half-heartedly and the man will not burn. Everybody is making all kinds of effort because they want to get away from there as quickly as possible; but the dead people are also tricky, they will try their hardest to keep you there as long as possible.

I told my parents, "It is not a question of being related to somebody. I am certainly related with death, that you cannot deny. It does not matter who dies – it is symbolic to me. One day I will be dying. I have to know how people behave with the dead, how the dead behave with the living; otherwise, how am I going to learn?"

They said, "You bring strange arguments."

"But," I said, "you have to convince me that death is not related to me, that I am not going to die. If you can convince me of that, I will stop going; otherwise let me explore." They could not tell me that I would not die, so I said, "Then just keep quiet. I am not telling *you* to go. I enjoy everything that happens there."

The first thing I have observed is that, even there, nobody talks about death. The funeral pyre is burning somebody's father, somebody's brother, somebody's uncle, somebody's friend, somebody's enemy: he was related to many people in many ways. He is dead – and they are all engaged in trivia.

They would be talking about the movies, they would be talking about politics, they would be talking about the market; they would be talking about all kinds of things, except death. They would make small cliques and sit all around the funeral pyre. I would go from one clique to another: nobody was talking about death. And I know for certain that they were talking about other things to keep them occupied so that they didn't see the burning body – because it was their body too.

If they had a little insight into things, they could see that *they* are burning there on the funeral pyre – nobody else. It is only a question of time. Tomorrow somebody else from these people will be there on the funeral pyre; the day after tomorrow somebody else will be – every day people are being brought to the funeral pyre. One day

I am going to be brought to the funeral pyre, and this is the treatment that these people will be giving to me. This is their last farewell: they are talking about prices going up, the rupee devaluating – in front of death. And they are all sitting with their backs toward the funeral pyre.

They *had* to come, so they have come, but they never wanted to come. So they want to be there almost absently present, just to fulfill a social conformity – they were present. That too is to make sure that when they die they will not be taken by the municipal corporation truck. Because they have participated in so many people's death, naturally it becomes obligatory for other people to give them a send-off. They know why they are there – they are there because they want people to be there when they are on the funeral pyre.

But what are these people doing? I asked people whom I knew. Sometimes one of my teachers was there, talking about stupid things – that somebody is flirting with somebody's wife. I said, "Is this the time to talk about somebody's wife and what she is doing? Think about the wife of this man who has died. Nobody is worried about that, nobody is talking about that.

"Think of your wife when you will be dead. With whom will she be flirting? What will she do? Have you made any arrangements for that? Can't you see the stupidity? Death is present and you are trying to avoid it in every possible way." But all the religions have done that. These people are simply representing certain traditions of certain religions.

The religions have first made you afraid of life; they have condemned it: everything that gives a sign of life in you is a sin. Love is sin, because it is a sign of life. It is life trying to reproduce itself; it is life's creativity.

Falling in love – what is it all about? It is life trying to go on and continue. It is a biological effort of nature to go on producing more bodies so more lives, souls, or whatever name you give to them, can get new houses, new vehicles. If biology stops producing bodies, where are you going to get new houses when the old houses topple down? And old houses cannot be continually renovated. A time comes when renovation becomes more of a trouble than to demolish the whole house and make a new house. Biology is trying to provide you with new houses. You fall in love because of a tremendous biological force.

All religions are against biology. Biology means the science of living, life. All religions are trying to prevent reproduction; their monks, their nuns, should not reproduce. In a way it is a very great crime against humanity.

It is one thing if somebody has no biological urge, that his urge has moved into higher realms of creativity. Then it is perfectly okay; he should be allowed to move. A poet may not feel like reproducing children. His poetry is enough, more than enough: he feels fulfilled. His biology has taken a new way, but his poetry will live, will have its own life. He has poured his life into it, just as a painter or a musician can pour his life into his music, into his dance, into his painting, and may not feel any biological urge. But he is not against biology, his energy is simply moving in a higher dimension. Then I say okay to it.

But what are your monks doing in the monasteries? What are your nuns doing in the nunneries? The people in all the religions are not creative at all. They are the most uncreative on the earth for the simple reason that the only creativity they knew was biology. Below biology there is no creative possibility; biology is the bottom. You can move upward but you cannot go downward. Once your biological reproduction is prohibited you are just a fossil, a dead person; you have a posthumous life. You have died already, because the moment your creative energy is prevented you cannot live. Living means creativity.

Even animals are living more than your monks. Trees are living more than your monks – at least they produce flowers, fruit. What do your monks produce? They simply go on repeating the Bible. It has already been produced. Keep it in the library, keep it in the museum, read it in the university, but why every day, go on repeating it like a parrot? Do you think these people are, in any way, living?

There are monasteries where once you enter, you never come out till you are dead. What does that signify? In fact you died the day you entered that monastery. You are cut off from life. You are not allowed to enjoy food because that is part of life. Religions teach that you should not be interested in food, in taste.

In India many religions teach how to destroy the taste of the food before you eat it. There are many traditions in India where the monk will beg and put all kinds of things in one begging bowl, because he is not allowed to beg from just one house. And even if he begs from just one house, then in one begging bowl there are sweet things, there are salty things, there are all kinds of spices, there is rice, there are all kinds of dhals, and they all get mixed up. But that is not enough! First the monk should go to the river and dip the whole begging bowl in the river – they don't take any chances – and then mix everything and enjoy it! Have a nice lunch, dinner, or whatever you call it.

In fact, it happened once that I was sitting on the bank of my village river, and a monk whom I knew – he used to beg from my house too, and he was very friendly with my father, and they used to chitchat – was doing this horrible thing of dipping his begging bowl.

I said to him, "Have you ever thought of one thing? The way you enjoy your food, even a buffalo would refuse it, a donkey would refuse it."

He said, "What?"

I said, "Yes." In India if you want to find donkeys, you will find them near the river because the washer men use donkeys to carry their clothes to the river. Only the washer men use the donkey. Nobody else even touches the donkey because the washerman is untouchable and his donkey is untouchable too. So while they are washing clothes their donkeys are just standing on the bank of the river waiting for the washermen to load them again, and then they will start moving home.

So I said, "There is a donkey; just give me your begging bowl. Don't be worried – if he eats it I will bring you a full bowl again from my house. If he does not eat it, you have to eat it.

He said, "I take the challenge."

I put the begging bowl in front of the donkey and the donkey simply escaped. He escaped for two reasons: one was the food, the other was me. It was not known to the monk that any donkey would have escaped. All the donkeys of my town were afraid of me because whenever I got a chance I would ride on them – just to harass my whole village. I would go to the marketplace sitting on a donkey. The whole village used to say, "This is too much!"

And I would say, "The donkey is a creation of God, and God cannot create anything bad. I don't see what is wrong. He is a poor fellow, and nice."

So all the donkeys knew me perfectly well. It became so that, even from far away, even at night, if a donkey was standing there and I was coming toward him, he would just escape. They started recognizing me. The monk was not aware that there were two reasons for the donkey running away, but he certainly saw that the donkey refused the food.

I said, "This is what your religion has been teaching you, to fall below the donkey. Even a donkey can sense that this is not food, not worth eating."

But everything that gives any hint of life has to be cut from its very roots. The monk should wear only rags that he collects from the street where people have thrown them. In India people are very generous about that, they throw things everywhere. Although the municipal committees have specific places to throw away things, nobody takes any notice of it. Who bothers to go that far?

It was too difficult for me to explain to my grandmother that throwing all the unnecessary things, clothes, dirt, from the window of the second story onto the street was not right. She said, "But I am seventy years old and I have been doing it for seventy years. Don't disturb me. I am not going to live much longer and I can't change my habits. I can't go downstairs and go to the municipal place, no. In seventy years no problem has arisen, so why should it arise for the next two or three years? I will manage."

I told her, "Every day a problem arises, but you don't think it is a problem. Your things sometimes fall on people and they shout."

She said, "That is their problem!"

People go on throwing things, and the monks have to collect clothes this way. They will make their robes, clothes out of small pieces, any kind of cloth. My father used to give new clothes to sannyasins he liked very much, but they would say, "We cannot accept new clothes. You can give us old clothes. First tear them into pieces, and then we will sew them." Whom are these people going to deceive? If their God is all-knowing he must know that these are new clothes made into rags. They put them in the dirt, rub dirt over them, and then they are perfectly good.

Religions have been against life because they know one thing perfectly well: if you live and live alertly, you don't need any religion at all. Religion becomes a need only when your life is cut off. Then you don't have any way except to be religious. If *this* life is cut off, then you will start thinking of *that* life: you have to think about something. You have to live at least in hope, if not in reality. To distract your mind and your being from this life to an imaginary life somewhere far away in heaven, the religions have used the most solid strategy: to condemn this life.

All religions are condemnatory but Jainas are superb. Jaina monks continually give sermons: "What is this body? – blood, flesh, bones, mucus, feces. What does this body consist of? – all kinds of dirty things just covered with a thin skin." This is described in such detail that you will think, "Have these people been butchers or what? Or perhaps they go on tearing apart dead bodies and finding every detail?" Because they are not doctors; it is very rare to find a Jaina doctor. It is only within the last twenty or thirty years that a few Jainas have become doctors; before that a Jaina would not become a doctor. Who is going to do this dirty surgery and go into men's bodies? The Jaina will faint, he will not be able to stand it.

They are not physiologists, they are not doctors, they are not butchers, but they have collected all the "dirty" details. For what? To create in your mind an image of dirtiness, so when you fall in love with a woman you know what you are falling in love with – with all the mucus, all the bones. Just think!

Just take the thin skin away and look at the woman – and you are falling in love with it! This bag – that is exactly the word they use – a *bag*, a *skin bag*. You are a skin bag, she is also a skin bag, and both are getting deceived by the skin. Just go a little deeper and what will you find? It will be nauseous. The Jaina monks create a continual idea of nauseousness about each other's bodies – about your own body too. Jaina scriptures are the most condemnatory of all the religions.

Life is possible only through the body. By their condemning the body so much, life becomes impossible. And once your whole energy is blocked it cannot move into life. But energy has to move: it is its intrinsic nature to move. It will find some other way to move. Religions immediately give you a substitute: love God. *He* is not a bag of mucus and blood and bones!

I used to ask the monks, particularly the Hindu monks, "You call human beings 'bags of every dirty thing'; then what are your incarnations of God? What about Rama? – no mucus?" Then he would be as dry as Oregon. He would have died, for the mucus is absolutely necessary. It keeps your body going. It is a kind of lubricant for your inner mechanism. Yes, once or twice a year you get a cold and you throw the mucus out. That too is necessary because that old mucus is no longer useful. It has to be thrown out so that new mucus is created and takes its place, which is just like changing the oil in your car.

Once in a while, the car has a cold; change the oil, otherwise it will stop. That oil is losing its quality of being a lubricant. It has been used enough. Were there no bones in Krishna and Rama? Then their bags would have just collapsed. Without bones, how could they manage to stand? Was there no blood? Then how can there be semen? – and Rama produced two boys! Great, a miraculous bag: no mucus, no semen, no blood, no bones – and he produced two children! This is a far bigger miracle than what the Holy Ghost did with Mary, because at least Mary was a real bag.

But in the story of Rama, Sita is also not an ordinary bag like you. Both bags were spiritual! Inside they were hollow. I asked these people, "Either you say they were hollow inside – hot air inside, what else? – or they were stuffed. There are only these two possibilities." And I said to them, "I would like to be just an ordinary bag, rather than a stuffed bag or a hollow bag with hot air. I simply refuse; I am perfectly okay as I am." Stupid ideas, but they have persisted for thousands of years just to make those people superhuman.

The first time I spoke in Mumbai – it must have been 1960 – I was invited by a Jaina committee. Mumbai has the richest and the biggest Jaina community of India. Their celebration for Mahavira's birthday is perhaps the best in the whole country. Everywhere the Jainas celebrate it really luxuriously because they are rich people, but Mumbai certainly has the climax.

They invite great monks, nuns, scholars, to address them. The first time I spoke in Mumbai was on Mahavira's birthday. At least twenty to thirty thousand Jainas were present. A Jaina monk who at that time was the top, the glory of Jaina monks – Chitrabhanu is his name – was invited. He is no longer a monk. He is also in America now, married to a Jaina woman; he escaped.

We had never met before and he had no idea what kind of man I am. Of course he was continually living in Mumbai, which is basically not allowed for a Jaina monk: he can stay for only three days in one city. So what have the Mumbai Jaina monks done? They don't go. Once a monk has entered Mumbai he never leaves, because life in Mumbai is comfortable, and who wants to go again into the villages, on mud paths with naked feet? Mumbai has every luxury for them, and every arrangement is made for them.

They have divided Mumbai into many cities; each section, each suburb is a city. From Vileparle they move to Dadar – these are just wards, these are not cities – from Dadar they move to Marine Drive. Mumbai is big; there are so many suburbs and so many different markets. It is one of the biggest cities in the world. So the monks go on moving round and round: three days in Vileparle, three days in Dadar, three days in Santa Cruz, three days in Juhu, and three days in Chowpatty.

This man, Chitrabhanu, had been in Mumbai for fifteen years. He was well respected, the most respected in Mumbai. He was the best orator among Jaina monks in Mumbai, so of course he spoke first. I was an absolutely unknown young man, and not a monk either. Nobody was even certain whether I was a Jaina or not.

Just one man was responsible for bringing me to Mumbai, and that was a coincidence. The man, Chiranjilal Badjatya, of Wardha, was the chief manager for Jamnalal Bajaj, who was one of the super-rich people in India. Chiranjilal Badjatya was the cause of bringing Mahatma Gandhi from Sabarmati near Ahmedabad, in Gujarat, to Wardha in Madhya Pradesh. Chiranjilal Badjatya was a unique man, very simple, very loving, and so simple and so loving that he never thought that two persons could be such opposites.

He brought Gandhi to Wardha because he persuaded Jamnalal Bajaj it would be for the best – Jamnalal Bajaj had branches all over India and his head office was in Wardha in central India. His son was here last year.

But the cause was Chiranjilal Badjatya who, although a poor man, impressed on Jamnalal: "It will be a great service to the country if we can bring Gandhi to Wardha, and it will be a great service to Wardha also, because Wardha will automatically become the capital of India." Certainly until freedom came to India, Wardha *was* the capital of India. Delhi remained the capital for the British Raj, but for all the Indian freedom fighters, Gandhi was the center, and his ashram was in Wardha. All trains and all roads for the revolutionaries were going to Wardha.

Chiranjilal Badjatya influenced Jamnalal Bajaj, and Jamnalal Bajaj used to respect the old man because he was really a lovely man. It was impossible not to respect him, although he was only his manager. He asked Gandhi to come to Wardha and told him,

"Sabarmati is not the right place because you have to depend on other people for each single paisa. I will give you blank checks. Whenever one of your checkbooks is finished, you will immediately get another, and blank. It is absolutely up to you: draw from the bank whatsoever money you want. You need not ask me."

Now Gandhi was also a born businessman and he saw a great opportunity. It was difficult to run Sabarmati even though it was not much of an ashram, only twenty people were living there. The way they were provided with food and clothes, any ordinary middle-class man could have run the whole show. But it was difficult for Gandhi.

Seeing this opportunity of a blank checkbook every month, Gandhi moved to Wardha. This was such a shock to Gujarat that one of Gujarat's very famous poets, Nanalal Bhatt, wrote a poem against Gandhi. He had been writing poems in praise of Gandhi, worshipping him like a god. And in his poem he said, "The man who was a saint in Sabarmati is just a sinner in Wardha." And this was from Nanalal Bhatt, who was a disciple of Gandhi: "The saint of Sabarmati has fallen so low, just for money." The whole of Gujarat was disappointed. But strangely enough Chiranjilal was also the cause of my going to Mumbai.

He met me in a Jaina fair which used to happen every year near Jabalpur. There is a beautiful temple in the hills, a temple made by a very poor woman who used to grind wheat and earn a little food for herself by grinding. The whole day she was grinding other people's wheat, and during her whole life she saved enough money to make this temple on the hill.

The temple is small. And in her memory, on top of the temple – the highest peak of the temple is called a *kalash*; it is made of gold – instead of a *kalash*, to respect the woman, people have put her grinding stone there. It is a primitive type of thing that is used in India. You cannot even call it a grinding machine, because there is nothing to it, just two stones: a round stone with another stone on top of it. The upper stone has a handle, and you move it on the stone underneath. You put whatever you want to grind between the two and just go on moving the stone; the two stones grind it.

Those two stones have been put on the *kalash* of the temple in memory of the woman because it was really a miracle: she was the poorest of the poor, and she managed to make this marble temple. Although the temple is small, and now many temples have been built around it, it remains the center. For thousands of years the fair has continued there in her memory.

I was speaking there and Chiranjilal heard me. When I came out of the crowd toward my car he was standing there. It was winter and he was standing there with a blanket around himself. He threw his blanket on the ground. I could not understand what he meant. He said, "Sit down just for a moment. I would love to sit down with you. I listened to you. What are you doing here? You are needed all over India. What you have said, I have not heard before in my whole life, and I have been in contact with all the great intellectuals and revolutionaries and mahatmas, because of Mahatma Gandhi."

Because he was the general manager for Jamnalal, of course without any formalities he became the general director of Gandhi's ashram. Jawaharlal, and Subash Chandra, and Maularia Azad – all the great leaders of India – were their guests, and he was taking care of them because he was the chief man. Jamnalal was old and too rich to bother about all this; it was Chiranjilal's responsibility to take care. They had made a very big guesthouse where at least five hundred great leaders, thinkers, philosophers, sages could be accommodated, because people were continually going there to meet Mahatma Gandhi. There were continually conferences: political, religious, literary – all kinds of gatherings. Because of Gandhi, it was the center.

So Chiranjilal said, "I know everybody in this country, and nobody speaks like you. What are you doing here? You have to come to Mumbai for this Mahavira Jayanti."

I said, "I don't know anybody there and nobody knows me."

He said, "Don't worry. Everybody knows me and I know everybody; I will arrange it. You have to promise to come."

I could not refuse that man. Tears were coming from his eyes just because nobody knew about me and because I didn't bother that my words should reach people – what a calamity! To *him* it was a calamity. He said, "I will do everything: what I have not done for Mahatma Gandhi I will do for you. But just once let me introduce you in Mumbai. From there things will begin on the right track."

I said, "Okay, I will come; don't cry." A crowd had gathered, and it looked so awkward – an old man crying – so I said, "I will come." I gave him the date of my train, but he was an old man with such thick glasses that I could not feel sure that he was able even to see my face rightly, because the way he was looking up and down, above the glasses... He was trying to look at me from the side, to figure out what kind of man I was. I said, "Don't be worried, I will come. And even if you don't recognize me, I will recognize you – don't worry."

I went to Mumbai and a strange thing happened because of this old man. Somehow he described everything rightly, but he said I wore a white cap. How did that come to his mind? Perhaps because all the people that he knew who came to Wardha all wore the Gandhi cap, the white cap. He had seen thousands of people in white caps; perhaps he had forgotten that there were a few people who didn't wear the cap at all.

He described me saying that I had a small beard, and I wore white clothes, a long robe; but somehow he got mixed up and said that I wore a white cap. I was standing at the door of the train, and people were running here and there. I could see they were looking for me, but I didn't see that old man.

I was waiting for the old man because if he didn't recognize me, I would recognize him. But I didn't see him: he had fallen sick and could not come, so he had simply described me in a letter. All the people were looking at my head. Nobody looked at my face; they looked at my head and just went on. Finally I was the only passenger left and they were the only people there – twenty or twenty-five people.

Finally I said, "What is the point now? I alone am left, and I can see that you are looking for something on my head, but there has never been anything on my head." They showed me the letter. I said "Yes, this man Chiranjilal Badjatya is the man who created the whole trouble for you and for me."

They said, "But he has written, 'a white Gandhi cap,' and we are puzzled because we found so many people with Gandhi caps but they didn't have beards. So we said, 'No, this is not the man.' We found somebody who did, but he was not wearing a long robe. You fitted perfectly but the cap was missing."

I said, "I was suspicious of that old man's glasses. Perhaps he saw the white cap because he has seen only white caps for almost his whole life. He has been taking care of thousands of Indian revolutionaries who were all white-cap people, so the white cap has become fixed in his mind. He must have seen it – I don't suspect his intentions or anything – but where is he?"

They said, "He has fallen sick. He is very sorry that he has not come, but don't be worried: he has talked about you to every man of any importance in Mumbai. But we were expecting that you would be very old because of the way he described you and said, 'Nobody speaks like this man.' We were not thinking of just a young man, a thirty-year old."

At that meeting naturally, among those twenty, thirty thousand people nobody knew about me. Chitrabhanu spoke first and he talked about one of the most significant things about Mahavira, the only thing that can be called a miracle in Mahavira's life. Mahavira is standing naked in meditation and a cobra bites him. Instead of blood, milk comes out of the wounds on his feet. Jainas have always believed that – there is no problem.

When I stood up I said, "This man Chitrabhanu seems to be a little nuts." A few people at that meeting later on became my sannyasins. They told me, "We thought that now there is going to be a riot. Who is this man? He looks like a Mohammedan, with a beard, and the way he is speaking, and the way he is hitting Chitrabhanu who is the confirmed leader of all the Jaina monks and the Jaina community...!"

I really hit him hard, because either I really hit or I don't hit; there is no third way. I said, "This man is mad. He will have to explain how milk can come out of the feet, because for milk a woman needs breasts, and a certain physiological arrangement that is in the breasts transforms her food, her blood, into milk. Either you have to prove that Mahavira had breasts on his feet, or you have to accept that he was a bag full of milk; otherwise take your words back."

There was pin-drop silence. I spoke for thirty minutes, hammering him as much as possible. And I said, "These types of stupid people are your leaders. Then who are you? If you accept these kinds of idiots as leaders, you are certainly far below them. This man is cunning and he is going to deceive you, because whatever he was saying was simply to buttress your ego. That should not be the way of a man of truth. A man of truth simply says the truth; whether it hits you, makes you an enemy, who cares? The man of truth only cares about truth.

"This man was lying; everything that he has said was a lie, although it is written in the scriptures. Those scriptures were also written by such people, so I don't take those scriptures as an authority. I don't take this man as an authority. He should stand up and answer my questions. He has to prove what he is saying; otherwise, tomorrow I am going to bring a cobra, and the cobra will bite this man, and blood should not come out; milk has to come out. He should make arrangements. I give him twenty-four hours."

Certainly that man finally deceived those people and escaped to America with a girl from a rich Jaina family. Now he is a professor in New York and teaches Jaina philosophy. What Jaina philosophy does he know? He still goes on pretending that he is a monk. In America nobody bothers to ask, "How can you be a Jaina monk?" He still continues to say that he is a Jaina monk, still carries the symbols of the Jaina monk.

The day he escaped from Mumbai he had to leave by the back door because thousands of Jainas were standing there just to kill him, because no Jaina monk had ever traveled by air before. And secondly, a Jaina monk escaping with a woman is just not heard of at all. It may have happened some time, but it is not known – and that too, so openly. The police were called because there was every possibility that if they could have caught him, they would have killed him.

Respect can turn into hatred so easily. It just moved to the other extreme because the reasons for which they were giving him respect were no longer there – in fact, what he was doing was just the opposite. This man who was escaping would pretend all over the world that he was still a Jaina monk and nobody would ever think that having a woman with him... They wanted to take away all his Jaina monk symbols: his bowl and other symbols that that particular sect has. Under police escort he was taken from the back door to the airplane, and since then he has not gone back to India. He cannot go: they are still waiting for him whenever he comes.

I had asked – and that was my only meeting with him: "In the twentieth century, you are still asking people to live against life? You yourself are not capable of living against life. All your desires are there as they are bound to be in everybody; it is natural. You have to accept that you are repressing them, if you are a man of truth. Or can you say that you have transcended them? Then I will make an effort to expose you."

He was getting red-hot with anger. I showed them, "Look at

his face. This man with so much anger can be without sex? This man with so much anger, can he be really nonviolent? What is his face saying?" He tried to kill me three times – while remaining a Jaina monk!

I was coming from Pune and an anonymous friend phoned just as I was getting into the car. He said, "Don't bring Osho by car because on the way Chitrabhanu's people are there and it may prove dangerous." So I had to fly, they had to arrange a special flight. But I told one of my friends to go in the same car in which I was going to travel, and see. They *were* there – with pistols, and the road was blocked with big stones. When they saw that I wasn't there they just felt embarrassed. But my friend said that the information was correct. This happened three times. That man was trying to kill me; this was his answer. And those people are nonviolent?

Violence goes on accumulating. Whatever you reject in your life you accumulate within yourself. Those people are more lustful than ordinary common people, more full of anger than ordinary people; because ordinary people become angry when they are angry, but it is momentary, it comes and goes. But those people go on accumulating anger. They are sitting on a volcano; they just need somebody to hit them at their weak point.

He never again spoke with me. He used to tell the organizers that only one person could speak, "Either he speaks or I. We cannot both speak from the same stage."

But I told the organizers, "I would love to speak from the same stage. He can choose. If he feels that speaking first is dangerous, because speaking after him I criticize him, I am ready to speak first; let him criticize *me*. I am ready for any situation. If he wants, he can speak first and then I speak, and then he can answer – for that I am ready. He can speak twice, I will speak just once; but I know my once will be more than his twice. I have seen him."

He was sitting there just like a stone, throbbing with anger, trembling, almost shaking. I told the people, "Look at his hands." He was holding a piece of paper and the paper was shaking. I said, "Look at the paper." On the paper he was taking notes to speak against me but finally decided that it was not going to be worth anything because what proof could he give? Nobody had argued about it before: in twenty-five centuries nobody had asked how it was possible for milk to be coming out of the feet.

No, followers don't ask. They are trained not to ask any embarrassing questions. They are asked to believe, because belief is going to pay, and doubt is sin. But *without* doubt there is no knowing; there is no possibility of you ever becoming aware, conscious.

These people are cutting the very roots from where you can become aware and conscious – it is life, living situations, challenges, opportunities. But if you simply shrink yourself and withdraw yourself from living, you will never attain to consciousness.

It is said of a Hindu monk, who for thirty years remained in the Himalayas…

The monk's problem was the ego. Some sage – I mean some fool – suggested to him, "Just go into the silent valleys of the Himalayas, and your ego will cool down. It will take some time, so don't come back in a hurry unless you are certain." And, of course, if you live in the Himalayas, in a deep, faraway valley where you never come to encounter another human being, how are you going to know that you have an ego? The ego needs another ego; then it immediately comes up. If there is no other ego, there is no challenge for it to come up. It goes fast asleep.

Thirty years is a long time, and the man became convinced that he had no ego. By this time his fame was spreading down onto the plains, and people had started coming to worship him. He was feeling even better: "I am so egoless," and certainly when people are touching your feet you can feel egoless. There is no problem in it because your ego will feel satisfied.

But the problem arose because there was going to be a Kumbha, a fair which is the biggest in the world: at least thirty million people gather for it. Nowhere else in the world does such a gathering happen as in the Kumbha, the fair in Allahabad, that happens every twelve years.

So the Kumbha was going to happen and people invited him: "You are absolutely needed there. Your being will be a blessing for the millions of people who travel from all over the country."

"Of course," he said. Now he knew that he had no ego. He came down from the Himalayas to the plains and when he reached this vast oceanic crowd – you could not see where it begins and where it ends, and nobody knew him in that crowd – somebody stepped on his feet, and thirty years disappeared in a flash! He clutched the man by the throat and said, "I will kill you!" But then immediately he remembered what he was going to do: "What happened to my thirty years? It was a sheer wastage – I am still the same man."

You can sit upon a certain thing for thirty lives; it won't make any difference. The only way to know who you are, of what your mind consists, is to be amid life and living in as many possible ways as you can find, opening all the doors and windows to every side of life so that you can become aware of who you are within, because each window will open into you and a certain hidden part will suddenly be exposed.

One story I have loved very much...

A man was a very, very angry type, as if all his energy was converted into anger. And it was not just verbal; he was really a strong man, and every day he was fighting and beating people for any small thing. One day it was too much; he threw his wife into the well and killed her. It shocked him.

He loved the woman. If he could do such a thing to someone he loves, what could he do to others? Now he was repentant and guilty. A Jaina monk was in the city and the man went to him because he had heard Jaina monks preach nonviolence, no anger, "So perhaps he can teach me a way."

The Jaina monk said, "It is simple: renounce life. Without renunciation you cannot get rid of these things because in life, every day your anger will be rubbed against others' anger, your ego will be rubbed against others' egos, and you will not find even a moment to relax and be silent. So renounce life. Renouncing life means getting out of all those situations which create trouble so that you can rest at ease and be silent. And I will give you a mantra to chant; do the mantra."

You can understand it. The angry type of person is very quick in taking any decision. They can kill – when he killed his wife it was a quick decision, he did not think twice over it. If he had thought twice, he would not have thrown her into the well. This type of person doesn't think twice. He said, "I am ready right now. Give me the initiation. I don't like the five stages, I simply want to be at the final stage from this moment."

The Jaina monk was very happy. He was a naked Jaina monk.

He was happy because now it is getting very difficult to find new initiates – there are only twenty-two left. There were thousands in Mahavira's time. Mahavira alone used to move with ten thousand naked monks; he himself used to move with that company. Now only twenty-two are left, and when one dies he is not replaced, because it is so arduous. First you have to pass the five stages, and that takes almost your whole life. You have to go on renouncing, and this is the ultimate renunciation: you renounce everything, even clothes. Then you don't touch anything.

"This man is a rare man," thought the Jaina monk. He said, "You are a unique person. You want to be initiated in the fifth stage right now?"

He said, "Right now" – and he dropped his clothes, the same way he had dropped his wife; there was no difference. But that Jaina monk could not see the point. It was so simple. If I had been there I would have said that what he was doing was the same, there was no difference in it. But the Jaina monk was very happy. He initiated the man and gave him the name Shantinath – Shantinath means "the lord of silence and peace" – just to remind him that anger had been dropped, violence had been dropped, and that from that day peace had to be his life, silence had to be his vibe.

After twenty years he had become very famous all over the country. A friend from his village came to see him. He was in New Delhi; he was staying in New Delhi because there the great leaders and the great scholars and great people from all over the world are available, so he had made it his place.

New Delhi is widely spread, the same way as Mumbai is: it does not have skyscrapers, so it does not rise vertically, but it spreads horizontally. You will need five to six hours to drive from one corner to another corner. And it has the worst traffic in the world, with all kinds of vehicles: bullock carts, camel carts, elephants, horse and carts, bicycle rickshaws, auto-rickshaws, cars, buses. All the centuries are together on those small streets of the old city, which were not made for buses and cars. It takes hours to cross – you can get stuck anywhere.

You can divide Delhi into many villages very easily, so Shantinath, the Jaina monk, was moving around, and remaining in Delhi. Ambassadors were coming, and it was greatly satisfying to see him, because a Jaina monk is really a thing worth seeing. Yes, I say a *thing* worth seeing: he is an exhibitionist. In the language of psychology, he is an exhibitionist.

There are a few people who, once in a while, are caught by the police because they exhibit their nudity to somebody on a street corner – these Jaina monks are exhibiting themselves to crowds of people. They should be behind bars or in mental institutions. They are perfect exhibitionists, and Delhi is the best place.

This friend from Shantinath's village, hearing that his name had become so famous and seeing his photographs in the newspapers, became very interested. He went to Delhi to see him. He was a poor man; it was difficult for him to get there but he borrowed money and managed it. He wanted to see his friend who had become such a great world-famous figure.

As the man entered the temple, Shantinath saw him and immediately recognized him, but it was below him by then to recognize such an ordinary person, so he pretended he did not recognize him. The man could see in his eyes that he had recognized him, and that he was trying to pretend. He went close by and he asked Shantinath, "Sir, can I ask you your name?"

Shantinath said, "Don't you read newspapers? I have never seen such a fool; everybody knows my name."

He said, "I am an ignorant person from a faraway village" – and he told him the name of the village. "I am just a villager, so forgive me, but please tell me your name."

He said, "My name is Muni Shantinath Deva." *Muni* is the Jaina word for monk.

The man said, "Shantinath?"

He said, "Yes! Are you in some doubt?"

And the man said, "No, I am not in any doubt, I was just thinking..." He said, "But just one more time because I forgot: what did you say your name was?"

Now Shantinath was enraged. He said, "Did you not hear me? You are really an idiot. My name is Shantinath Deva!"

The man said, "I will try to remember it. It is so big, and I am such a fool." He went a few feet away and then came back and said, "Just one more time."

Shantinath Deva took his staff and said, "You will not understand easily; you will understand only the right language. Come here close to me and I will tell you who I am."

The man said, "I have understood – there is no need. I understood from the very beginning, just as you have understood from the very beginning. You were pretending, I was pretending. But Shantinath Deva, nothing has changed; only the name is new, your whole personality is the same. I have simply been asking your name and you have taken your staff in your hand. If there was a well nearby you would have thrown me into it just as you did your wife."

Nothing changes if you withdraw from life. Nothing can change. Life has to be lived to be known. And if you live life without any inhibition, without any fear... There is nothing to fear – it is *your* life; it has been given to you to live. It is a gift of nature to you. It is not a punishment; it is simply a gift from existence. Rejoice in it, and burn your life's candle from both ends together. Live as intensely as possible, and the very taste of life will give you the clue why death is not to be feared. Once you have known your life, its fire, you will know that there is no death.

This life that one comes to know by intense living is eternal. The feeling of its eternity arises simultaneously as you live. The deeper, the more intensely you live, the quicker you feel there is no death. In my religion, death is celebrated because there is no death; it is only an entry into another life.

We celebrate birth – people think we are celebrating death – because there is no death as such. Nothing dies, only forms change. Life transmigrates from one form into another; it should be a moment of rejoicing for all concerned when a person dies, because he is only apparently dying. From our side it feels as if he is dying; from the other side he is being born. Yes, he goes out of one house – and we live in this house so we think he is finished – but he enters another house immediately. Or he may stay a little longer without a house, but there is no death.

Ninety-nine percent of people are instantly born into another form of life. The higher their consciousness, the higher will be the form; the lower their consciousness, the lower will be the form. It depends on you, how capable you have become of being aware and responsible. That much responsibility will be given to you by existence – you deserve it. You have proved yourself worthy of being given a better gift. You used the last gift so beautifully that you deserve a reward.

And it is all automatic. Nobody is there deciding; otherwise he could be bribed, he could be persuaded. You could just cling to his feet and say, "Lord, forgive me. You are a great forgiver, and I am a sinner and nothing, but forgive me."

The Sufi mystic Omar Khayyam says, "Don't stop me from sinning. Don't stop me from drinking. Don't stop me from going to women, because your stopping me shows that you doubt God's compassion. I trust in God's compassion." Now, he is saying not to be worried: when you meet God just hold his feet; harass him till he forgives you. It is a single man's monopoly. Nobody is above him, nobody is going to question him; he is not answerable to anybody. He will forgive you.

No. It is not a one-man dictatorship: existence is autonomous. Here, when you put your hand in the fire and it is burned, it is not that some God decides that you, somewhere in existence, are putting your hand in the fire and that now you have to be burned. Or, if he sees that you are a saint, then you have to be saved, not burned. For thousands of years man has believed that if you are telling the truth, fire will not burn you. In many countries the fire test has been prevalent to know whether a man is speaking the truth or untruth.

But it is so easy. I can ask you, "What is the time on your watch?" and you say, "9:05." Then I tell you, "Just put your hand on a candle and we can see whether you are speaking the truth or an untruth." Do you think you won't be burned because it is 9:05? And if you are burned, then what about other things, other great problems where truth is not so easily decided, things where truth can be in question? Here there seems no problem, but perhaps there may be a problem; perhaps your watch is slow or fast – it is not 9:05, it is only 9.00 – and you may be burned. Then I can just ask something else: who is sitting by your side? Or how many hands do you have? – even simpler, so no problem arises. Or just, how much is two plus two? – and put your hand in the fire.

All these people were so against life that they have forced ugly, inhuman, unscientific things on you in the name of God, telling you that if you are true then God will save you. But you can check on it: there is no God and there is nobody who is going to save you; if you put your hand in the fire, you will be burned. You may be true, you may be untrue; it does not matter at all. Knowing life, slowly your awareness grows.

With awareness growing, you start feeling that you are not the body. You are *in* the body, but you are not the body. With awareness growing still more, you start feeling that you are not the mind either; you are *in* the mind, but not the mind. Slowly you are coming to your very center.

That center is simply awareness, from where you can watch your mind, your emotions, thoughts, body, pain, pleasure – everything. But you are simply a watcher, unidentified with anything else that you are watching.

Now this watcher remains watching even in your sleep. The day you can feel your watcher even in your sleep, that day you know: now death is nothing but a longer sleep. For the body it is eternal sleep, but the watcher simply moves forward, enters another womb, another body. And this movement continues, this transmigration of the soul continues till your watchfulness is absolutely pure.

When the flame is without any smoke, then you disappear into the universal, into the existential. Then you are not going into another house; you don't need any house any more, you have learned the lesson. That was a school: moving from one house to another was moving from one class to another. But one day you graduate – you become part of existence.

That's why we celebrate, because there is no death. Either the man is going into a new house – a good time to celebrate – or the man is going into the eternal existence. That is the best time to celebrate, and the last time to celebrate.

Celebrating death will help you to understand that there is nothing in life to be afraid of. If death is a celebration, then what else can be a cause of fear? If you can celebrate death, you have attained a maturity. It is possible only to those who live life as a rejoicing, a constant celebration. Then death is not the termination, but only a small incident of changing your clothes, your house, your body. But you remain exactly the same forever – nothing changes in your intrinsic being.

From eternity to eternity you are exactly the same.

CHAPTER 3

The New Man: Intellect in Harmony with the Heart

Osho,
How can we believe that the soul exists after death and transmigrates to another form of life, or dissolves into the universe?

I have never asked you to believe in anything.

It is my *experience* that the soul exists after death, that it transmigrates into other forms of life, and finally when there is no more to learn, no question to be answered, no search, no desire – when that ultimate point of absolute contentment, fulfillment, enlightenment arises – then the soul simply dissolves into existence. To transmigrate you need to have a desire to live, a desire to be fulfilled; that's a basic necessity.

It is not *you* who go on being born again and again; it is your desire that goes on and on, never being fulfilled. You are simply following your desire like a shadow. I have not said that you have to believe it. I would rather like you to be skeptical about it, to doubt it, and to inquire into it. I am simply provoking you into an inquiry, not into a faith.

My religion is not a faith; it is an inquiry into the ultimate truth.

So whatsoever I say, the basic reason behind it is always to inspire you – not to believe in a dogma, but to go on in search. If I say the soul exists after death, it is only a hypothesis for you. For me this is an experience. I don't believe in it: I know it, and I will tell you how I know it.

When I say that the soul finally dissolves into the universe, it is not a hope for me. I know it; it has happened. I am no longer separate from existence. As far as I am concerned I do not exist at all as an individual entity. I have not been there for many years. But I am not saying to you to believe it. Again I am provoking you, challenging you to inquire.

Perhaps I am wrong – I am not an infallible pope, I don't have any divine authority to impose a belief on you; I hold no power, and I am not in any way programming you. I am simply trying to create a longing in you that is sleeping, dormant. I am trying to wake it up so that you start inquiring.

The people who say to you to believe and to have faith are the people who themselves do not believe and do not have faith. Because I know what I am saying to you is my experience, I can challenge you to doubt, to be skeptical, to try in every possible way to prove that it is wrong – because I know you cannot prove it wrong. The more you try to inquire, the more you will become convinced of the fact.

I am not saying that you *have* to become convinced, I am saying you *will* become convinced. Even against your whole mind, in spite of all your doubting, skepticism, inquiry, when the truth comes as a revelation, all doubts, all disbeliefs, simply disappear like shadows You have brought light in, the shadows start disappearing; they never existed.

So only the man who knows can have the guts to say to you, "Doubt me, question me."

There is one question that a sannyasin has asked: "Osho, before, you used to talk about the beautiful way of trust, love, the way of the heart. Now your emphasis seems to be more on reason, questioning, skepticism, intelligence. Has your work changed or is it a new phase of your work?"

No, it is not a new phase, it is just the other side of the first. I was teaching about trust because you had come from a world which knows nothing of trust. You had come from a world which has trained you intellectually and tried to deny you the existence of your own heart, to deny that feeling is also a way of knowing. I was talking about trust so that I could open the new door of the heart. Without opening the door of the heart I cannot say to you, "Doubt, be skeptical," because then I am sending you on a dangerous path which leads nowhere. It is a little complex but try to understand.

A man who knows nothing about feeling, nothing about trust, who has never experienced anything like love – his heart has never jumped with joy, danced with joy in someone's presence – can go on doubting, but he will not find the answer because his doubt will be very shallow. He will not trust his own doubt. His inquiry will be just so-so. He will not trust his own inquiry – he knows nothing of trust. Inquiry will need trust because you will be going into the unknown. It will demand tremendous trust and courage because you are moving away from the conventional and the traditional; you are moving away from the crowd. You are going into the open sea, and you don't know whether the other, further shore exists at all.

I could not send you into such an inquiry without preparing you to have trust. It will look contradictory, but what can I do? – this is how life is. Only a man of great trust is capable of great doubt. A man of little trust can only doubt a little. A man of no trust can only pretend that he doubts. He cannot doubt. The depth comes through trust – and it is a risk.

Before I send you into the uncharted sea, I have to prepare you for this immense journey on which you will have to go alone – but I can lead you up to the boat. I was trying to teach you about the beauty of trust, the ecstasy of the way of the heart, so when you go into the open ocean of reality you will have courage enough to keep on going. Whatever happens, you will have trust enough in yourself.

Just see it: how can you trust me if you don't trust yourself? It is impossible. If you doubt yourself how can you trust me? It is *you* who are going to trust me, and you don't trust yourself – how can you trust your trust?

It is absolutely necessary that the heart should be opened before intellect can be transformed into intelligence. That's the difference between intellect and intelligence. Intelligence is intellect in tune with your heart. The heart knows how to trust; the intellect knows how to seek and search.

There is an old Eastern story:

Two beggars lived outside a village. One was blind and one had no legs. One day the forest near the village where these beggars lived caught fire. They were competitors of course – in the same profession, begging from the same people – and they were continually angry with each other. They were enemies, not friends.

People in the same profession cannot be friends. It is very difficult because it is a question of competition, clients – you take away somebody's client. Beggars label their clients: "Remember that this is my man; don't bother him." You don't know to which beggar you belong, in which beggar's possession you are, but some beggar on the street has possessed you. He may have fought and won the battle and now you are his possession.

I used to see a beggar near the university; one day I found him in the market. He had been constantly near the university because young people are more generous; older people slowly become more miserly, more afraid. Death is coming close; now money seems to be the only thing that can help. And if they have money, then others may help also; if they don't have money, even their own sons, their own daughters, won't bother about them. Young people can be spendthrifts. They are young, they can earn; there is a long life ahead.

He was a rich beggar because in India a student reaches university only if he comes from a rich family, otherwise it is a struggle. A few poor people reach but it is painful, arduous. I was also from a poor family. The whole night I was working as an editor of a newspaper, and in the day I went to the university. For years I could not sleep more than three or four hours – whenever I could find time in the day or in the night.

So this beggar was very strong. No other beggar could enter the university street; even entry was banned. Everybody knew to whom the university belonged – to that beggar! One day suddenly I saw a young man; the old man was not there. I asked him, "What happened? Where is the old man?"

He said, "He is my father-in-law. He has given the university to me as a gift." Now, the university did not know that the ownership had changed, that somebody else was now the owner! The young man said, "I have married his girl."

In India a dowry is given when a daughter marries. Your father-in-law, if he is very rich, has to give you a car, a bungalow; if not very rich then at least a scooter; if not that, then at least a bicycle. But he has to give something or other – a radio, a transistor set, a television, and some cash. If he is really rich then he gives you an opportunity to go abroad, to study, to become a more educated person, a doctor, an engineer.

This beggar's daughter had married and in dowry the young man had been given the whole university. He said, "From today this street and this university belong to me. And my father-in-law has shown me who my clients are."

I saw the old man in the marketplace so I said to him, "Great! You have done well in giving a dowry."

"Yes," he said, "I had only one daughter and I wanted to do something for my son-in-law. I have given him the best place to beg. Now I am here trying again to arrange my monopoly in the market. It is a very tough job here because there are so many beggars, senior ones who have already taken possession of clients. But there is nothing to be worried about. I will manage; I will throw out a few beggars from here" – and certainly he did.

So when the forest was on fire those two beggars thought for a moment. They were enemies, not even on speaking terms, but this was an emergency. The blind man said to the man who had no legs, "Now the only way to escape is that you sit on my shoulders; use my legs and I will use your eyes. That's the only way we can save ourselves."

It was immediately understood. There was no problem. The man without legs could not get out; it was impossible for him to cross the forest – it was all on fire. He would have moved a little bit but that would not help: an exit, and a very quick exit, was needed. The blind man also was certain that he could not get out. He did not know where the fire was, where the road was, where the trees were burning and where they were not: as a blind man, he would get lost. But both were intelligent people; they dropped their enmity, became friends and saved their lives.

This is an Eastern fable. It is about your intellect and your heart. It has nothing to do with beggars, it has something to do with you. It has nothing to do with the forest on fire, it has something to do with you – because *you* are on fire. Each moment you are burning, suffering, in misery, anguish. Alone your intellect is blind. It has legs, it can run fast, it can move fast, but because it is blind it cannot choose the right direction in which to go. It is bound to be continually stumbling, falling, hurting itself and feeling that life is meaningless. That's what the intellectuals of the whole world are saying: "Life is meaningless."

The reason life seems meaningless to them is that the blind intellect is trying to see the light. It is impossible. There is a heart within you which sees, which feels, but which has no legs; it cannot run. It remains where it is, beating, waiting: someday intellect will understand and will be able to use the heart's eyes.

When I say the word *trust* I mean the eyes of the heart. And when I say doubt I mean the legs of your intellect. Together they can come out of the fire; there is no problem at all. But remember, the intellect has to accept the heart above its shoulders. It has to. The heart has no legs, only eyes, and intellect has to listen to the heart and follow its directions.

In the hands of the heart the intellect becomes intelligent. It is a transformation, a total transformation of energy. Then a person does not become an intellectual, he simply becomes wise. Wisdom comes through the meeting of the heart and the intellect.

Once you have learned the art of creating a synchronicity between your heartbeats and the workings of your intellect, you have the whole secret in your hands, the master key to open all the mysteries.

I could have taught you doubt, but that would have changed you into intellectuals. I would have defeated my purpose and I would have destroyed your life. And there is no contradiction in what I am doing. First I had to teach you the way of the heart because I wanted you to understand that the heart is higher than your intellect. I had to deny the intellect completely so you forgot all the doubting and skepticism that you acquired from your schools, colleges, universities – which know nothing of the heart, which depend only on the intellect. They create the intelligentsia.

Even their greatest intellectuals, like Bertrand Russell, Jean-Paul Sartre, Martin Heidegger, are poor, blind; they know nothing. They have immense knowledgeability, but they know nothing. They have not experienced anything at all, because experience is something that happens through the heart.

The intellect can take the heart into that space where experience happens. The intellect cannot experience it; the experiencer will be the heart, but the intellect can be a good vehicle. If the reins are in the hands of the heart, then the horse of intellect is of tremendous beauty. This is the harmony which creates a real, authentic seeker.

It was a problem for me: from where to begin? I had to begin somewhere; either I had to begin with doubt or I had to begin with trust. I contemplated and weighed both for years. You cannot teach both together; it will simply confuse people. The best is to teach one first and then the second. Even then it creates trouble: there is the question that these two things seem to be contradictory. They are not.

Is the friendship of the blind beggar and the beggar without legs contradictory? What can be more harmonious? Two people functioning like one person – what can be more harmonious? The eyes belong to one person, the legs belong to somebody else; but eyes and legs belonging to two different people are functioning as if they belong to one person.

I would have loved to start with doubt because that is easier; you are already trained in it. That's what J. Krishnamurti has been doing all his life, and he has proved an absolute failure. Now there is no possibility for him to change his way of working. He has worked hard – ninety years of continual teaching of doubt, skepticism, intellect, reason – one feels sad for him, but all that he has been able to create are doubting Thomases all around the world. Those doubting Thomases are blind, and perhaps J. Krishnamurti also cannot see clearly. He is not blind, but his heart is not on top of his intellect; his intellect is sitting on top of his heart. He has not moved anywhere either: whatever he was saying in 1925 he is saying the same in 1985.

Just now Sheela was telling me that one of my sannyasins, Deeksha, went to see Krishnamurti in England. At first he was not ready to see her, but Deeksha is not the type to leave anybody so easily. She pestered him, and she wouldn't leave; finally, poor Krishnamurti had to encounter Deeksha.

But the first thing she did, she should not have done. She wanted to take over J. Krishnamurti's kitchen – it was a good idea, she is a perfectly good cook – but what she did wrong was to mention she had been with me. That was not the right certificate to produce. That was not the right qualification; that was absolutely the wrong qualification, the wrong certificate.

If she had asked me I would have told her how to approach J. Krishnamurti: at least don't mention my name, ever, because my working is totally opposite to his; he immediately gets enraged. The moment she mentioned my name – you cannot believe that a man like J. Krishnamurti would say such a thing – he said, "Yes, Osho was enlightened, but now he is no longer."

Now this is something great! Nobody has ever heard that somebody who has been enlightened can also become unenlightened. Nobody can fall from there because there is nothing to fall, nowhere to fall, nobody to fall; not a single ingredient exists. Where can you fall? The whole universe is in you, and you are in the whole universe. Where can you fall? There is no other space. And who can fall? – because the one who could fall has fallen long ago: it is his fall that makes enlightenment possible.

A person exists before enlightenment, not after enlightenment. After enlightenment, enlightenment exists. No person, no ego, no "I" – so who can fall? To fall from enlightenment is one of the impossible things in existence.

Yes, one man has been doing it, and that is one of my sannyasins, Gunakar; Germans can do impossible things. He has become enlightened many times. He declares *himself* enlightened: he cannot wait. He used to become enlightened and then he would write, trying to show his enlightenment in the letter – and it was all rubbish.

He wrote to all the government heads of the whole world; he wrote letters to all the members of the U.N. declaring his enlightenment. Those letters were all rubbish, but he was advising everybody. I asked him to come so that I could see his enlightenment. He came, very nervous, and as he sat down in front of me, I said, "Now become unenlightened again!"

So he said, "If you say so, Osho, then I am unenlightened again. In fact I was so impatient: I want to become enlightened."

I said, "It is perfectly good that you want to become enlightened, but you need not declare your enlightenment without becoming enlightened. When you become enlightened, you will be recognized. I will write a letter to *you*, you need not write a letter to me. Just wait!"

So he would say, "Okay, so I am not enlightened."

This has happened three or four times. Since I came to America he has not come here because he does not want to become unenlightened again. But this is the only case in the whole history of humanity. Gunakar is unique! Otherwise, once a person becomes enlightened he is no more.

Now, Krishnamurti saying to Deeksha, "Osho *was* enlightened; now, since he moved to America, he is no longer enlightened" – that too is strange. Krishnamurti *lives* in America; his whole life he has lived in America or in England, but his home base is America. I have been here only three years, and I have become unenlightened in three years. What to say about him? He has been here his whole life, almost eighty years – at least twenty-five times longer. He *must* have become unenlightened! How can America make a person unenlightened? Yes, it is possible that if you are a born Oregonian you may never become enlightened; that is possible, I don't see much hope. But even Oregon cannot do the miracle of making an enlightened person unenlightened.

Krishnamurti is really angry with me. I simply laugh at the poor old fellow. He is nice, but why does he get so angry? And only with me? There are so many gurus around the world, and he is not angry with any of them, so why with me? The reason is very clear, but perhaps not so clear to him. The reason is clear: what he has been trying to do and has been constantly failing to do, I have managed in a very short period. The same profession – either of beggars or of masters, it makes no difference. He has no clients, and I have so many clients that I go on chopping and dropping and somehow sorting out the wrong ones.

He has been looking for people like you, but he cannot find them because of his own strategy. He has chosen doubt as the first step – that's where he missed. He missed the first step.

I have chosen trust as the first step. And once you have felt the taste of trust then doubt is impotent. It cannot destroy your trust. It will destroy your beliefs, which are needed to be destroyed. It will destroy all that is not authentic – and that is needed to be destroyed. What it cannot destroy is trust. When doubt comes face to face with authentic trust, then doubt accepts the trust – its eyes, its way of feeling – as higher than it. It is so clear, there is no other possibility.

Your doubt bows down to your trust, and a friendship happens in you. Your heart is the master, your intellect becomes the servant. And that's what I mean by intelligence. It is intelligence which will ultimately become enlightenment.

So I started with trust because I wanted people who can take the risk of trusting, who are confident enough to take the risk. Trust is risky, doubt is not risky. Doubt is really trying to defend yourself; it is a defense measure so that you are not cheated, you are not exploited, so that somebody does not befool you, you don't fall into the hands of a con man. Doubt simply prevents you from being cheated. But if you don't have anything, and doubt goes on protecting you, what is the point of it all? It is like a man who goes on guarding his safe and knows perfectly well that there is nothing in it. Then what are you guarding? Have a good sleep, because there is nothing! What do you have that can be exploited?

Yes, a man of trust has something: he has a throbbing, living, feeling heart. He has a treasure house. Now doubt can be put on guard. First I tried to create the treasure in you; now I am telling you that you need a guard. You have something to lose, and you should be alert. There is no contradiction at all. Only for intellectuals will it seem that there is a contradiction; for intelligent people it will be immediately clear that there is a synchronicity. I may look mad – one day teaching you trust, another day starting to teach you about doubt – but my madness has a method in it. It is not just madness, but madness with a method.

I don't say to you, "Believe me." I say to you, "Take this hypothesis" – and now I *can* say to you, "Take this hypothesis" because you have this much trust in me. I am not asking for belief or faith, I am simply saying, "I know something which I cannot make you know; I know something which I cannot even express to you. But I can give you a hypothesis just to begin with, so that you can inquire."

When I say the soul transmigrates, to me it is an experience: I remember my past lives. I have transmigrated; there is no question of doubt for me, but I am not saying for you to believe it. What I am conspiring is to make you interested in this strange inquiry into past lives. If I can know my past lives – because they are all imprinted in the unconscious, nothing is ever lost – you can descend the staircase and go into *your* unconscious, and you can start knowing about your past lives.

When you know, there is no need to believe – because then you *know*. When you don't know, never believe, because if you believe you will never know. So belief is not needed at any stage of life. When you are ignorant, belief is not needed; it is very dangerous, because if you start believing then who is going to inquire? Belief stops inquiry, kills inquiry. And when you know something, it will be simply foolish to believe in it. What will be the point of believing? You know. You don't believe in the sun, you don't believe in the roses – you know. You believe in God because you *don't* know. You believe in the soul because you don't know.

I am trying to destroy all unnecessary hypotheses, so you are not diverted; then you can move into an inquiry for God. One thing is certain: if God wants to meet you, he will look for you. In this vast universe you should not be so insane that you can search for God.

Man has reached only up to the moon. That is not very far; it is the nearest planet. The nearest star is four light years away. If some day we can invent a vehicle, a rocket which moves with the same speed as light – it is impossible but just for argument's sake – then we will reach the nearest star in four years. That is a one-way journey; the return journey would be eight years. In the first place the problem is the speed, because at the speed of light everything becomes light. No matter what metal is used, at that speed everything is transformed into light – just as at a certain speed fire is created.

In olden times in India – in my childhood I have seen it in my village – people who smoked used to carry two stones, the white stones which are available on the shore of any river. They would put a little cotton between those two stones and hit the cotton between them; that hitting would create fire, the cotton would burn up. That was perhaps the most primitive lighter. Perhaps they are still doing it. I have not been to my village for many years; they must still be doing it today. Who will bother about a modern lighter? – you need petrol and you need this and you need that. Those poor people can just get two stones from anywhere, and carry the stones with them. It is the simplest and cheapest way, and they can create fire anywhere.

I have seen people creating fire by rubbing two bamboos together. In the aboriginal state of Bastar in India there is perhaps an even more primitive method: fire is created by rubbing dry wood together. That is how forests catch on fire, because in strong winds trees rub against each other and their rubbing creates fire. Just the other day I was telling you that meteorites fall from the sky and burn up. You see a star falling: it is a stone burning because its speed creates great friction with the air. The friction at that speed creates fire.

Light travels at the ultimate speed. At that speed everything is going to turn into light: the vehicle, the passengers, everybody. You won't reach the nearest star in four years. And if we move at the same speed as we have gone to the moon, it will take perhaps thousands of years one way; a round trip, thousands more. You will not find the people you left behind when you left the earth, on your return – nobody at all. In those years all those people have gone; generations have passed. When you come back you will not be able to recognize a single face.

Even the hazards of the journey to the moon were tremendous, anything could have gone wrong; but it was only a question of a very short time. Still things were going wrong: machines are, after all, machines. And you don't have a workshop and mechanics, engineers and scientists; they are all here on the earth with remote controls, and the remote controls sometimes just don't work. To depend completely on machines for all those years seems to be impossible.

One thing more: God is not on that star, because that is the nearest star. If he wants to avoid man he has so many stars, so far away – stars for which this Earth has never existed. Their distance is such that if on the day the Earth came into existence their light started traveling toward the Earth, by the time that light reaches the Earth, the Earth will be gone. The distance is such that Earth's few million years of life are not enough for the light to reach here. And there are stars further away than that.

If God wants to meet you, the only way is for him to look for you, and he has not bothered at all. It is man who is bothering about God by looking above. It was good in Jesus' time to look above because it was thought that the stars were very close by, just lamps for the night that God had created to give you some light. The world was very small, the stars were very close. Now we know that they are not lamps created to give you light, and that there are millions of stars, expanding continuously with the same speed as light. The universe is an expanding universe. If God wants to meet you it is up to him – but I don't think he is interested.

You unnecessarily get involved in a search for God. All that you will end up with will be your own hallucination, your own imagination. That's why I want to drop all unnecessary hypotheses, so you can focus yourself on the most necessary hypothesis – your being, your soul.

Please first find yourself, then try to find God; otherwise you will not even be able to introduce yourself. Who are you? If by chance, by accident, you come across him somewhere and he asks, "Who are you?" you won't be able to answer him: you don't know. Your name will not work, your religion will not work, your degrees will not work; because you are not your name, you are not your degrees and you are not your profession. He will not ask, "Are you a doctor or an engineer or a plumber?" He will ask, "Who are you? Engineering may be your education – forget about it! Just tell me who *you* are." And you don't know. This is the basic question.

I say to you, you *are*; but don't believe me, just take it as a hypothesis. That's why I needed first your trust, a little trust: the trust that this man is not going to give you a wrong hypothesis. This much trust – I am not asking much.

Jesus and Krishna asked for total surrender. I am just asking for a very simple thing, a thing that any scientist will ask of you: "This is the hypothesis – work on it." You cannot doubt a hypothesis, remember, because a hypothesis is not a belief, so the question of doubt does not arise. A hypothesis means something temporarily assumed, to inquire about. Once you find it, you can see whether the hypothesis was right or wrong. You can put your experience against the hypothesis and judge. And if this hypothesis has given you the experience, then the hypothesis was right. If the hypothesis just leads you into a desert land, and no oasis appears, then drop that hypothesis – and the sooner the better. Find something better. But I tell you I have found it.

In a master you need only hypothetical trust, not a total surrender. How can you surrender totally? I sometimes feel simply surprised that Krishna told Arjuna, "Surrender to me totally." Now, if Arjuna is asking a thousand and one questions about everything, is it possible for him to surrender totally? And Krishna tells Arjuna, who is continually doubting everything that Krishna is saying and raising question upon question, "Just surrender totally to me."

Do you think it is a child's game? How can this man surrender? Arjuna was a great intellectual: all the questions that he had raised before Krishna are relevant. And all the answers that Krishna had given him are just to explain *away* his question, not to explain. There is no way to explain, he is simply trying to explain them away. But Arjuna is insistent: Krishna tries to escape from one question, Arjuna brings another. This goes on and on, and in the middle of it, Krishna suddenly says, "Just surrender to me, and leave everything to me."

I am surprised by Krishna's demand, and that too of an intellectual like Arjuna. Can't he see that this man is not a gullible type? Even if you can find a gullible type – a man who cannot live totally, cannot do anything totally, can he be expected to surrender totally? Moreover, can surrender be an act on the part of the disciple?

One young man who was a very gullible, believing, devotional type used to come to me. The situation between me and him was just the reverse of that between Krishna and Arjuna. He would just hold my legs and sit on the floor and say, "Accept me. I want to surrender totally to you."

Once I said, "You want to surrender totally to me, but I don't want your surrender! Are you going to force your surrender upon me? What am I going to do with your surrender? – I don't need it. You may need it somewhere else; don't waste it totally. Save it for some emergency. Somewhere somebody may demand surrender with a gun, then what will you do? You will say, 'I don't have any surrender left, I have surrendered all to one person.' You will be in danger – you keep it."

He said, "You are strange. Every master says, 'Surrender.' And I come to you; I believe in you, and I *want* to surrender."

I said, "Listen, today you have come to surrender; tomorrow you can come and say, 'Give my surrender back.' I will unnecessarily have to take care of your surrender so that it is not lost. I may put it somewhere, and one day you may appear and suddenly ask, 'Give my surrender back.'"

He said, "You are joking."

I said, "I am not joking! If *you* are surrendering, *you* have the right to take it back. *You* are the master, I am not the master. You are surrendering to me – who is the master? It is *your* act, I am simply outside your act. I am not doing anything, you are doing it – but tomorrow you can cancel it. You can find a better master; you can find some fault in me, and you can take your surrender back.

"I don't ask anything from you. I don't need your surrender, all I need is a hypothetical trust. Do what I say; it may prove right, it may prove wrong. So there is no need to trust me, just do it with a 'perhaps.' I have no interest in deceiving you. By your sitting in silence, meditating, I am not going to gain anything. So let it be clear that I am not going to gain anything by your sitting in silence, by your becoming enlightened; I am not going to have any share in it.

"Why should I send you in the wrong direction? I have no investment. I am not a priest, I don't live on any priesthood. How in the world, for what reason would I misguide you? So just hypothetically, that's enough; more than that I don't want, because more than that is dangerous. Today you say, 'I surrender totally,' and then you think you need not do anything. What else can you do? – you have done all, you have surrendered totally."

Krishna is saying to Arjuna: "Surrender totally, and I will take care of you." This is certainly destroying the other person's independence, individuality, his freedom to inquire; you are completely killing the person spiritually. But this has been the way of all the religions. Hence, you see some contradiction between trust and doubt. There is none.

I have taught you trust and the way of the heart so that your heart is open, available; your eyes are there, available. Now I have to train your intellect. Before I leave I have to complete my work. I have to train your intellect, sharpen it. I have to teach you doubt because doubt is not a simple thing.

Doubt needs great courage because you will doubt everything possible. You will be surrounded by all kinds of doubts. All consoling beliefs will be taken away, beliefs which gave you a certain confidence, a certain stability, a certain feeling that you belong to a big tradition, a well-respected religion of holy scriptures, messiahs, representatives of God. You had all those things surrounding you. They gave you a cozy feeling that you are not alone. I am trying to do just this: cut away everything that gives you a false, cozy feeling and that keeps you dozing all your life.

Belief is the opium which all the religions have been giving you in good doses. I am trying to destroy your addiction to that opium. My whole effort is to leave you alone. Yes, you will feel fear, you will feel a certain trembling, you will feel all is lost; but this is just in the beginning. A little patience – it is a passing phase. Soon you will feel a tremendous energy arising in you which would never have arisen in the crowd, with its beliefs, because there was no need: you were spoon-fed, there was no need for you to think about your food on your own.

I am taking away every consolation, every comfort – I mean spiritually – so you are completely alone in your being. And then take the hypothesis: meditate, be silent, just watch yourself.

Somebody has asked, "How can we be certain that the watcher is not part of the mind?" It is a relevant question but only intellectually. It is not out of meditation because the man is bringing into his question three things of which he is not aware: the mind, the watcher – and who is this third who is thinking whether the mind and the watcher are one thing? There is a third entity which is raising the question. I say to you: the watcher, your watcher, is part of your mind. And not only that, the second watcher behind it is also part of your mind.

When you realize silent watching, you don't see any mind anywhere; all thoughts stop. That is the beauty and the revolution of the watcher: when you are in a watching state there is nothing to be watched.

This is the trouble: when there is everything to watch, the watcher is not there; when the watcher comes in, there is nothing to watch. Only one can exist, both cannot exist together. The presence of the watcher simply disperses the mind; it is no longer needed. It was just functioning because the watcher was absent.

Gurdjieff used to tell a story:

A very rich man went on a pilgrimage. He had many servants and a very big palace where he lived alone with all these servants. He called all the servants and told them he was going on a journey: "One by one, on rotation, you have to be on guard. I don't know how much time I am going to take, it may be many years; the journey is long, the pilgrimage is hazardous. I may come back, I may not come back, but the palace and the garden all have to be present as they are now."

They said, "Of course. Whatsoever you say we will do."

The man went away. Months passed, years passed. By and by the servants started to completely forget that they were servants because the master had been gone so long. Man's memory is not that long, and there are things which one does not really want to remember. Who wants to remember being a slave and that somebody is the master?

Each servant had to guard the palace in rotation, and when each servant was guarding, he would pretend that he was the master. Anybody coming to the palace or passing by would ask, "Whose palace is this?" The servant would answer, "It is my palace, my garden. Don't you like it?"

This was happening with all the guards. Years passed and the guards completely forgot about the master and that he was going to return. "By now he must be dead, something must have happened. And it is good that we got rid of that fellow – now we are the masters." They declared to the whole town, "We are the masters." The town had also forgotten the master; it was long ago. Only old people remembered that somebody had been there, but only very vaguely. Nobody was aware of when he went, where he went, and what happened to him.

But one day, the master appeared; he knocked on the door. The slaves looked at him and suddenly fell at his feet: "Master, you are back!"

He said, "I told you I would come back, even though it may take a long time."

They said, "Forgive us, because the city people will say we have committed a crime against you. We had forgotten you completely; we enjoyed being the master so much that we declared that we were the masters – and the city believes that we are the masters."

Gurdjieff used to tell this story, saying that the same is the case with the watcher. The watcher is absent; the mind – which is just a slave – is pretending to be the master. And it is not a question of a few years – for millions of years the master has been absent. Perhaps the master has never been home; there is no question that he had gone, because once he arrives he never goes. So your thoughts, and the combination of thoughts which you call your mind, certainly, confidently believe that they are the master.

Just try to watch your thoughts.

Remember one thing: thought itself cannot watch another thought – that is impossible. A thought cannot become a watcher of another thought; so when in your mind the thought arises, "I am watching," you have missed, because it is a thought. When the watcher is there you will not even have the idea of "Aha! Got it!" Lost it! You were just on the verge of getting it and Werner Erhard entered, and EST finished everything: "Got it!" Even that much, just two words, is enough; the mind is back.

It is always the mind that gets it, or does not get it; the watcher simply watches. No idea is formed, just absolute silence prevails. In that moment is the seeing, knowing, experiencing – without any thought. Can't you experience something without any thought? You will have to learn, because mind has been trained for centuries to think every experience in words. You see a beautiful roseflower: immediately the mind says, "How beautiful!" You may not say it aloud, you are not that insane, but silently you will say, "How beautiful!" But in saying it, you miss the experience of the beauty of the flower.

The moment you said, "How beautiful!" you went far away from the flower. You have already compared it with your past experiences of the flower. And remember, your past experiences must have been just like this: they were not experiences because those times too, you would have missed in the same way, by saying, "How beautiful!" You have always been missing the train!

Standing by the side of a roseflower, just stand there. Can't you keep for a few seconds just a watching state of consciousness, with no interference of words – *beautiful, ugly, red, yellow*? No, just stand by the side. It is not difficult; it needs just a little knack, and you can practice it anytime, doing anything. Just don't allow words to come in between you and what is happening.

Once this knack is learned, the same is the situation inside. Of course, the inside experience is inexpressible, and tremendously more vast and profound than the beauty of a roseflower or the sunset; but what you have to do is the same. Just relish it, drown in it, and if for a few minutes... Mahavira has counted exactly – and I agree with him because I have counted it also – it is exactly forty-eight minutes. If you can manage this state of watching without any word interfering for forty-eight minutes – I am not asking much... It is something of a law of existence that within forty-eight minutes the experience is complete. Then nobody can take it from you, you cannot fall from it. You can come to America, you can come to Oregon – you cannot fall from it.

I really enjoyed it when Sheela told me that J. Krishnamurti thinks that I have lost my enlightenment. He must be furious! He cannot be joking, that much is certain. He is not a man to be non-serious, no; he is continually serious. He must have been serious. But what is troubling him? – he started with the wrong step. That is not my fault. If you get out of your bed with the wrong foot, what can I do? It is your bed and your foot, and you go on doing that for eighty years; I have nothing to do with it!

I was also in a dilemma in the beginning, but sometimes things which are not appreciated prove tremendously helpful. My laziness proved tremendously helpful. I went on sitting on my bed, figuring out which foot to put down first. I would have waited there my whole life. For almost seven years I never told anybody, "I am no longer part of you." Yes, a few people came to suspect – those who had the experience. One was Magga Baba, a very poor man, a beggar. He was the first to take hold of me – with both his hands he shook me – and he said, "You cannot befool me!"

I said, "I have not done anything."

He said, "You haven't *done* anything, that is true, but you have been someplace which you are hiding."

I said, "That's true, but please don't tell anybody because I don't want any harassment. I will get out of the bed, but I have not yet decided which foot is the right one to get out with."

I am a lazy man, bone lazy. My physician, Doctor Devaraj, wants to give me Vitamin D because I am bone lazy. Calcium is missing he thinks – perhaps! But it has been tremendous; it is good that it was missing. If I had jumped out of bed, I would have been in the same mess as J. Krishnamurti. I got out of bed only when I had figured out everything completely. And since that moment I have been moving with every step calculated.

First I taught you about trust, the heart, feeling, love; and now I am teaching you about doubt, skepticism, reason, intellect, because I would like you to be a *whole* man. You can be completely satisfied with trusting, with the heart, but you will not be a whole man.

I would not call Meera a whole person, I would not call Ramakrishna a whole person. They are beautiful, but the intellect is missing; it is all heart. It is too much sugar, it creates diabetes. I am diabetic. Too much of the heart, too much sweetness, and you suffer from diabetes – and I don't want any of you to suffer from diabetes. Yes, just living by the heart you will have spiritual diabetes. Intellect is salty, spicy; it is not all sugar.

I would like you to enjoy the wholeness of your being, when your body, your heart, your intellect, all fall in tune. I have called that the new man – Zorba the Buddha.

CHAPTER 4

The Only Hope: The Enlightenment of Humanity

Osho,
Wouldn't it have been much easier for you to work without being associated with the word *religion*? What is the secret behind your choosing to do it this way?

I would have loved not to be associated in any way with the word *religion*. The whole history of religion simply stinks. It is ugly, and it shows the degradation of man, his inhumanity, and all that is evil. This is not about any one single religion, it is the same story repeated by all the religions of the world: man exploiting man in the name of God. I still feel uneasy being associated with the word *religion*. But there are a few problems: in life sometimes one has to choose things that one hates.

In my youth I was known in the university as an atheist, irreligious, against all moral systems. That was my stand, and that is still my stand. I have not changed even an inch; my position is exactly the same. But being known as an atheist, irreligious, amoral, became a problem. It was difficult to communicate with people, almost impossible to bridge any kind of relationship with people. To commune with people, the words *atheist*, *irreligious*, *amoral*, functioned like impenetrable walls. I would have remained so – for me there was no problem – but I saw that it was impossible to spread my experience, to share.

The moment people heard that I was an atheist, irreligious, amoral, they were completely closed. That I don't believe in any God, that I don't believe in any heaven and hell was enough for them to withdraw from me. Because I was a professor in the university, I was surrounded by hundreds of professors, research scholars, intelligent, educated people – and even they simply avoided me because they had no courage to defend what they believed; they had no argument for themselves.

I was continually arguing on street corners, in the university, in the pan wallah's shop – anywhere that I could get hold of somebody. I would hammer religion and try to clean people completely of all this nonsense. But the total result was that I became like an island; nobody even wanted to talk with me because even to say hello to me was dangerous: where would it lead? Finally I had to change my strategy.

I became aware that, strangely, the people who were interested in the search for truth had become involved in religions. Because they thought me irreligious, I could not commune with them; and they were the people who would be really interested to know. They were the people who would be ready to travel with me to unknown spaces. But they were already involved in some religion, in some sect, in some philosophy; and just their thinking of me as irreligious, atheistic, became a barrier. They were the people that I had to seek out.

There were people who were not involved in religions but they were not seekers at all. They were just interested in the trivia of life: earning more money, being a great leader – a politician, a prime minister, a president. Their interests were very mundane. They were no use to me, and they were also not interested in what I had to offer to them because it was not their interest at all.

The man who wants to become the prime minister of the country is not interested in finding the truth. If truth and the prime ministership are both presented to him, he will choose the prime ministership. He will say about truth, "There is no hurry. We can do that – the whole of eternity is available – but the opportunity of the prime ministership may or may not come again. It rarely comes, and only to very, very rare people, once in a while. Truth is everybody's nature, so we can find it any day. First let us do that which is momentary, temporal, fleeting. This beautiful dream may not happen again. Reality is not going anywhere, but this dream is fleeting."

Their interest was in dreaming, imagination. They were not my people, and communication with them was also impossible because our interests were diametrically opposite. I tried hard but those people were not interested in religion, not interested in truth, not interested in anything significant.

The people who *were* interested were Christians, or Hindus, Mohammedans, Jainas, Buddhists: they were already following some ideology, some religion. Then it was obvious to me that I would have to play the game of being religious; there was no other way. Only then could I find people who were authentic seekers.

I hate the word *religion*, I have always hated it, but I had to talk about religion. But what I was talking about under the cover of religion was not the same as people understood by religion. Now, this was simply a strategy. I was using their words – *God*, *religion*, *liberation*, *moksha* – and I was giving them my meaning. In this way I could start finding people; and people started coming to me.

It took a few years for me to change my image in people's eyes. But people only listen to words, they don't understand meanings: people only understand what you say, they don't understand what is conveyed unsaid. So I used their own weapons against them. I commented on religious books, and gave a meaning that was totally mine.

I would have said the same thing without commenting – it would have been far easier because then I would have been speaking directly to you. There was no need to drag in Krishna, Mahavira, and Jesus, and then make them say what they had never said. But such is the stupidity of humanity; I was saying the same thing that I had been saying before and they were not ready even to hear it, and now thousands started gathering around me because I was speaking on Krishna.

Now, what have I to do with Krishna? What has he done for me? What relationship have I got with Jesus? If I had met him while he was alive I would have said to him, "You are a fanatic and you are not in your senses. I cannot say that the people who want to crucify you are absolutely wrong, because they have no other way to deal with you."

So this was the only way. When I started speaking on Jesus,

Christian colleges and Christian theological institutes started inviting me to speak, and I was really continually giggling inside, because those fools thought that this was what Jesus had said. Yes, I used Jesus' words – one has just to understand a little game with words and one can make any word mean anything – and they thought that this was the real message of Jesus: "Our own Christian missionaries and priests have not done as much for Jesus as you have done."

I had to keep quiet, knowing that I have nothing to do with Jesus, and that what I was saying Jesus might not have been able to even understand. He was a poor fellow, absolutely uneducated. Certainly he had a charismatic personality so it was not difficult to gather a few uneducated people, fear-oriented and greedy for the joys in heaven. This man was making promises and asking nothing. So cheap: what was the harm of believing in him? There was no danger, no harm. If there was no heaven and no God, you were not losing anything. By chance if there were, and this man was the begotten son of God, then you were gaining so much for nothing: simple arithmetic!

But it is significant that not a single educated, cultured rabbi became Jesus' disciple, because those rabbis knew far better expressions, far better ways of philosophizing. This man knew nothing; he was not giving a single argument, he was simply stating things which he had heard from others; and he was a stubborn type of young man.

What I said in the name of Jesus, I had been saying before also, but no Christian community, no Christian college, no Christian theological institute would have invited me. What to say of invitation? If I had wanted to even enter they would have closed the doors! That was the situation: I was prohibited from entering my own city's central temple, and they had the support of the police so that I should not be allowed in. So whenever there was a Hindu monk speaking inside, a policeman was on guard outside to prevent me coming in.

I said, "But I want to listen to that man."

The police officer said, "We know, everybody knows, that when you are there, everybody has to listen to *you*. And we have been called here just to prevent you, not anybody else; everybody else is allowed. If you stop coming we would not be bothered because we are unnecessarily standing here for two or three hours every day. While the discourse session continues I will be standing here outside the temple just for you, one person."

But now the same temple started inviting me. Again the police were there – to prevent overcrowding! They said to me – one officer who was still there said to me – "You are something! We were standing here to keep you out, now we are standing here because too much crowding is dangerous – the temple is old."

It had balconies and at least five thousand people could sit inside. But when I used to speak there, nearabout fifteen thousand people would turn up. So people would go on the balconies which were usually never used. One day it became so serious that it was almost possible the balconies would fall down – there were so many people on the balconies, and it was an old temple. Then naturally they had to arrange that from the next day only a certain number of people were to be allowed in.

That created trouble. That officer said, "Now new trouble! You speak for two hours, but people start coming two hours earlier, because if they come late they won't get in." He said to me, "But you are something! You *were* against God."

I said in his ear, "I still am – don't tell anybody because nobody will believe it. I will always remain against God. Before I depart from the world I will expose everything. But you are not to tell because nobody is going to believe you, and I will flatly deny that I have ever said anything to you."

He said, "You are something. You are against God and speaking on God?"

But then I had to find my own ways. I would speak on God and then tell people that *godliness* was a far better word. That was a way of disposing of God. But because I was speaking on God, the people who were involved – who were true seekers being exploited by the religious priesthood – started becoming interested in me. I found the cream from all the religions.

There was no other way because I would not have been able to enter their folds, and they would not have been able to come to me: just those few words would have been enough to prevent them. I could not have blamed them, I would have blamed myself. I had to find a way so that I could approach them, and I found the way; it was very simple. I simply thought, "Use their words, use their language, use their scriptures.

"If you are using somebody else's gun, it does not mean you cannot put your own cartridges in it. Let the gun be anybody's, the cartridges are mine! The real work is going to happen through the cartridges, not the gun, so what harm?" It was easy, very easy, because I could use Hindu words and play the same game; I could use Mohammedan words and play the same game; I could use Christian words and play the same game.

Not only were those people coming to me, but Jaina monks, nuns, Hindu monks, Buddhist monks, Christian missionaries, priests – all kinds of people started coming to me. And you will not believe it: you have not seen me laughing because I have laughed so much inside that there was no need. I have been telling jokes to you, but I have not been laughing because I have been playing a joke my whole life! What can be funnier? I managed to befool all those priests and great scholars so easily.

They started coming to me and asking me questions. I just had to be alert in the beginning to use their vocabulary, and just between the lines, between the words, to go on putting the real stuff in which I was interested. I learned the art from a fisherman.

I used to sit by the bank of the river for hours because that was the most beautiful place in my village. The morning was beautiful, the evening was beautiful; and even in the hot summer there were spots where there were thick trees leaning over the river. You could just sit in the river, in the water, and it was so cool you could forget it was summer.

I was just sitting looking at the morning sun, and fishermen were there. In India they put out bait for the fish. Everywhere fishermen put out bait, but in India it has to be non-vegetarian, because the people who are catching fish and the people who are going to buy fish are both non-vegetarians. So the fishermen will cut small insects into pieces, which are delicious to the fishes, and hook them to their fishing lines. The fish will come and catch the insect and with the insect there is a hook; the hook will catch the fish. The fish will come to get the insect, but inside the insect the hook has been put, so once she swallows the insect, the fish is caught by the hook and she can be pulled out immediately.

Looking at this fisherman I thought, "I have to find a way that I can catch my people. Right now they are in different camps, nobody is mine." I was alone: nobody was courageous enough even to associate with me or to walk with me because people would think that he was also gone, was lost. I found the bait: use their words.

In the beginning people were really shocked. Those who knew me for years, who knew that I had always been against God, were really puzzled, absolutely puzzled. One of my teachers, whom I had tortured for three years continually in my high school because he was a very pious type of man: praying morning and evening, and continually keeping on his forehead the symbol of his religion... I was continually harassing him about everything; he was incapable of answering any question.

In fact nobody can answer questions relating to fictions. If reality is there, some way can be found and any question can be answered. But if there is no reality at all and you are just feeling high on something fictitious, you will be afraid even to listen to a question from somebody because that brings doubt to your mind.

This teacher lived not very far from my house, so I used to go to torture him there – because in class he would simply say, "Get out!" before he took the attendance. I would say, "Please, first take my attendance; otherwise, I come every day, but at the end of term you will say that my attendance is not good enough and that I cannot appear in the examinations. So please, first take the attendance."

He said, "That I will do – you need not even come." He gave me exactly one hundred percent attendance, but he said, "Before I start my work, you get out!"

I used to go to his house, and I would say, "Here you have to treat me like a god because that is what scriptures say: *atithi devo bhava* – the guest is equal to God. Here you cannot tell me to get out; and English is not allowed at all because it is a religious conversation for which I have come."

He would keep both his fingers in his ears. His wife would ask, "Why are you so afraid of this boy?"

He would say, "I don't want to listen to what he wants to say. I cannot throw him out of the house. He is right, he is saying, '*Atithi devo bhava*: a guest is God, nothing less; treat him as if God has come.' But no scripture says that you cannot put your fingers in your ears. I won't listen to a single word from him because he creates doubts in me. His whole purpose in coming here is to create doubt."

Once his wife asked, "Why do you unnecessarily take the trouble to come when he does not listen?"

I said, "But do you see? Do you think your husband is a religious man?"

She said, "Since you started coming I don't think that he is a religious man. What kind of faith does a man have who is afraid of even listening to anything that goes against his beliefs?"

One day, when I was talking to his wife, he must have taken his fingers out of his ears to listen to what I was saying. When he heard that his wife was saying that he was not much of a religious man – "Perhaps you are right: he is such a coward, and I never knew"– he came running into the house because I was in the kitchen talking to his wife.

He said, "Now you are spoiling my wife! Can't you leave me alone? Now she is saying that I am not a religious man. You have planted the idea in her mind; she will torture me. From you I can manage to escape, I can throw you out of the class, but where am I going to throw my wife?"

His wife said, "Whatsoever the boy says is significant. You have to answer him if you are a real believer."

This teacher met me almost twenty years later in a discourse in Mumbai. I was speaking on the most popular Hindu scripture, the Shrimad Bhagavadgita. He could not believe it: thousands of people, and I was speaking on Bhagavadgita! And not only thousands of people, but hundreds of sannyasins too. He came to the back and waited there for when I came out.

He said, "What has happened? You are transformed!" And he touched my feet.

I said, "Don't touch them. I am not transformed, I am the same man. And I am very stubborn: I am going to remain the same man to the last breath. Don't touch my feet" – but he had already touched them.

He said, "You must be joking! If so many sannyasins..." That's why I had chosen the orange robe, just to sabotage the whole idea of ancient sannyas. There was now no difference between my sannyasins and their sannyasins: it was difficult to figure out who was who. And my sannyasins were increasing every day, in every place all over the country. When he said, "So many sages are also sitting there," I said, "None of them is a sage! Keep your eyes open and close your ears. You should not come here – you are a simple person, this is not for you."

But he said, "I have heard you – the whole lecture – and I have been reading the Gita my whole life. Nobody has ever interpreted

Krishna's words the way you have. I have read many commentaries, but listening to you I found that all those were third rate."

This was happening again and again. Once I was speaking in a Mohammedan institute in Jabalpur. One of my Mohammedan teachers had become the principal of this institute; he was not aware that I was the same person he knew. Somebody told him that they had heard me speaking on Sufis and that it was something incredible: "We had not thought about Sufis that way, and our institute will be honored if he comes."

In India, or in any other country, if a Mohammedan comes and speaks on the Bible you feel very flattered, your ego is tremendously strengthened; or if a Mohammedan, a Hindu, a Buddhist, is speaking on Jesus, praising him and his words. Particularly in India where Mohammedans and Hindus are continuously killing each other, if somebody who is not a Mohammedan can speak on Sufism... My old teacher was very happy; he invited me to talk.

I was in search of all these invitations because I wanted to find my people, and they were all hiding in different places.

When my teacher saw me he said, "I have only *heard* of miracles, but this is a miracle! You are speaking on Sufism, on Islam, on the fundamental philosophy of Islam?"

I said, "To you I will not lie – you are my old teacher. I will be speaking only on my philosophy. Yes, I have learned the art of throwing in the word *Islam* to people once in a while, that much I will do."

He said, "My God! But now we are caught: people are waiting in the auditorium, and you are the same mischievous person, you have not changed. Are you kidding or something? – because one of our trusted teachers who is an authority on Sufism has praised you. Because of his praise I have invited you."

I said, "He has spoken rightly, and you will also praise what I say. But remember always, I will say only what I want to say. It does not matter, it is so simple a thing: if a Buddhist calls me I have only to change a few words, and from Sufism I talk about Zen, not about Sufis. I say the same thing; it is just that Sufism is changed a little here and there. I have to be alert not to forget about whom I am speaking, that's all."

And I spoke. Of course he had been sitting there very sad, but when he heard me he was so joyous. He came and hugged me and he said, "You must have been joking."

I said, "I am always joking – don't take it seriously."

"You *are* a Sufi," he said.

I said, "That's what people say!"

I was speaking in Amritsar in the Golden Temple, which is now creating great trouble in India. This is the Sikh temple, and because of this temple Indira Gandhi has been assassinated; the whole country is shaken. I was speaking in that temple. Everywhere, all around the country, people had asked me thousands of times, "Why do you grow a beard?" I had become accustomed to the question and I enjoyed answering in different ways to different people. But in the Golden Temple when I was speaking on Nanak and his message, a very old *sardar* came to me, touched my feet and said, "*Sadarji*, why have you cut your hair?" That was a new question, asked for the first time. He said, "Your beard is perfectly okay, but why have you cut your hair? – you being such a religious man."

Only five things are needed to be a Sikh, very simple things; you can manage them, anybody can. They are called the five *K*'s because each word starts with *K*. *Kesh* means hair, *katar* means a knife; *kachchha* means underwear – that I have not been able to figure out. It is the only question I cannot answer. What philosophy is being taught? Strange, but there must be some reason. I inquired of the Sikh priests and their high priest, "Everything is okay – grow your hair and have a sword or a knife – but this *kachchha*...? What theological, theosophical, philosophical meaning does *kachchha* have?"

They said, "Nobody has ever asked about it; we just have to follow these five *K*'s." In Nanak's time, when he chose the *kachchha*, it was a time of continual war between Mohammedans and Hindus. He changed the whole caliber of the Punjab. He gave them almost a new energy with which to fight; certainly a martial race was born out of the Hindus, who cannot fight, who don't want to fight – they were all Hindus. Perhaps in a fight the Hindu clothes were not fitting. A loose dhoti, a loose gown, are comfortable, very comfortable, and in a hot country, very airy and comfortable; they remind one of a time when people did not need to work hard. But you cannot give that kind of clothes to soldiers, so Nanak changed it: instead of the dhoti he created the *salwar*, which is a kind of pajama. But in a war, at any time your pajama can go bananas because there is only a small thread that is holding it up.

Now Neelam is enjoying this because she is a Punjabi. She

knows the Punjabis – they are all bananas! So Nanak must have thought that it was better to give them some underwear also, because their *salwar* could drop any moment, and then it would look a real mess and be embarrassing – a soldier need not stand naked in the field! Something like that must have been behind it.

This old *sardar* thought that I was a *sardar* because nobody who was not a *sardar* had ever spoken in the Golden Temple; it was unprecedented. He was certainly puzzled why I, such a religious man, had cut my hair. And I was only thirty at that time.

So I told him, "There is a reason in it. I don't feel yet a perfect *sardar*, and I don't want to claim anything that I am not. So I have kept four things but I have cut my hair. I will grow my hair when I am a perfect *sardar*."

He said, "That's right. It is tremendously significant that a man should think about this, that he should not pretend to be a perfect *sardar*. You are a better *sardar* than us: we think we are perfect because we have all five things."

From among these people I found my people. It was not difficult, it was very easy. I was speaking their language, their religious idioms, quoting their scriptures and giving *my* message. The intelligent people there immediately understood and they started gathering around me.

All over India I started creating groups of my own people. Now there was no need for me to speak on Sikhism, Hinduism, Jainism; there was no need, but for ten years I had been continually speaking on them. Slowly, when I had my own people, I dropped speaking on others. After traveling for twenty years I stopped traveling also, because there was no need. Now I had my people: if they wanted to come to me they could come.

So speaking on religion was an absolute necessity; there was no other way to hook my people. Everybody is already divided. It is not an open world: somebody is a Christian, somebody is a Hindu, somebody is a Mohammedan. It is very difficult to find a person who is nobody. I had to find my people from these closed flocks, but to enter their flock I had to talk their language. Slowly, slowly, I dropped their language. As my message became more and more clear, proportionately I slowly dropped their language.

After my years of giving sannyas, I gave this three-year period of silence, a gap when anybody who wanted to leave me, could leave because I don't want to interfere in anybody's life. If I can enhance, good. If I cannot enhance you and your being, then it is better that you move away from me. The people who were with me just because they enjoyed my discourses could not stand silence: they have left. Of course when somebody leaves he has to find some excuse just to justify himself; he *has* to justify himself. He cannot just say, "I am going because Osho no longer speaks." That would simply show that he was here not for me but only to listen to me. And he could have done that through a tape recorder, through a video; he could have read the books – that was not the problem. He was not with me. He was enjoying what I was saying, but it was not his search, it was only his entertainment.

This gap helped. First I had to find my people; but it is natural when you collect a large mass of people around you that a few unwanted ones are bound to enter accidentally. For example Neelam is with me whether I am speaking or not speaking, but her husband escaped. He was accidental; a nice person, a loving person, but he was only interested in my speaking. He used to come from the Punjab to Pune to listen to me; he came here too, but he could not find what he was seeking. It was just an entertainment. But to Neelam it was her life. He simply posed the question to her: "You can choose either to be here with Osho or come with me; I am going."

It was hard for Neelam, difficult, but she chose me, dropped her husband and forgot all about her family life. There she was rich, had her own beautiful house, had her own car, and everything. Here I see her working hard in the garden, on the road; but she is immensely happy and radiant as she has never been before. Her husband waited a few months – perhaps she would come; her daughter is also here, but her daughter also refused to go. Her daughter, Priya, chose me, whom she can only see on the drive-by, and dropped her father who loved her very much. Priya is their only child, but she refused to go. Even if Neelam had gone, then too she was going to remain here. Neelam's husband got married again, to a very rich widow. He was accidental: sooner or later, some way or other, he had to leave. He had just come following Neelam because he loved her.

So these three years helped: we have dropped all the unnecessary baggage – because as you move higher you have to drop more luggage. On the plains you can carry much luggage, but when you start moving uphill you will have to choose what is unnecessary and drop it. Still higher, a few more things have to be dropped.

When Edmund Hillary reached the peak of Everest he had no luggage at all. He was simply standing there with nothing, because everything had to be dropped by and by. When he started there had been so many things and equipment – this machine and that machine, and oxygen tanks... He was a scientific mind so there was all that luggage, with fifty servants carrying it. But by and by, at each camp something had to be dropped because it was becoming impossible. Just to carry yourself was enough. Standing on Everest, he was absolutely without luggage; one has to be weightless.

These three years have helped to drop much luggage; hence the difference you will see in my speaking. You will see many things; those who have heard me before and are hearing me now will feel in a great difficulty – so many shocks. But now I am simply speaking the truth that is mine, because now I can trust that you will understand, that you don't need some via media: Jesus, Mahavira, Buddha, Krishna. I can talk to you directly, immediately. I don't need to play a game with words.

So this gap was a discontinuity in a way. The game that I had to play was a necessary evil, otherwise it would not have been possible to find you. Do you think you would have come to an atheist, an amoralist, a godless, irreligious person? If you ask yourself that question you will understand why I had to use religion and religious terminology. I was using it against myself just for you. It was for your sake that I have been doing that whole number, but now there is no need.

Somebody has asked if people are sending me jokes the way they used to in Pune. They started sending jokes. I said no, because now I don't need jokes. I needed jokes at that time because it was an entertainment. It is no longer entertainment. If a joke comes on its own, just by the way, I am not averse to it. But now I want to speak spontaneously, directly, immediately, the simple truth that is mine.

That's why the lectures have become so long, because to talk on others was tedious for me, to tell you the truth. I managed to tolerate sixty minutes, seventy minutes, at the most ninety minutes. With more than that it was possible I may have forgotten on whom I was speaking! I had to keep questions and notes in front of me so I could remember that this was a Zen series, that this was a Sufi series, that this was a Hassid series, and didn't get mixed up. Teertha read the story and I kept another copy with myself so I didn't forget the story and get lost, because I could have easily moved in any direction.

Now there is no problem. I don't have to remember anybody, I can simply say whatever comes; hence the lecture has become too long. People have inquired as to why sometimes I finish abruptly – I never used to do that. That is true. When I was just entertaining you I gave the right beginning, gave the right middle and gave the right end; rounded, complete. But right now it is all raw, uncut – unpolished diamonds from the mine itself.

So there is no beginning in fact, and there is no end. Abruptly, I start. So as not to shock you I have persuaded Sheela to begin with a question. Otherwise if I begin speaking abruptly you will think I have gone completely out of my mind! Nobody is asking and I am answering! But that's actually the case: nobody is asking the questions, most of the questions I have to tell Sheela to write down. They are not somebody else's. So poor Sheela has to write down a question, then ask it, and because it is my own question I don't need to keep it in front of me. I am free to move in any way. Abruptly I start, and abruptly I stop – that's truly existential!

In life things start abruptly, things end abruptly, and you don't ask why. If somebody suddenly dies in the middle of the road, you don't tell him, "At least you could have waited till you reached the other side. In the middle of the road – is this a way to die? You could have chosen a weekend. Now people will have to ask for leave to come. You have raised all kinds of unnecessary problems. Could you not have waited a little – for Saturday or Sunday?"

But life ends abruptly, there is never a full stop, it is always a semi-colon. Not a single life has ever ended with a full stop – cannot. Something is always incomplete. Something is always growing and has not come to its full flowering; something is always on the move, and then there comes the abrupt end.

Beginnings are abrupt. If you look closely existence is abrupt, sudden – and I want these discourses to be existential. Yes, I will stop anywhere I feel to stop; there is no other consideration. You can see clearly now why I had to use religious language, and why now I am continually telling you to flush God down the toilet, to forget all about heaven and hell, and that the law of karma is nothing but *boo boo*. I am no longer showing any respect to Jesus, or Buddha, Mahavira, Krishna. I am just treating them as a headmaster treats his children. If they behave rightly then they will not be punished, that's all. If they don't behave rightly, then I am going to give them real hits that they will never forget.

Now I have no need for any camouflage. I can stand fully naked, as I am, open to you. There is no desire anywhere in me to say a single word that I cannot authenticate on my own authority. That's why I am saying my religion is godless, religionless. It looks strange to say a religionless religion, but the word *religion* in itself is beautiful. People have used it, abused it – that's why I said I hate it. The original meaning of the word is really beautiful, but who cares about the original meanings?

The original meaning of the word *religion* is "to bring all the parts together, to make it whole." As man exists he is many, a crowd. Religion means to put the crowd in such a harmony that it becomes one individuality. Literally so, because individuality literally means indivisibility: that it cannot be divided, that you are no longer fragments of a jigsaw puzzle, that every fragment is put where it should be and the puzzle disappears. The puzzle was there because fragments were in places where they are not supposed to be. Where your heart is supposed to be, it is not there. Where your intellect is supposed to be, it is not there. Where your emotions are supposed to be, they are not there. Everything is misplaced; your house is in a chaos. Religion means to create a cosmos within a chaos.

The word is beautiful in its original sense; hence I still use it. But to avoid misuse and the wrong associations, first I say religionless and then I say religion. All that you have understood about religion up to now, all that religions have been saying, I am denying in the word *religionless*. And all that has to be said and has not been said, I am saying in the word *religion*.

Those who are in search of truth will understand it, love it, enjoy it, will be nourished by it, because it is no longer intellectual entertainment; it is spiritual nourishment. I am pouring my heart into you. And now the time is ripe. Before it is too late I have to convey all that I have been waiting for years to convey.

I had to avoid a thousand and one things because they would have created immediate trouble. I said a thousand and one things because that was the only way to catch hold of my people. But now, allow me to relax so I can simply say whatsoever comes on its own. Not even I know what the next sentence or the next word is going to be. That's why many times I simply stop in the middle of the sentence. I have to wait. If it comes, it comes; if it does not come, I look at the clock. Whenever I look at the clock you can understand that I am waiting for the word and it is not coming.

Vivek was saying to me, "You go on criticizing J. Krishnamurti; Krishnamurti goes on saying things about you. You must both be giggling inside."

I said, "As far as I am concerned, I am certainly giggling. About Krishnamurti I cannot say that." He is incapable of giggling, absolutely incapable. He has forgotten to laugh; he is too serious, and as he becomes older he goes on becoming more and more serious, I can understand, and I could have been of immense help to him, but he cannot even tolerate seeing one of my sannyasins; otherwise I can give him a whole commune.

Krishnamurti has been looking for people who can understand him and do what he wants them to do. Now I have so many communes around the world, I can give him a whole commune. It will be a joy to me if he can get a little satisfaction in the last years, perhaps the last days of his life. He is ninety, any time he will pop off. Before he pops off I offer him any commune. If he wants this commune he can take this commune – I will withdraw. If he can manage my people... It is up to him. But he could not even manage Deeksha, although she tried hard to convince him: "I have left Osho, I am no longer with him."

He said, "It is good that you have left him, but I won't allow you in my kitchen – just get lost!" Why? Deeksha is such a good cook, she would have managed his kitchen perfectly; and he has not much of a kitchen anyway.

In his school, in Brockwood, where he stays in England, there are not more than a dozen boys and girls. They are the problem children; no school accepts them. When parents are tired, fed up, they send them to Krishnamurti's school because he allows anybody who comes. In fact not many come; I think not more than a dozen. Last time one of my friends visited, there were not more than eight children of all ages. And Krishnamurti lives there.

For Deeksha this would have been a very small job, but poor Deeksha would have felt good: if she has missed me, she has at least got hold of J. Krishnamurti. But he does not allow my sannyasins in his kitchen. He does not want to see any of my sannyasins sitting in front in his discourses. But that is his problem, it is not my problem. Many of his followers have become my sannyasins, many of his followers have been my lovers. Many of his lovers, many of his followers have been immensely interested in me. I don't see any problem.

So I said to Vivek, "I giggle – the whole situation is so absurd. Poor Deeksha asking to be allowed in the kitchen! He should have allowed her. This is just inhuman, to tell her to get lost. As far as I am concerned I am willing: he can take any of my communes. If he wants people who can risk everything, then I have got the people." But he cannot tolerate, he cannot risk being among my people. He is so enraged because what he wanted to do he has not been able to do, and I have managed to do it without much doing.

I don't do anything. I have told you, I am just a lazybones. That's how I have been my whole life: I don't do anything. But there is something in me that attracts people who do – and for no reward except that they are with me, except that they can bathe, be showered, in my presence, in my love. What other remuneration have they got? They are risking their whole lives.

I can give him the people he has not been able to find because he moved wrongly. He missed the train; but I am in the train and I can pull the emergency chain. If he wants me to get down I can get down and be in his place and he can take my place; there is no problem in it. But that will be a great problem to him because this world that I have created around me can be managed only by a non-existent manager like me.

He is after people too much. To each single person he will talk for three hours. He is after you too much – he will drive you nuts. One interview will be enough, you will not ask for a second interview. You may ask one thing and he will answer something else – completely, totally different. He is not listening to your questions; he is full of his own ideology. Your question is just a jumping board and then he starts throwing his ideology over you. Basically what he is doing is a contradiction: on the one hand he teaches that there is no need for a guide, no need for a master; and on the other hand he continues guiding people.

What is it all about, to go around the world, if you are not teaching people? Are you mad or something? You *are* teaching people. Perhaps you are teaching them to be against teaching but that does not matter; it is still teaching. You may be saying that there is no master, no disciple, but they start following *that*: "Yes, there is no master, no disciple; but we are Krishnamurti-ites, we follow you." You become the master, they become disciples. You get angry because you put people in a dilemma.

It is a very complex dilemma. If they really understand you, nobody should come to listen to you. That should be tried sometime: he comes to speak in Mumbai or New Delhi, and he simply sits there and nobody comes – because there is no master and there is no disciple, no teaching, no philosophy, nothing.

So he sits near Jehangir Art Gallery in Mumbai where all the crows of Mumbai gather in the evening – a great place he has chosen! Those crows must have been religious masters in their past lives because they are all teaching simultaneously, all the crows, while Krishnamurti teaches. And he tells people, "If you are attentive and aware, don't be bothered by the crows, you just listen to me."

But why? They are attentive and aware, and they are listening to the crows and not to you. Why should they listen to you? The crows are creating such chaos! That is their place: they are doing that every day, whether disciples come or not. You come only once a year for a few days; you are just an intruder in their territory. One day nobody should go, then his teaching will be fulfilled. But will he feel happy? No, he wants more people to come. And that's what goes on troubling him.

So I said to Vivek, "I can giggle because to me he is not a problem; to me nobody is a problem." But to him, somehow my existence hurts because *this* is what he wanted.

Just a few days ago Somendra wrote to one of the sannyasins here. The sannyasin had written to Somendra, "I am here in the commune, blissful as I have never been. I don't think I want to be anywhere else; this is the place." Somendra must have been trying to pull her away, because he is trying to create a commune in Switzerland.

Seeing by her letter that she is out of reach, he wrote, "If you are feeling happy there, then I am happy. God has given Osho what he wanted. I hope that one day God will give me also what I want."

Now, Somendra is naive. Compared to Krishnamurti, Somendra is naive. He does not know what he is writing. He does not know that deep down he is trying to compete with me. One day God will give him too, he hopes. Now, poor Somendra, nobody is preventing him. I can give him one of the communes in Switzerland – we have a beautiful commune. Why give it to him? – because there is no God, I know, and his hope will not be fulfilled; so when I can give him one, why bother God?

Just a single hint from your side, and I give the commune to you, and you do whatsoever you want to do. But no, he thinks it is God who has given me what I wanted and he is hoping that God... Do you think God will help *me*? I don't think so. God, if he is somewhere, must be trying hard to destroy everything: he must be entering the governor of Oregon, the attorney-general of Oregon, Senator Hatfield – or is it Fatfield? God must be getting into all the idiots of Oregon, the 1000 Friends of Oregon, all the watchdogs. God is barking from everywhere! And Somendra says that he has given me what I wanted. No, nowhere, in no scripture is it mentioned that God is so generous!

I am not a god, I am a human being: I can be generous. I have always been joking with Somendra; he was one of my patent fools – he could not understand it, he does not even understand now. A commune is not created by your effort or God's help. A commune is a spontaneous phenomenon. I have never asked you to come to me, I have never written letters to you to come to me. You have found me on your own. It is your search that has brought you to me.

Now, Somendra is writing to all the sannyasins everywhere, "Come, we are going to create a great commune." Nobody seems to be listening, and nobody seems to be coming. This is not the way. In the first place, he betrayed me. I had immense trust in him, and still have the same trust. I loved him as I love you. It makes no difference whether you are a sannyasin or not. What difference does it make?

But people who drop sannyas get into a very difficult situation. They cannot come back because they feel embarrassed: what to say now? – because when they dropped, people were asking, "Why are you dropping sannyas?" Then they were saying many things against me or against the commune or against the organization. Now, if they want to come back they have closed their doors on themselves. People will ask, "What happened? You were speaking against all these things; now is everything alright again?" With what face...?

I want to tell all of the sannyasins who want to come back that they will be welcomed with great joy. It is human once in a while to go astray. It is not something very serious at all, and with me nothing is serious. You wanted to taste the world as a non-sannyasin – perfectly good. Now you feel that it was not worthwhile, and you want to come back. It is your home – come back.

Why should this poor Somendra ask God? Because I know God is not there, nobody is going to answer. And if Somendra tries to create a commune on his own, he will get into a mess, into trouble, into all kinds of problems. He himself is not yet in a state where he can be of any real help to anybody. He himself needs help. His creating a commune is just like a blind man collecting other blind men and saying, "Come follow me."

Perhaps a few blind people may start following you, but sooner or later you will find yourself with your whole group in a ditch. One should be absolutely aware: do you have eyes? Can you see the light? Do you have that energy that you can share with people? If not, then don't try such an idiotic act because you are playing with people's lives. You are in darkness and you will lead those people into more darkness.

In those days I had to speak in the name of religion, in the name of God. It was compulsory. There was no alternative: it was not that I had not tried it. I had tried it, but found it simply closed people's doors. But I could see a simple way out. Even my father was puzzled, more so than anybody else, because he knew me from my very childhood – that I was an atheist, a born atheist; that I was against religion, against the priests. When I started speaking in religious conferences, he asked me, "What is happening? Have you changed?"

I said, "Not a bit, I have just changed my strategy; otherwise it is difficult to speak in the Hindu world conference. They won't allow an atheist on their stage. An amoralist, a godless person, they won't allow. But they invited me – and in the name of religion, I said everything against religion."

The Shankaracharya, the head of the Hindu religion, was presiding over the conference. The King of Nepal – Nepal is the only Hindu kingdom in the world – inaugurated the conference. The Shankaracharya was in great difficulty because what I was saying was absolutely sabotaging the whole conference. But the way I was presenting it, people were getting impressed. This old man became so angry that he stood up and tried to snatch away the microphone.

While he was trying to snatch it away, I said, "Just one minute and I will be finished." So just for one minute he stopped – and in one minute I managed!

I asked the people – there must have been at least one hundred thousand people – I asked them, "What do you want? He is the president, he can stop me if he wants, and certainly I will stop. But you are the people who have come here to listen. If you want to listen to me, then raise your hands; and to make it clear raise both your hands."

Two hundred thousand hands; I looked at the old fellow and said, "Now sit down. You are no longer president: two hundred thousand hands have canceled you completely. Whom do you represent? You were president – these people had made you president, now these people have canceled you. Now I will speak as long as I want to speak." It would have been impossible otherwise. I found hundreds of people from that gathering: Bihar became one of the most potential sources of my sannyasins.

In the same way I moved around the country going into religious conferences and catching hold of people. Once I had my own group in that city then I never bothered about their conferences; then my group was holding its own conferences, its own meetings. But it takes time.

Now I am not searching for anybody. I have found the people who are enough for my work to spread worldwide. That's why I want to complete the circle. Now I want to say things which I wanted to say in the beginning but which were difficult to say because nobody was ready to listen.

Now I have my people, whose hearts are open to absorb me, to take me in. And before I depart from the body, I would like to pour all that I have in you. It is almost like lighting one candle with another candle. You can go on lighting one candle with another candle: you can light millions of candles. The first candle does not lose anything, remember. It is not that it has lost so much light because now a million candles are burning. No, it has not lost anything, it has gained.

It was a lonely candle in a dark world. Now, millions of candles are showering their light all over the space. Their light is the same. Their flames are different. Each sannyasin has to be a flame unto himself, but the light of all the sannyasins will be the same: the light that I want to be spread all over the earth – because that is the only hope. Without it humanity cannot last more than fifteen years. But if we can create the light I am talking about, if we can make this whole world afire – and we *can*.

I started the journey alone. People went on coming and joining me; now there are thousands of sannyasins. And do you see? – I have not been on the road very long, just twenty-five years. The difficulties that I have been facing you will not be facing. The problems that I had to face, you will not be facing. One day, alone, I started. Now my candle is burning in thousands of candles.

Each candle has the same potential: it can light up millions of candles.

In the coming fifteen years everything will become intense: the danger will become intense; the challenge will become intense; the possibility of ultimate destruction will become intense. And the possibility of ultimate transformation will become intense. In these fifteen years everything is going to take the most intense form possible, because a planet that has been working for millions of years to create human consciousness has come to a space where either death or total transformation will be the only alternatives.

Old religions are just dead. They don't give any option; they are dying with the dying society, and there is nobody except you. You should understand the gravity, the significance, the responsibility. There is nobody on the whole earth like you, nobody who has dropped all the old rubbish and who is ready to become a new kind of man.

Don't be worried that you are such a small minority. The day I started I was alone. Even at that time I did not think that I was a minority, because truth is never a minority. Truth is always the whole – not even the majority but the whole, one hundred percent.

My grandfather used to ask me, "You are thinking to transform the whole world alone?"

I said, "With just a small candle I can burn the whole forest. An atom bomb is not needed; one just has to choose the right timing. If the wind is blowing toward the forest, then just a single candle and the whole forest will be afire. So don't think that I am alone, and what can I do?"

My grandfather was not alive when I started initiating people into sannyas, otherwise he would have been immensely happy that what

I had said to him had happened. You are not a small minority, don't think in those terms. A single sannyasin – even a single sannyasin – is not a minority, because the truth that burns in him and the light that he holds in his hands, the torch that he holds in his hand, is enough to create the whole face of the earth.

It is going to happen – and not with God's help, because God's help has been coming for thousands of years and you see what has happened. This time, without God – at least give it a try this time without God, without heaven, without hell, without all that crap!

Just give a chance to pure humanity, to the ordinary, natural human being.

And I say to you it *is* going to happen – no God can prevent it.

CHAPTER 5

Superman: The Fantasy for the Inferior

Osho,
Isn't the vision of the new man somehow similar to the idea of the superman?

The idea of the new man is not only *not* similar to the idea of the superman, it is just the very opposite. The superman is a continuity with the old man; the new man is a discontinuity with the old man. The superman is superior, higher, but still belongs to the same world of the old man. He is better, stronger, more beautiful, more powerful, more intelligent; but the difference is only of degrees, of more or less.

The new man is absolutely unrelated to the old man. The superior man, the superman, is a refinement of the old. The new man is the death of the old man. The new man comes into being when the old man dies, hence they cannot be similar at all. They may sound similar to those who think only intellectually. I am not an intellectual, neither am I a thinker. I see things; I am a seer and in my eyes the superman and the new man are just the contrary to each other.

The old society, culture, religion, philosophy are not against the superman; in fact the superman is their projection, their desire, their hope. They have been working for thousands of years to produce the superman. And in the name of the superman they have tortured the poor common man so much: it is almost impossible to believe how much humanity has been sacrificed in order to bring the superman onto the earth.

What was Adolf Hitler doing? He was fascinated with the idea of superman. He got it from Friedrich Nietzsche. Now, it is a strange thing to understand that the people who have been interested in the superman were very inferior kinds of people. Strange, but not irrelevant. Somehow, deep down, you feel yourself inferior, and to forget that inferiority you start imagining, projecting, just the opposite of it: the superman.

Nietzsche was in love with a woman, Wagner's wife. Wagner was one of the great musicians, a great master as far as music is concerned; and he was tremendously charismatic. He was not only a maestro of music but his playing had some touch of magic too. That's what makes a difference. The same music may be played by many people – it may be the same instrument, the same music, the same notes, but somebody simply gives wings to it and it goes on soaring higher and higher. It takes you beyond yourself into unknown spaces.

With someone else it is just ordinary music. It takes you nowhere; at the most, it is a kind of entertainment. You have nothing to do so you listen to the music. At least it keeps you occupied in the same way that smoking keeps somebody occupied, or gossiping keeps somebody else occupied. But when a man like Wagner plays music he gives a new dimension to your being, he opens up new doors. You start moving into dimensions you have not even dreamed of.

Nietzsche was learning music from the master and fell in love with the master's wife, not thinking at all that he had a very poor personality, in no way to be compared with Wagner. Of course Wagner's wife was not interested; she had not even thought about Nietzsche. He was ugly looking, not even physically attractive like Wagner – what to say about the spiritual quality of Wagner and his artistic mastery of music? In the whole history of man there are not many names which can be compared to Wagner's, not more than you can count on your fingers. He is one of the greatest musicians.

The woman had fallen in love not only with the man but with the music which surrounded that man and the magic that was somewhere absolutely present, almost tangible. There was no question of comparing Nietzsche with him. When Nietzsche approached her, she simply laughed and said, "You must be a fool! Even if God were standing before me my choice would be Wagner, because I cannot believe even God can be so charismatic.

"When Wagner plays I cannot believe that I am his wife and so fortunate to be so close to him. He is so far away and yet so compassionate that he allows me the intimacy. I know that I am not worthy; it is his compassion. Far more beautiful women are mad about him. Anybody who has any sensitivity to music and to the charismatic personality of a person is bound to fall in love with him.

"How could you think," she told Nietzsche, "that I could even think about you? Simply forget all about it. You are nowhere. And it is disgraceful: you are a student of my husband and he trusts you, that's why you are allowed in the house. You are just like a son to him, and I am just like a mother to you – age does not matter."

This was such a shock and such an exposure of Nietzsche's own inferiority that never again in his life did he approach another woman; he lost his nerve. But after that day he started thinking of a new race of man: the superman. He wrote against Wagner, he became an enemy. Wagner could not understand why, because he had no idea of what had transpired between his wife and his disciple; why Nietzsche had left and gone to the mountains.

Nietzsche took the wound really seriously. It created an immense hatred in him for women and for all the qualities that are womanly. For example, he started hating compassion, love, sympathy, kindness – these are all womanly qualities. He started hating Jesus, he started hating Gautam the Buddha, simply because they were teaching womanly qualities. Nonviolence is womanly, violence is manly; to be a real man you have to be violent. His mind became completely perverted from the shock.

Jesus is talking about humbleness and meekness; those are womanly qualities. Jesus has destroyed man's manliness. It is womanly, that when somebody hits your face you have to give him your other cheek. What else can be more womanly? But can you see how things are associated? One woman's rejection caused his rejection of all womankind, and not only of womankind but also of qualities which have something in them which can be called womanly.

He condemned Gautam Buddha, saying, "It is because of Buddha that India became cowardly – he taught India to be womanly." He said, "All these saints are not even worth comparing with soldiers. Even a third-rate soldier is better than a first-rate saint." Now, the soldier! – and he himself was not a soldier; he himself was not even tall enough to be accepted in the army. He had tried and was rejected because he was not tall enough. There is a possibility that somewhere in his parentage some crossbreeding must have happened: he was not Nordic German – neither was Adolf Hitler Nordic German. Nordic Germans, if they are pure blood, are tall, blond, strong people. But neither Nietzsche was strong and tall nor was Adolf Hitler.

Nietzsche says, "The only beautiful thing that I remember in my life is when one morning as the sun was rising I saw a long brigade of soldiers marching on the street. Their naked swords were shining in the morning sun, almost like lightning. Their boots falling in tune were so musical that I have never heard any music comparable to it. Their uniforms and the harmony and the early morning sun...!" People have talked about lotus flowers in the early morning sun, of roses in the early morning sun, but Nietzsche is the only one in the whole history of man who talks about soldiers in the early morning sun and the beauty of the swords shining and the music of their boots: right, left, right, left, in harmony – the music! He says, "I never came across such a beautiful experience again."

Now he himself was not an athlete, he was not a soldier. I don't think he would have been able to hold a sword rightly, or know how to keep hold of it. He was a man who knew how to hold a fountain pen, not a sword. For his whole life he was simply writing; he had never fought. But he started projecting the idea of the superman.

Nietzsche started condemning the old man without ever thinking that he belonged to the old. It happens: one can put oneself aside, and put the old man on this side and the superman on that side; then you think you are not part of the old man. But because you are creating the idea of the superman, you start believing yourself that superman is your projection, your idea: you are giving birth to superman – then of course you belong to the superman. That's how one tries to forget one's inferiority.

Nietzsche never attempted to approach another woman for the simple reason that it might again provoke the feeling of inferiority;

once was enough. He was a very egoistic type of man. It is a rare phenomenon: if a woman says "I am not in love with you," that does not mean that there will never be a woman who will accept you. And he had qualities of his own; there was no need to be another Wagner. He was not a musician, but he had his own qualities: he was a great philosopher. But the insult went so deep he forgot all about his qualities and started comparing himself only with Wagner.

He influenced many people – all of them strange in a certain way. He influenced George Bernard Shaw – similarly a very egoistic man, a showman. If you read George Bernard Shaw's books you will be surprised that the book is small but the preface is big. That has happened for the first time in the whole history of the world of literature: the preface is big and the book is small! Why? The book should be enough to explain itself. That's what art, creativity, means.

The best painters have not titled their paintings, what to say of a preface? They have realized that if the painting is not explanatory itself, a title will not help. It should be left to the person who is seeing the painting to understand it according to his capacity, understanding, intelligence.

To put a title on a painting means you are worried that your painting is not going to be understood so you have to give a hint. But to give a title to a painting is to make it small and closed; it is a way of framing it. You have framed it with the title. Now you are telling the person this painting only means this, nothing else. You have taken the multidimensionality of the painting and given it a very small frame. You have destroyed it.

Bernard Shaw's books are not difficult; you don't need to be a genius to understand them. He wrote only dramas, and even those not of a very high quality. Anybody with a little bit of intelligence, even if below mediocrity, would be able to understand them. But perhaps he suffered from some inferiority himself. Perhaps he thought that nobody would understand the drama, perhaps he himself did not understand it rightly.

He had written it but he was not certain whether he had written that which he wanted to write, whether he had given it the right expression, the right words. Is it certain that it will be understood? He was in a confusion, hence the long preface. The preface destroys the whole drama because he tried to explain everything in it. When you have understood everything about the drama, what is left in it?

It is as if somebody tells you the whole story of a movie and then gives you a ticket, saying "Go, I have brought a ticket for you." He has destroyed everything by telling you the whole story; now the ticket is absolutely useless. You will simply be bored because there is not going to be any excitement. You know already what is going to happen, you know already the end from the very beginning.

Bernard Shaw did exactly that, and did it to such an extent: one-hundred-page, two-hundred-page prefaces for a twenty-page drama. I don't think that any psychoanalyst has tried – I have never come across anything – but Bernard Shaw needs to be psychoanalyzed. Why did he write these long prefaces to ordinary dramas? He simply projected himself. It seems that if the drama were written by somebody else he would not understand it, he would need a big introduction. That's what he was doing.

George Bernard Shaw was impressed by Nietzsche's idea of superman; he wrote a drama on superman too. Strangely enough, he was also rejected by a woman. The name of the woman was Annie Besant. She was the godmother – is it okay to use "godmother" as well as "godfather"? – of J. Krishnamurti. She was the president of the Theosophical Movement for the whole world. She was a very beautiful woman with great charisma of her own, very intelligent, and one of the greatest orators ever. If she had remained in England she would have become prime minister anytime, because none of the prime ministers of her time had the same charisma, or the art of speaking that she had.

Bernard Shaw heard her for the first time in a Theosophical conference and he immediately fell in love. When he approached her she said, "Please excuse me, I have far bigger things to do." And certainly she had far bigger things to do than to be the wife of George Bernard Shaw. But George Bernard Shaw thought that he was the greatest man on the earth: "And she has far greater things to do...?" The wound remained with him.

Annie Besant became more and more popular. It is simply unbelievable that she became the president of the Indian National Congress. When India was under the British Raj, a British woman was accepted by Indian revolutionaries – who were fighting the British Raj – as their president! You can understand her charisma. Even the white skin was hated because that represented the rulers, the oppressors. And to accept a woman who comes from the same country with which you are fighting... The Indian National Congress was the party struggling with Britain to get independence and it accepted her as president. She must have had a magic personality. So if she refused Bernard Shaw, I don't think that she did anything wrong; she certainly had much bigger things to do.

She made the whole Theosophical Movement for the first time into a worldwide movement. She created the idea that a world teacher is going to be born and made the idea worth believing by millions of people. It is not so easy. Even Jesus was not able to convince his own people that he was the messiah. But this woman was saying, "I am going to introduce to you, at the right moment, the messiah who is going to save the whole world," and millions of people believed in her word. *She* was not the messiah, but she had some quality of creating trust in people.

Bernard Shaw was rejected by Annie Besant; he carried that wound his whole life and started projecting the idea of the superman.

Adolf Hitler was the second person who became a disciple of Friedrich Nietzsche, and he was in every way intellectually inferior. Even to call him mediocre does not feel justified; the word falls short, he was far below mediocrity. He had no intelligence of any kind; he was absolutely an idiot. He should have been born in Oregon; it was just an accident that he was born in Germany. Germany is not the right place for such great idiots.

He was rejected from the school of architecture – he wanted to become an architect. He was rejected from art school – he wanted to become a painter. He was rejected from the army because he could not prove his mettle in the First World War. He was a coward: he used every excuse to hide and keep himself behind, and not go forward and rush toward the enemy. Whenever it was time to fight, he would fall sick. He would manage to produce a stomachache, a headache, backache – anything which cannot be proved.

Now there is no way to prove whether a headache is there or not. One of my teachers used to begin his class every day with this ritual: "First listen to my conditions. I don't accept a headache, I don't accept a stomachache. Things that I cannot find, I don't accept. Yes, if you have fever, I accept it because I can check that your temperature is high. So remember, nobody is to ask leave for things which are unprovable. Even a doctor cannot prove whether there is a headache or not." He prevented almost everything because you had to produce a visible disease, only then could you get out; but I had to find some way around it because this was unacceptable.

He was an old man, so all that I had to do was in the night... He was old, but very strong and very particular about exercise, about walking, so he used to get up early, at five o'clock, and go for a long walk in the dark. So I just had to put a few banana peels in front of his door. In the morning he fell, and had a bad back. I was available immediately because I knew about it.

He said, "My back is hurting so much."

I said, "Don't mention anything which you cannot prove."

He said, "But whether I can prove it or not, I am not able to come to school today."

"Then," I said, "you will have to stop your conditions from tomorrow, because I am going to spread the whole thing to the whole school, that if a bad back is accepted... What proof have you got? Then why not a headache? Why not a stomachache?"

He said, "I think you have something to do with these banana peels here."

I said, "Perhaps you are right, but you cannot prove it, and I believe only in things which can be proved."

He said, "You can at least do me one favor: you can take my application to the principal."

I said, "I will take your application, but remember, from tomorrow stop those conditions, because sometimes I have a headache, sometimes I have a stomachache, because I am accustomed to eating all kinds of unripe fruits – when you are stealing from other people's gardens, you cannot ask that they should be ripe. You can get them only before they are ripe; once they are ripe the people take them. So I suffer from stomachache." From that day he stopped the conditions. He just looked at me, smiled, and started his class.

The students were simply shocked: "What has happened to him? What about the conditions?"

I stood up and said, "I have a lot of pain in my stomach."

He said, "You can go." He told me in the evening when he came to see my father, "This is the first time I have given leave to anybody for a stomachache, because these people are just so imaginative and inventive." He told my father, "Your boy is dangerous."

I said, "Again you are trying to do something which you cannot prove, you are just assuming. I was simply going for a morning walk and I saw you fall, and I just went to help you to get up. Do you think it is wrong to help somebody?"

He said, "No, it is not wrong to help somebody; but who put those banana peels there?"

I said, "That, you have to find out – it is *your* house. It was just coincidence that I was going for a morning walk; and my father knows that every day I go for a morning walk."

My father said, "That's true, he goes every day. It is possible he may have done it but unless you prove it, it is no use: we have to prove things to him. If argumentatively he wins, then even though we are right, he is the winner and we are the losers. He has told me the whole story about your bad back, and that since then you have stopped your two conditions."

My father had also been his student. He said, "This is strange, because you never began without those two conditions."

My teacher said, "Never before did I have this kind of student. I had to change my whole plan because it is dangerous to be in conflict with him; he could have killed me."

When Adolf Hitler was in the army he continually had headaches, backaches, stomachaches – any excuse to get into hospital just so that he did not go on the battlefield. After the First World War he was refused by the army. Now, this man was unemployed with no qualifications. He gathered seventeen other unemployed soldiers who had been rejected by the army, and those eighteen people created the National Socialist Party – the Nazi Party. Their ideal was: "We have to conquer the whole world because that's God's mission given to the Nordic Germans, the purest Aryan race. The mission is to rule the world. The world consists of pygmies."

Now, Adolf Hitler was a pygmy in every way; in no way can you find anything which has any value. But he got the idea moving, and the Nordic Germans started feeling that they had a certain mission, that they were the chosen few of God. Why was he so much against the Jews? One of the reasons was that the Jews have been saying since Moses that *they* are the chosen few of God.

Now, there cannot be two races chosen by God; so either the Nordic Germans are the chosen race, or the Jews. It had to be proved. Hitler started killing the Jews. He said, "The Jews have to be completely erased because they have been pretending that they are the chosen few – while we are the chosen few and have not been even aware of it." And it got into the minds of people. The mind gets such ideas very easily and makes you afire because you suffer from so many inferiorities.

Everybody in life comes across boundaries he cannot cross over and feels inferior; comes against walls, gets hit and has to turn back. Everybody in life some way or other has to face the problem of inferiority. If somebody gives you the idea that you are one of the chosen few of God, you are going to buy it. And Hitler was giving it free, he was not charging you anything; he was making you the very top. Nietzsche's books became Hitler's bible.

The third man who was impressed was Sri Aurobindo in India. He was also suffering from a tremendous inferiority complex. Sri Aurobindo was educated in England. He belonged to a rich family and was going to become an ICS, a member of the Indian Civil Service, which was the topmost bureaucracy in India, created by the British. To be an ICS one had to pass many examinations in England, and naturally it was very difficult for Indians to pass those examinations. The examinations were such that Indians were not accustomed to them.

For example, Aurobindo failed in only one subject – horse riding. Indians are not interested in horse riding; English people are. Indians are not interested at all in horse riding, nobody thinks it of some great value; in fact Jainas prohibit it because to ride on a horse is to be violent. Who are you to ride on the horse? If horses start riding on you would you like the idea? Jainas are averse to it. And in India nobody is interested in horse riding the way British are.

So, of course, Aurobindo was not a good horse rider compared with British students, but in all other subjects he passed. One wonders what an ICS officer has to do with horse riding, but you don't know the ways of imperialism. Horse riding had a certain purpose for the ICS officer. In India, the moment you saw a white man dressed in army uniform with a gun, and riding on a beautiful horse, it was the symbol of imperialism and its power.

Now, Aurobindo was a Bengali, so I don't think he could have managed even to ride a donkey! Donkeys are also very clever; I have been riding on them so I know. You can try it, and you will find that donkeys have a special trick. They will never walk in the middle of the road; they will always go to the side and rub you against the walls of the houses. It is impossible to keep them in the middle of the road: they will simply move either to this side or to that side and rub against the wall. Of course they will damage your leg and you will have to get down. They are simply saying, "Get down, get lost!"

Aurobindo was very shocked because he came back having failed, and to be an ICS was his ambition. Inferiority always has great ambitions; the inferiority complex is the base of all ambition. Now, to be an ICS officer was the greatest ambition any Indian could have in the British regime because it was the topmost position you could reach; more than that was not available to Indians. One Indian might succeed in reaching it out of thousands of ICS officers, so it was really something superior.

Aurobindo came back frustrated, with great anger, jealousy, rage; and he joined the Indian National Congress – the party that was trying to throw out the British Empire. Just look at the facts. He had gone to join the British Empire, and if only he had succeeded in horse riding he would have been a supporter of the British Empire; he would have been killing those people whom he was now joining. Now he wanted to *destroy* the British Empire. Can you see how people's minds work?

He was not a nonviolent revolutionary, no. He did not believe in Gandhi, he was not a follower of Gandhi. He was a believer in violence: he wanted the British people to be killed, burned, destroyed. He was trying to make bombs and was caught red-handed, and suffered a few years in jail.

It is very interesting to look into people's lives. If you have an unprejudiced mind then strange facts start coming up. When Aurobindo was in jail he suddenly became a religious man. From being thrown out of the ambition that he was trying to fulfill, he moved to the opposite extreme: he wanted to take revenge, but now in the name of revolution. Then, when he was put into jail, he saw the whole thing: that it was not so easy to overthrow this great empire with just creating hand bombs; it was just befooling yourself. You may kill one or two persons or you may destroy a bridge, but that is not going to destroy the empire; it is not possible. The empire has tremendous power.

Then how to fulfill the ambition? He had seen that he could not succeed in Britain in becoming an ICS officer; he had seen that he could not become the great leader of the Indian revolution.

He turned to religion. He could become a great saint; at least nobody could prevent him doing that. That is the cheapest way in the whole world. Who can prevent you? There is no competition either.

Aurobindo became a religious person. He started writing a commentary on the Shrimad Bhagavadgita in jail. When he was released, the first thing he did was to escape from the British Empire. Pondicherry was not part of British India; it was a small place under the French empire. It is part of India now, but three hundred years ago when all European powers were struggling to capture India, Britain succeeded in capturing almost the whole of India: France only succeeded in capturing a small place, Pondicherry, and Spain succeeded in having only one small place, Goa, and two small islands, Daman and Diu.

Why did Aurobindo escape to Pondicherry? It was just close to Bengal. He was a coward; now he was afraid to face his revolutionary friends. He could not say to them that now he was no longer a revolutionary, that he wanted to become a saint – which is the safest way to fulfill your ambition to become respectable, honorable and great. He created his ashram in Pondicherry.

He was immensely interested in the idea of the superman. In fact he made it his life's ambition. He said, "I am going to bring the superman into myself. The superman will descend from heaven into my body, so I am trying to purify my body so that the superman will descend." For thirty years he remained in a closed house, and his followers believed that he was purifying his body. Now, if you look at his literature you can see perfectly well that for all those thirty years he was continually writing, because that literature is not spoken, it is written. The volume of literature is so big that I suspect he had no time left to purify his body. And what purification? – the body *is* pure. What can you do with it? What is wrong with the body? For anything that is wrong you need medical science to help you. In a closed room how are you going to purify your body?

He became fatter and fatter, that's all. He had been a very lean and thin young man, but just reading and writing, reading and writing... And his writing is the worst possible. One sentence will continue for almost the whole page. You will forget about the beginning of the sentence by the time you have reached the end. By the end of the page you will have to go back again to the beginning to see what words the sentence had started with.

Aurobindo's books are unreadable, pedantic, verbose. He uses big words because he thinks the bigger the word, the more unused it is by people, the more mystified they will be. And it happened – people *were* mystified. People are very strange: they get impressed by things which they cannot understand. If they can understand, they don't get impressed. Their logic is simple: "If I can understand it there is nothing in it." Unless they feel "I cannot understand it," they cannot believe that something higher, something of the beyond, is there. The way he has written is just to mystify. There is no need to write a paragraph or a page as one sentence. It is simply ridiculous if you want your word to reach to people. But no, he wanted to mystify.

I have gone through all his books and I have suffered so much. You cannot believe how much I have suffered through such people. I had gone through all his books simply to see what this man was trying to do. In those books there is nothing. You dig up a whole mountain and you don't find even a rat! But they are big volumes, one thousand pages; and there are big words. He was clever enough to make and create big words, for example, *supramental*. And he would create categories.

For the superman to arrive, first you have to create the state of *supramental*, and for that you have to purify your body. He declared that he was going to be physically immortal. Up to now Mahavira, Buddha, Krishna, Christ, Mohammed have all said that the soul is eternal. Aurobindo said, "I am going to prove that only an eternal body can contain an eternal soul. My body is going to live forever, it is immortal."

Now this kind of thing is simple nonsense. But there is one good thing about such statements: you can never prove such statements wrong because if the man dies, to whom are you going to prove he is wrong? And if he lives, of course he is immortal. This is the trick behind the statement, "I am going to be immortal. I have purified my body, and the superman is descending, slowly, slowly coming into this body. This body is going to be immortal, and then I will teach my disciples to be immortal."

Hundreds of people, hoping to be physically immortal, followed Sri Aurobindo their whole life. The day he died, one of my friends was in his ashram; he was his follower. I had been telling him again and again, "Don't be a fool! The body cannot be immortal, it is made of mortal things. Perhaps one can live a little longer, but to live eternally...! You can see the body is continually changing: the child is becoming a young man, the young man is becoming old, the old man is becoming older. Death does not come suddenly, it is coming from the very day you were born. Somebody who says his body is going to be immortal has to prove that his body has stopped changing.

That was my argument to my friend: "If you can manage to send a message" – because Aurobindo used to see his disciples only once a year, and that too simply for *darshan*. He would not talk, he would not answer; he would simply sit there and people would pass by him in a line – you could see him just for a moment. So I said to my friend, "If somehow you can send a message..."

There was a way. The woman who was in charge of the ashram was called "the Mother." People have completely forgotten her name, they have forgotten even her profession. She was a film actress who fell in love with Sri Aurobindo. She dropped her husband and became a disciple – because obviously the idea of physical immortality will appeal more to women than to men.

Women are more physical, more grounded, and have more of a sense of their body. I don't think women believe much in the soul, because they cannot see any soul in the mirror. What they cannot see in the mirror is just a stupid men's idea. All women know that men go on playing with words and philosophy and religion. The woman is not interested in these things. She is more interested in gossip, in juicy things; what is happening in the neighborhood, who has purchased a new car and who has purchased new clothes and who has made a new house. They are not worried about God at all. It is not their concern. If they become concerned it is because of men. Because men are continually worried about God and soul and heaven and hell, the woman thinks, "Perhaps there is something in it; if so many men are interested in it, who knows? It is better at least to keep quiet about it, not to say anything." But I know every woman feels that all this is simply jargon.

This French actress became interested in the idea of physical immortality. She was a powerful woman and really capable of organizing, so Aurobindo could withdraw – he had a good organizer at hand. He wanted all his time to write. He was trying to create the whole philosophy of the superman: all the stages, methodologies to purify the body and the mind, what stages you will reach, what lights you will see and what colors will appear at what stage. If you read him you will think, "Perhaps this man is talking sense, because he talks like somebody talking about geography. He can show you everything on the map."

But looking at his books, all I can say to you is that he was a good linguist and knew how to play with words and language. For thirty years he was in isolation. Nothing was being purified; it was just that he needed time to study and to write. And his voluminous literature is proof enough – nobody could produce that much literature if he were not continually working at least twelve or fourteen hours a day. The sheer volume is proof enough.

So I told my friend, "Send this message to Aurobindo: 'If you say you have attained immortality physically, then one thing can be the proof. If you die then whom are we going to ask? If you don't die and you continue not to die, of course you are right – because you are living. But I have found a criterion of immortality: the criterion is that your body should not change anymore – because death is only a change. If you are young, then you should not become old; if your hair is black it should not grow white. That will be proof enough.'"

But my friend said, "His hair is gray and he is looking older and older every year. We can feel it more clearly because we see him only after a year." When you see a person every day you cannot detect that he is becoming older. But if you see him after a gap of a year you can immediately see how much change has happened, how much his hair has gone gray, how much his face has wrinkled, how much older he is looking.

So I said, "If he cannot prevent old age, then be certain that he cannot prevent death, because old age is just a preparation for death." And that's what happened: one day Aurobindo died. When he died it was a great shock to his disciples who lived in his ashram and to his followers who were all around the earth, because who does not want to be physically immortal?

There are people in America, at least ten of them, whose dead bodies are preserved – those bodies belong to multi-millionaires – in the hope that within the coming ten to fifteen years, science will be able to revive a dead man. Those people have put all their money into a trust so that their bodies should be preserved exactly as they were when they died. So if, after ten or fifteen years, science becomes capable of reviving the body, their bodies will be revived.

Do you see man's ambitions, his poverty, his inferiority, his fear of death, his lust for life? Even after death they are hoping...! Millions of dollars are being wasted on their bodies because they have a trust; it is their money. They are being preserved, frozen, completely frozen. Even if they come back after fifteen years, what are they going to do? They won't see anybody around whom they had left. Their wives may have gone, their children may have died. And even if the children are there, who will want them? Who would like to have them back? Just think: your father comes after fifteen years of being a ghost; one day he suddenly comes home. You may die just with the shock of seeing your father standing before you.

People are talking about the generation gap – have you thought about the gap between the dead and the living? If after fifteen years a person comes back to life, he will not find anything recognizable, everything will be different. Perhaps he will not find the same world at all; perhaps the Third World War will have happened and he may wake up to start the whole game again: to go in search for Eve! If by chance he finds an Eve, then they will both have to think twice before they take the jump: should we start that whole thing again? If they have any intelligence they won't because once was enough – look what happened to it!

But people are interested in immortality. Aurobindo exploited the idea of the superman: physical immortality was his contribution. Nietzsche was not thinking of that, neither was Bernard Shaw, nor was Adolf Hitler. But Aurobindo, being an Indian, contributed to the idea. He was not very original because the immortality of the soul has always been talked about. He simply transferred it to the body: immortality of the body.

When he died, they kept it a secret for three days because the Mother, the organizer of the ashram, said, "He cannot die, that is impossible. It must be a certain stage when he is going out of the body, and the superman is getting into the body. It is just the interim stage, the interval.

"Of course if somebody is getting out of a house he has to take his luggage and furniture and mattresses; and there are so many things to move out of the house. Then the other will bring his own mattresses, his own furniture. And who knows what kinds of things that superman needs? He will bring his own paraphernalia. So it is just an interval." People are so foolish. That's why I ask what kind of humanity we have, that people believed that it was an interval?

The body was kept in secret, and they were praying and waiting for the superman to descend. They were rejoicing because they thought, "Now it is happening" – and all that was happening was that the body was deteriorating: it started to stink. Then the Mother became afraid, so she said, "It seems it will take longer for the superman to descend, so we have to preserve the body inside a marble grave." You will not believe it: there are still people in Aurobindo's ashram who are waiting, thinking that one day he will knock inside the grave and say, "Now please open up: the superman has arrived."

The man died. Then the Mother started pretending the same role: that her body had become immortal. Of course she lived for long, almost a century, but if you had seen her face before she died, you would have thought that this face could only be of a ghost: she was just a skeleton, with wrinkled skin. You could count, even from a photograph, how many bones there were in her neck, and how many blood vessels were going down her neck. There was no need for any X ray, just seeing her was enough. You could have seen everything that was in her – nothing was left. The same people who had seen Aurobindo dying started to believe that she was immortal. Then she died and again the same stupidity: three days' interval, then the stinking body, then again another grave – and waiting. People are still waiting.

The idea of the superman is basically rooted in your feeling of inferiority, of fear, of death. But the new man has nothing to do with all this. The new man is the very ordinary man: nothing special, nothing superior, *supramental*.

The new man is the first man who recognizes that it is enough to be human. There is no need to be a superman. There is no need to become gods and goddesses. It is so fulfilling just to be an ordinary human being. I declare to you: there is nothing above human consciousness. Everything that is possible is within you. You are not to become special, superior; you have to become absolutely simple, ordinary, just nobodies.

One day I had a small meeting with Sheela and the group that works with her, and Hasya, John and their group. They were somehow feeling that they were not joining together and that somehow the gap was increasing. I had called a meeting of all and I also called Hanya.

Hanya is neither of this group nor of that. She is a simple woman, and I had especially called her to see the reaction of a simple nobody.

What I expected happened: Hanya freaked out. She could not understand. What politics? Why should these people be quarreling or arguing or creating a gap? They are both working for me – all are working for me. But I wanted to see the reaction of someone who has no political mind, no kind of division, who is simply in love with what I am doing; someone who has no ambitions, no ideas to make into a reality. She freaked out – that was expected.

Sheela told me, "Hanya is very disturbed and wants to leave."

I said that there was nothing to worry about; I knew that that was what was going to happen. I was expecting that she would not be able to understand. Sheela and her group understood, Hasya and her group understood and the gap has been dropped. The only person who was at a loss was Hanya.

I would like you all to be like Hanya – so simple, so innocent, that you cannot even understand what politics is, why people go on fighting, quarreling. For what? It is such a small life; we cannot be certain even of tomorrow and we are wasting it for some great ideals in the future, we start fighting about those ideals.

There was a case in an Indian court: two friends were brought into the court. The whole court knew they were great friends, but they suddenly started beating each other. The police came, the friends were caught and taken to the court. The police asked, "Why were you fighting?"

One said to the other, "You say it," and the other said, "*You* say it" – and both felt embarrassed.

The judge said, "Enough! You simply have to answer: what was the reason you were fighting? Why were you creating a nuisance in the village? You were so angry and violent you could have killed. You both have to say what the reason was."

They said, "We feel very embarrassed to say it, but now if you force us, we have to."

One said, "We were both sitting by the side of the riverbank on the sand, and I was saying to my friend that I was going to purchase a buffalo, and he said, 'Nothing doing. You are not going to purchase a buffalo, I won't allow it.'

"I said, 'This is something! Who are you to prevent me? I am purchasing the buffalo with my own money; I am not asking you to give me money. Who are you to decide it?'

"Then my friend said, 'I have told you this is not going to happen because my farm is at the side of your field. If your buffalo enters my farm, I am telling you, I will kill it. I don't want any nuisance around my farm.'

"I said, 'You will kill my buffalo? Let us see.'

"My friend drew his farm on the sand with his finger and said, 'This is my farm; now I will see. Bring your buffalo in' – so with my finger I drew my buffalo coming."

And that was the point when they started beating each other; and that's why they were feeling embarrassed, because there was no buffalo, no field, and they were almost on the verge of killing each other!

All the politics of the world is like that. Why are people fighting in the name of religion, in the name of a political ideology: socialism, Communism, democracy, Fascism? – just words, just fingers drawing lines on the sand. What are your maps but lines drawn by fingers on the sand? If I say I am coming into your land without a passport, without a visa, immediately your army and National Guard are ready to kill me. Just on the map: I cannot even *say* it – it is a criminal act.

Strange: the earth has no boundaries, but you cannot get into Russia, you cannot get into America. Although I have been here for four years, I am not here. Rajneeshpuram has been here for four years; there are seven thousand people living here – enjoying, dancing, doing all kinds of things that should be done, and should not be done. But for the government there is no such thing. You don't exist!

Your city is really unique in the whole history of humanity. There have been cities and there have been no cities; but an illegal city? – never heard of before. It is a city, but illegal. It is not recognized that you are here. Ignored, you don't exist.

I am here, and I am going to be here. There is no way to send me back because I have my own arrangements. I persuaded the Indian government to reject me, so where are you going to send me? You can only deport me to India. I persuaded India beforehand; they are not going to accept me at all. Now I am stuck here in the Big Muddy Ranch. There is no way, no crane to get me out.

But these fools are in power. They have removed even the name of Rajneeshpuram from the Wasco County city project. In the Wasco County files, Rajneeshpuram does not exist. If seven thousand people suddenly disappear, the Oregon government will not be able even to say that they have disappeared, because then they will have first to accept that we were here – and we are not here!

But in a way it is perfectly good: if we are not in Oregon, then of course we are not in America. This seems to be the birth of a new nation. Soon we will have to make our own constitution and declare our independence. What else to do? We are big enough to be a nation. Just the other day Sheela showed me the list of all the nations who accept and respect patents made in America. The Vatican City is one of the countries listed, and the Vatican City is only eight square miles. We are too big – we are almost a continent compared to Vatican City. We can do it.

These lines are just drawn on the sand. The wind comes and all the lines are erased. And the wind of the new man is going to erase all these lines.

The new man will be simply man – not American, not Russian, not Indian; neither Hindu, nor Mohammedan, nor Christian; neither democrat nor republican, nor liberal, nor independent. All these non-sense words will not exist for the new man.

The new man will be simply man. I repeat again: I don't accept anything higher than man. I am talking about the ordinary, simple man. There is nothing higher than that. The idea of being higher than that arises out of inferiority. I would like you to be just like Hanya: ordinary, no politics. But I will tell Hanya there is no need to go anywhere: this is your place, and you are the type of person I want all my sannyasins to be. Superman is just rubbish.

The new man is the birth, for the first time, of man without any ideology, without any ideals – just the way Adam and Eve entered the world. Was Adam Communist, Fascist, socialist? Was he Hindu, Mohammedan, Christian? Was he superior or inferior? He was simply what he was: there was no question of superiority or inferiority. I want you to be again Adam and Eve, to go back to your authentic nature, to your original face.

CHAPTER 6

Holy Scriptures: Wholly Bullshit

Osho,
What is the difference between madness and enlightenment?

There is a great difference and also a great similarity. The similarity has to be understood first, because without understanding it, it will be difficult to understand the difference.

Both madness and enlightenment are beyond the mind. Madness is below the mind; enlightenment is above the mind. But both are out of the mind. Hence, you have the expression for a madman "out of his mind." The same expression can be used for the enlightened person; he is also out of his mind.

Mind functions logically, rationally, intellectually. Neither madness nor enlightenment functions intellectually. They are similar: madness has fallen below reason, and enlightenment has gone above reason, but both are irrational; hence, sometimes in the East a madman is misunderstood as being an enlightened man. The similarities *are* there.

Once in a while in the West – it is not an everyday phenomenon, but once in a while – an enlightened person has been thought to be mad, because the West understands only one thing: if you are out of your mind, you are mad. It has no category for above the mind; it has only one category, that of below the mind.

In the East the misunderstanding happens because for centuries it has known people who are out of their minds and at the same time above the mind, hence the similarity. For the Eastern masses it creates a confusion, it creates a problem. They have decided it is better to misunderstand a madman as being an enlightened man than to misunderstand an enlightened man as being a madman – because what are you losing by misunderstanding a madman as being an enlightened man? You are not losing anything. But by misunderstanding an enlightened man as being a madman you are certainly losing a tremendous opportunity. The misunderstanding is possible because of the similarities.

I have come across a few madmen who were thought to be enlightened. One man was just thirty or thirty-five miles away from Jabalpur. Nobody knew his name – he was very old. He used to keep a bell in his hand and – nobody knew for what reason – sometimes he would ring the bell, sometimes he would not ring the bell. Because of the bell he was called Tuntun Pal Baba: the bell made the sound *tuntun*, and nobody knew his real name.

He never talked intelligibly; he uttered sounds but not words. He remained sitting in one place and never moved from that place. In his village people had known him for sixty years. There were old people who knew that this man had come when they were very young, and since that time he had been sitting on a cot in the porch of the house of the landlord, the richest man in the village. He had not moved from the cot, and for sixty years all that they had heard from him was his bell.

I went to see him many times, at different times, to figure him out. He used to drink tea continually; it was almost his only food. He would drink half the cup and then offer the other half to anybody who was there to see him. This was thought to be *prasad*, a gift, and people enjoyed it because it was very rare. Hundreds of people were seeing him every day; to only a few people would he offer the cup. But always first he would drink from the cup itself, then the remaining he would offer. People thought he was enlightened, so something that he had tasted was blessed.

The more I watched the man, the more I was convinced that he was simply mad; and not totally mad either, because his madness had a certain consistency. It was not without any purpose that he was ringing his bell; it was always to attract the attention of people. Slowly people started understanding that he needed something, perhaps a cup of tea – that was the most needed thing – so immediately they would bring tea.

Those who had been serving him for years had even started understanding the language of his bell: how many times he rang when he wanted tea; how many times he rang when he wanted the crowd to leave him alone, how many times when he wanted people to be allowed to see him, how many times when he wanted to go to sleep. It was a language, a code language that the disciples who lived with him knew.

Now this man was not totally mad, although certainly a little insane. As I watched him I found that he was half-paralyzed too, because when I saw him sipping the tea it was always from one side of his mouth; the other side never moved. One day, when he was alone, I took his bell from his hand and put it in his other hand. The bell fell, because the other hand was paralyzed. Now it was clear why he was not moving from the cot; it was nothing to do with any austerity.

People thought that it was some ascetic practice; perhaps he had taken a vow that he would remain sitting in the same posture for so many years, or his whole life. But it was simply that he was paralyzed. In fact, that seemed to be the clear reason why he was not able to utter intelligible sounds: half of his mouth was paralyzed. With half of your mouth you can make sounds, but to make words is very difficult, almost impossible. You may try but the other will only hear some unintelligible gibberish.

But gibberish has been thought to be one of the methods used by enlightened people. You may be surprised to know that the English word, *gibberish*, is not English, it is Arabic; and it comes from an enlightened man, Jabbar. Jabbar was certainly an enlightened man, but he spoke so fast that his words would run over each other. It was impossible to make any sense out of what he said because there were no full stops, no commas, no indication of where the sentence began and where it ended. Jabbar simply did not believe in all these mannerisms.

It is because of Jabbar that people started calling his language gibberish, but by and by the word gibberish became completely disassociated from Jabbar. Nobody would think that the English word *gibberish* is from a Sufi word and has come from a man who was enlightened. Gibberish, in the East, is thought to be a way of enlightened people. They are saying to you: nothing can be said through words; you will have to understand something besides the words.

But mad people also do the same. And this man Tuntun Pal Baba was simply paralyzed, retarded; you could see it in his face. As I went again and again to him and he became more and more familiar with me, and I became familiar with him, we started some kind of communication. I started using his bell, and I made a few code signals with the bell.

I tried writing, asking him, "What is your name?" and I would ring the bell two times. I knew that he could read because he looked at the slate on which I had written, "What is your name?" and his eyes had the flash showing that he could read. I made the signal three times and wrote on the slate: "I understand that you can read." He looked at it and smiled with half his face. I put the pen in his hand and made the sign of ringing the bell two times, and he wrote his name, Tuntun Pal Baba.

I said, "This is not right – you can't deceive me that you are enlightened. You have deceived thousands of people for sixty years, but this is not good; you have not gained anything out of it. The poor people from the villages have lived with the belief that they are under the guidance, under the blessings, of an enlightened man. This is criminal. And on the other hand you could have been cured, because there is not much of a problem; paralysis can be cured."

I could see the flash in his eyes that he understood that he had made a mistake. If paralysis could be cured... It was perhaps because of paralysis that half of his brain also had gone numb and created the madness. He wrote on the slate: "Is it possible that I can be cured?"

I said, "Perhaps now it is too late. You have been paralyzed for sixty years, your brain has been numb for sixty years; I don't think that after sixty years of paralysis the brain cells can be alive, can function again. And now, what is the point? You must be nearabout ninety, ninety-five, or a hundred: what is the point now? Now it is better you remain enlightened – at least people are happy. And you are not feeling in an inferior state: that you are paralyzed, that you cannot speak, that half your brain is not functioning."

So I said to him, "I am not going to say anything to anybody. I will keep your secret. Remain enlightened; it is doing good both to you and to people. People need somebody: they are in constant search to follow somebody. At least you cannot indoctrinate them, you cannot give rubbish to their minds. In a way you are innocent. You have not done anything. You have simply offered gifts, whatsoever you had. You don't have anything other than that tea." That was all that he was using, that was all his food.

"And you are feeling in good spirits. Thousands of people gather, and on particular festival days the village becomes a big city. People are enjoying, you are enjoying – I am not going to disturb the game. I simply wanted to find out if it is possible that something which is not enlightenment can be misunderstood as being enlightenment. That is proved by you. I am grateful to you that you were sincere with me; you did not hide anything."

A tear came into one of his eyes – the other eye was paralyzed – a tear of thankfulness. I continued to go to see him once in a while; it was not far away. Once in a while, whenever I had time, I would go; and he started to love me. Perhaps I was the only person who had sat on his cot. With one of his hands he would pull me up and make me sit by his side on his cot.

People would touch my feet also, and I would say, "You are already mistaken; now you are again making a mistake. At least don't commit this mistake." But they never understood me when I said, "You are already mistaken. At least don't commit the same mistake again."

A madman can sometimes have glimpses which the rational man cannot have because the madman has stepped out of the mechanism of mind; of course on the wrong side, from the back door, but still he is out of the mind. Even from the back door he can have some glimpses which are not available to the people who never come out of the house. Certainly he is not so fortunate as to have come from the front door, that needs tremendous effort. Madness is a disease. It happens to you – you don't have to make an effort to be mad. It is a sickness and it is curable. Enlightenment happens through tremendous awareness and arduous effort.

Enlightenment is the supreme health.

You should understand the word *health* carefully. It is not only physiologically meaningful. Of course physiologically it is meaningful, but not only physiologically; it has a far higher meaning too. *Health* means healing the wounds. It comes from the root which means healing. If your physiology needs some healing then medicine is offered. If your spirituality needs some healing, then meditation is offered. Strangely, *health* comes from the same root from which the word *wholeness* comes.

Health means the body is whole, nothing is missing. And from *wholeness* comes the word *holy*: the spirit is whole, nothing is missing. Similarly, the word *medicine* and the word *meditation* come from the same root – that which cures. Medicine cures wounds in your physiology, and meditation cures wounds in your spiritual existence, in your ultimate being.

The madman, if in the hands of enlightened people, can achieve enlightenment faster than your so-called sane people. In the East there has been a long-standing tradition, and in this century one man revived it again – his name was Meher Baba. He went all over India seeking and searching for mad people. Anywhere that he heard there was a madman, he would go. He traveled all over India his whole life, searching for mad people.

His disciples asked him, “Why are you wasting your time with mad people when sane people are available to work upon, and they want your time?”

Meher Baba said, “You don’t understand. To bring a sane person out of his sanity is very difficult. But to bring out a madman is very easy because in a way he is already out, but from the back door. He has tasted something of the outside; we have only to show him the right door and say, “Please don’t go out of the wrong door, go from the right door. Being out is perfectly right, but choose the right door.” And Meher Baba turned many mad people into enlightened people.

It is a strange world. Here, really great things are never rewarded. Nobody has bothered about Meher Baba. Mother Teresa will get a Nobel Prize because she looks after poor orphan children, and nobody thought of giving a Nobel Prize to Meher Baba who really did a miraculous job – and he was the only man, after centuries.

Sufis call the madman *mast*; *mast* means intoxicated. The madman and the enlightened man both have to pass through a certain stage: getting out of reason, out of their minds. They have to cross the same boundary: by the wrong door or right door, they both cross the same boundary, and while they are crossing the boundary they both become *masts* – intoxicated.

But the enlightened person soon regains his balance because he has made an effort to get out of the mind; he is prepared to get out of the mind, he is ready to get out of the mind. The madman has got out of his mind unprepared. He was not ready. He has simply fallen out of his mind – it is an accident. Enlightenment is never an accident. But both the madman and the enlightened man pass through a certain state called *mast*, the intoxicated, where they behave similarly; hence the necessity of a master has been absolutely accepted. When one gets into the state of *mast*, then only a master can take one out of that intoxicated state – because that intoxicated state itself is immensely beautiful.

You must have seen mad people very happy. You can't find a madman unhappy. That does not happen at all; a madman and suffering don't coexist. A madman always enjoys. Perhaps he has nothing to enjoy, but he enjoys. It does not matter whether he has something to enjoy or not, but he is always happy. To be unhappy you need reason, thinking, worrying. Now he is incapable of worrying and thinking. He cannot be bothered with tomorrow; he has no tomorrow and he has no memories of yesterday. The madman also exists herenow – that is the similarity. But he is not aware that he is herenow – that is the difference.

The enlightened man is also always blissful. I am using a different word just so you don't get confused. The madman is always happy. But there is a possibility he can be cured; then he will become unhappy, then he will start worrying. He will worry more than you because he will see that he had gone mad: now he will worry about madness. When he was mad he had no worry at all, he could not care less. Now he will worry that he had gone mad and he will worry that tomorrow it could happen again because it *has* happened.

I had a friend who was a doctor. His father was a very miserly person, rich but very miserly, and he had a very tight hold on the family. He was a politician; his name was Shri Nath Bhatt. He was a Gujarati, and he had a very beautiful jeweler's shop. He was the president of the local Indian National Congress, the party that was fighting for India's freedom against the British Raj. His son, whose name was Shyam, and I were friends from our very childhood. I hated Shyam's father more than Shyam hated him, because he was such a miser. Of course his son could not do anything about it but I said, "Don't be worried; I will do something about it" – and I did.

It was an everyday phenomenon during the British Raj that there were continual processions against the government, strikes against the government – and Shri Nath Bhatt was the leader. There were the two slogans. One slogan was: *Bharatmata zindabad* – Long live Mother India. *Zindabad* means long live. And: *British Raj murdabad* – *murdabad* means die quickly, as soon as possible."

I would start the slogan, "British Raj," and people would repeat "*murdabad*" – "die soon." Three or four times I would say, "British Raj," and the fifth time I would say, "Shri Nath Bhatt." Because people were continuously saying "*murdabad*," they would say "*murdabad*."

Shri Nath Bhatt called me to his home and he said, "You are tricky; you always used my name after 'British Raj,' never after '*bharatmata*.' If you had used my name after '*bharatmata*' they would have said '*zindabad*' long live.' But you are mischievous."

I said, "No, I was not doing it knowingly. One thing you have to promise: you have to drop your miserliness toward my friend, your boy, Shyam. If you promise me that, then your name will come after '*bharatmata*,' I promise you that; otherwise your name will always come exactly in the middle of 'British Raj.' Five times it will be, 'British Raj,' and then you; then again five times, 'British Raj,' so people get mixed up." And I was always on the mike.

So he said, "Okay, it is a pact: I will not be miserly." But he was miserly – it was very difficult for him not to be. Shyam became a doctor and I became a professor. Once Shyam became a doctor his father wouldn't allow him to join the medical services. He wanted to join the medical services to somehow get away from his father and his family, but his father wouldn't let him go.

Shri Nath Bhatt opened a shop for Shyam just by his own shop so he could keep an eye on him. He put a compounder of his choice, who was his man, and a nurse of his choice, in that shop. They had to keep an eye out to see that no money went anywhere, and every evening all the money that Doctor Shyam had earned went to Shri Nath Bhatt.

Shyam got married, and one day his wife sent a telegram that she was very sick, and that it would be helpful if Shyam came because he understood her more than any other doctor, although the doctors were doing their best.

She was at her father's place because she was pregnant. In India it is a tradition that the first child is born at the house of the wife's parents, because of course your mother will take more care than your mother-in-law. A mother-in-law is only a mother-in-law. There is no mother – it is only law. So this is traditional, at least for the first child. By the second child the woman will be capable of understanding many things on her own, but with the first child she is completely unaware about the pain and the trouble.

So Doctor Shyam told his father, "This telegram has come and my wife is sick." Now, from my village, Nagpur is not very far away. In those days it was two rupees for a one-way ticket, and at the most it was a ten-hour journey. So two rupees to go and two rupees to come back meant four rupees. And perhaps his wife was seriously sick, so Shyam would spend something there. It meant nearabout fifty rupees would be gone – and fifty rupees would give Shri Nath Bhatt a heart attack.

Shri Nath Bhatt simply said, "In Nagpur there are better doctors than you" – Nagpur was the capital, in those days, of central India. "And there is a medical college with every kind of facility. So what are you going to do there? You have been a student in Nagpur, your professors are there: send a telegram to any one of your famous professors, to some gynecologist, and he will take care of her.

"There is no need to go, and I am not going to spend money unnecessarily. Fifty rupees, and who knows? – you may spend more. And how many days will you be away? The fifty or sixty rupees that you earn here every day also has to be taken into account. If you are there for a week causing me such a loss – and for no reason at all, because it is simple: I will send a telegram. Just give me the name of your professor in the medical college."

But Shyam was very attached to his wife; he escaped. He tried to travel without a ticket, and because he was without a ticket he was nervous. For the first time in his life he was traveling without a ticket – and he, a doctor, a well-educated person. If he were caught it would be really shameful. He was very worried about his wife, about his father, and what would happen the next morning when his father found that Shyam had escaped.

About the ticket... In India, trains are very crowded and Shyam was standing just by the door because it was so crowded. Particularly in those days they were even more crowded; now there are more trains. So he was just standing there, holding onto the bars on the door as a handle, with such worry in his mind about whether he would be able to see his wife or not – because she was not the type of woman who, knowing his father, would call him unless it were absolutely necessary.

While Shyam was in this tension and worry and the crowd, somebody pushed him, and he fell out of the train. Physically he was not harmed, but psychologically he accidentally went out of his mind. This is what I mean by falling out of the mind. Suddenly he crossed over the line of the mind. With too much worry, tension, fear, nervousness, the mind was as if in a cyclone. And with this shock of falling from the fastest-moving train, he simply slipped out of his mind.

People recognized that he was a doctor and he was brought home. By chance I happened to be in the village. I heard about the accident and I went to see him: he could not even recognize me, and he had forgotten his language. There was no harm to the body at all – small bruises here and there, nothing to be worried about – but he just looked vacant, empty. That's the way the enlightened person looks. If you look in his eyes they are empty, vacant. You may get afraid.

Shyam was in such a shock, not knowing what had happened – but not worried, smiling. I had not seen him smiling for years, because of his father; nobody could smile in his house. There were five sons, five daughters-in-law and many grandchildren, but Shri Nath Bhatt was such a Tamerlane that it was impossible for anybody to smile, because even a smile meant an unnecessary waste. Preserve everything!

It was Sigmund Freud's insight that the people who suffer from constipation are miserly people. They preserve everything, they can't allow anything to go out. Naturally, how could Shri Nath Bhatt allow anybody to smile? But now he could not do anything: Shyam was out of his mind. He laughed, he smiled – I had never seen him so happy.

He remained mad, and for the first three years he really enjoyed it because no patients came to him anymore. Who would go to a madman? He would sit in his dispensary every day absolutely ready with his stethoscope and bag, and nobody would come except me, once in a while. He wouldn't recognize me, but it was a joy to be with him, just to laugh and enjoy. And he would try his doctoring on me.

I said, "Okay, you can, because you cannot find anybody; just no injections, because if your father comes to know that you are giving injections free, then he will create trouble for me. I can lie down and you can do a check, you can do any kind of work that you want to do." I would lie down and he would take a cardiogram and all that, but he wouldn't recognize me. I would say, "Shyam?" and he would listen as if I were calling somebody else; he had forgotten his own name too. Those three years were really of great happiness.

His wife was in a terrible mess, but I told her, "One thing you should see: with Shri Nath Bhatt alive there was no chance to be happy. But this man, by accident, by God's grace, has slipped out of his mind. Don't feel sorry for him. Can't you see? Yes, he is mad, but what is wrong with it? – he is happy. He was sane but unhappy and miserable. Now he goes into the market and purchases the best clothes possible because he does not have to pay – Shri Nath Bhatt will have to pay!"

His father used to tell me, "You are spoiling him. First, he is mad; then you take him to the market, and people come to me with their bills. I have to pay. Please leave him."

I said, "This is not possible. Everybody has left him; now I am the only person. And I am immensely happy that he became mad because in this house you are all mad except him; you are all in misery. He is happy, so what is wrong with being mad? If he had not gone out of his mind by accident then I would have tried my way, but he had to go out of his mind. Now that he has slipped out, let him enjoy it But remember, once he gets back into his mind I am going to help him to get out again – of course from the right door."

But that Shri Nath Bhatt was really a dangerous miser. He was afraid that I would do something, and that perhaps my association was encouraging Shyam to remain mad, because I used to take him to the hotels, to the restaurants, and I told him, "Enjoy yourself. Don't be worried about money – whatsoever you want is yours."

And he said, "Is it so?"

I said, "Just enjoy!"

He wouldn't enjoy himself alone; he would ask anybody, say to any stranger, "Come on!" The whole town was happy, the shopkeepers were happy, but Shri Nath Bhatt was really enraged. After three years he forced Shyam into a madhouse just so that I could not visit with him. And he made it a point to the authorities in the madhouse that I should not be allowed in. He gave my name and my photo to the authorities saying, "This man should not be allowed to meet my son. Anybody else is allowed, but you have to remember this photo."

When I went to see him, the officer showed me the photo and the statement that the father had given. He said, "I am sorry, I cannot help if his father does not want you to see him. He has given us a written statement and this photo, so that we recognize you and don't allow you in. Otherwise you may come in some other name."

I told him the whole story. I said, "First listen to the story, and if you are a man at all you should throw away this letter and this photograph. What proof has he got that he gave you a letter? The reason he does not want me to see his son is that he would prefer him to remain mad, rather than become sane and start understanding me and what I want him to do." I told him the whole story.

The man could not believe that Shyam's father could be so cruel. He didn't say anything; he simply tore up the photograph and the letter and threw them in the bin, in the wastepaper basket, and told me, "Come in – you are always welcome." So I saw Shyam: he was so happy there in the madhouse with almost three hundred mad people. He was in rags, unclean – perhaps he had not taken a bath for a few days, he was stinking – but immensely happy. He was not able to recognize me.

Then I moved from Jabalpur. Shyam is still in a madhouse, and perhaps will be in a madhouse his whole life, but he is in a better position than any sane man. I saw those three hundred mad people – many times I went to see him – they were all happy. One thing is sure: a madman is never in anguish. Why should he be? He has no problems.

Just see the point: even if you fall below the mind you are happy. It is the mind that is causing you all kinds of misery, suffering, jealousies, hatred, anger, violence, greed. They all go on making you more and more a pain to yourself. You start hurting all over; everybody is hurting all over. Even to fall below the mind – which is falling below humanity, because that is the only difference between you and the animals... A madman is really back in the world of animals. He has dropped out of evolution. He has gone back; he has turned his back on Charles Darwin. He has said, "Good-bye. Good-bye to your evolution!" He has simply fallen back to a subhuman level.

Animals are not happy, but they are not unhappy. Have you seen any animal unhappy? Yes, you will not see them happy – they cannot be happy because they don't know what unhappiness is. But when a man falls from the human level to the subhuman level, he becomes happy because he knows what unhappiness is. So he is not exactly the same animal that he was before he became man. He is a totally different kind of animal; a happy animal. There is no happy buffalo, no happy donkey, no happy monkey, no happy Yankee. Animals are not happy because they don't know unhappiness. But a madman is just happy for no reason at all.

That gives tremendous proof of what I have been teaching you, that if you can get out of the mind – but not by an accident, not by a shock – you will be blissful.

It is possible, more than possible – perhaps unfortunately it is going to happen – that in Communist countries they will start giving people electric shocks to bring their suffering to the subhuman level; then they will be happy. And the shock will be given in a certain scientific way so that they will not be mad either. They will be functionally sane, like a computer – but just functionally sane, like a mechanism with no soul. They cannot rebel. They will be very happy, and if they are happy why would they rebel? There will be no question of revolution; they will exist like robots.

There are many experiments going on in the Soviet Union and in China to make it possible that a man remains reasonable enough to be able to function in society, in the office, and yet is free of all worry, of all tension, all problems: he is happy. This will be the greatest crime against humanity; but there are scientists who are working on those lines. Even in America the famous psychologist, Delgado, is doing the same thing in a different way; he puts electrodes into your head and he has succeeded, he has shown his experiments to be absolutely successful.

One of the strangest things about your skull is that inside it there is no sensitivity. Even if a stone is put inside your skull and the skull is closed, you will not feel the stone because there is no sensitivity. The inside of the skull is absolutely insensitive, for a certain reason: it has the most precious instrument in your body. The brain is such a complicated mechanism, with ten billion cells, that if your skull were sensitive you would not be able to live, there would be so much noise coming inside your head. And if something went wrong – some cell died, some part became nonfunctioning – you would become aware of all those things, which would drive you nuts.

It is such a complex mechanism that many things can go wrong. Even if nothing is wrong, already half of your brain is not functioning. Fifty percent of your brain is absolutely in a state of paralysis. Perhaps that is the part of the mind that starts functioning when you become enlightened. The enlightened man can use his mind more efficiently than the greatest intellectual can, for the simple reason that he is outside the mind and has an overall view. Perhaps the half of the brain that is not functioning in normal human beings starts functioning when your consciousness goes beyond your normal reason, as you transcend your rationality. The other part functions only with your transcendence.

This is the experience of all those who have become enlightened. And when I say this, I say it on my own authority. I would not believe it if Buddha had said it: perhaps he was lying, perhaps he was misguided; perhaps he was not lying but was not right; perhaps there was no intention to lie but he could be confused, he could make a mistake. But I know it from my own experience because it is such a tremendous change that you cannot miss it. It is almost as if half of your body was paralyzed, then one day suddenly you feel you are no longer paralyzed; both your sides are functioning. Can you miss it? If a person who has been paralyzed suddenly finds he is not paralyzed, can he miss it? There is no possibility of missing it.

I know perfectly well the moment before enlightenment happened to me, and the moment after, knew with absolute certainty that something within my mind – which I was not even aware existed – had stirred and had started functioning. Since then there has been no problem for me. Since then I have existed without a problem, without a worry, without any tension. All these qualities come from the other part of the mind which is not functioning. And when the whole mind functions and you are out of it, you are the master. The mind is the best servant you can find, and the worst master you can find. But ordinarily the mind is the master – and that too, only half of it. The master – and half paralyzed! When you become the master, the mind is the servant and fully healthy, fully recovered.

Delgado put very small electrodes into the head. In the mind there are seven hundred centers – exactly the same number as acupuncture had discovered five thousand years ago in China.

Acupuncture had discovered seven hundred centers on the body; those seven hundred centers on the body are connected with the seven hundred centers in the mind. So it looks strange – acupuncture's way of treating a patient is very strange.

You have a headache and they may push their needles into your knee. You will say, "What are you doing? I have a headache and you are bothering about my knee." They will say, "Don't interfere; we know what we are doing."

Over those five thousand years they have found which center in the body is connected with a corresponding center in the head. And strangely enough, by pushing a needle into your knee or your thigh, your headache disappears. There is a current of electricity – now it is called scientifically bio-electricity – which is a very mild current of electricity but is still electricity. And sometimes very subtle things work miracles.

You have so much electricity always running in your body that you can put a five watt bulb in your hand and it can light up. It ordinarily does not happen, otherwise you would start giving shocks to people. But once it happened that a woman, somehow a freak of nature, started giving shocks to people. First her husband got shocked; he escaped from the house, screaming. Then the neighbors tried, but just to shake hands was enough. Then doctors were called in, and it was found that somehow her body electricity, which moves in a circle, had freaked out; somewhere her inner mechanism had gone wrong.

It was actually tried: a five watt bulb was put in that woman's hand and it lit up! Now, it is a scientifically established fact that subtle currents of electricity are continuously moving in the body, just like the blood. Each center is connected with other centers in the body. The real thing happens always inside the skull, but it immediately reaches the body.

In the Second World War, a man's leg was cut off – it was so damaged that there was no other way, and it was so terrible a pain that as he was coming to consciousness, the moment he felt the pain he would become unconscious again; it was unbearable. Consciousness could not survive; he could bear that pain only in unconsciousness. There was no need to give him any drugs, just the pain was enough to force him to go into unconsciousness. So they had to cut off his leg. But the strange thing was that when he became conscious again he was still complaining about the pain in the leg. He was covered with a blanket so he had no idea that the leg had been removed. The doctors said, "It is impossible."

He said, "I am suffering, and you say 'Impossible'?" Most of the pain was concentrated in his toe: he said, "My toe is hurting so much."

The doctor said, "Just look," and he uncovered his body: the leg was gone, the toe was gone. They brought his leg from the lab and said, "This is your toe and this is your leg. Now how can your toe give you pain? You are just hallucinating, imagining."

The man said, "I can see you have cut off my leg. I can see the leg, and that it *is* my leg – I know it is, I realize it, I recognize it – and that is the toe that is hurting. But it is hurting *here*."

This was the first case to give an indication that the toe is connected to a brain center. The brain center was still vibrating in the same way it was vibrating while the leg was still connected. You have disconnected the leg but the center connected with the leg is still vibrating in the same way. That started great research work on how to get to the centers of the head – because perhaps the leg could have been saved if they had stopped the vibration of the particular center in the head. Then even if the toe were damaged the man would not have felt any pain, because every experience happens in the head although it may be coming from another part of the body.

This research finally ended up in Delgado's hands, and he managed to find all seven hundred centers in the mind. Now, he puts an electrode in a particular center in the mind – for example, your happiness center – and he has a remote control. He just puts an electrode there and whenever he wants you to be happy he just pushes a button – it is a remote control, no wire is connected to you so you cannot see anything – and you start laughing, enjoying, giggling as if somebody is tickling you. You don't see anybody – what is happening? The man may be miles away but he can still control you.

Delgado showed his experiment first in Spain with a bull. He had put an electrode into the bull's head and he went into the field. Spaniards are strange people. They enjoy a bullfight just as the Americans enjoy football. Strange people, I simply wonder... There are a few idiots running with a ball, a few idiots returning the ball, and millions of idiots jumping up and down and fighting! It seems to be that Charles Darwin is not right: man has not evolved, he is still a monkey. Now, a man fighting a bull, putting a man in danger of death...

Delgado proved that the bull can be controlled; there was no problem. The strongest bull was given to him and he put an electrode inside it. He waved the red flag, and the bull came rushing – just like J. Krishnamurti seeing orange clothes. Jiddu Krishnamurti – that is his full name; Jiddu Krishnamurti. "J. Krishnamurti" saves him from some trouble because *jiddu* means stubborn; he *is* stubborn.

The bull came rushing toward Delgado who was standing there waving a red flag. When he was just one foot away and ready to push his horns into Delgado, Delgado pushed the button of the remote control in his pocket and the bull stopped so suddenly that the millions of people who were watching it could not believe it: what happened to the bull? He just stopped, frozen, as if he were practicing George Gurdjieff's "Stop" exercise. He remained like a statue, he would not move.

Delgado said, "We can control every man," and there is a possibility that sooner or later totalitarian governments are going to do it. Perhaps they have already started, because in the Soviet Union you cannot give birth to a child in your home – it is illegal. Every child has to be born in a government hospital.

Now, when the child is just born is the best time to put an electrode into his skull. The skull is very soft and the centers are very alive; if they grow with the electrode there, the electrode will become almost part of the brain. The child will never suspect throughout his whole life that everything that he is doing is manipulated from the switchboard in the central office of the Communist Party. It can make you happy, it can make you unhappy; it can make you rebellious, it can make you obedient. Obviously, they don't want any disobedience; they don't want any revolution, any rebellion, any doubt. Naturally, only those buttons will be used which make you a slave – but a very happy slave. They have reduced you to a robot.

The madman falls out of the mind, but he is better than a robot because the robot is controlled from the outside; somebody else has the remote controls. The controls can be given to you too, that is a possibility. You can be given a small switchboard: if you are feeling angry and you don't want to feel angry, you just push the anti-anger button and you are no longer angry.

Now, what is the need of Buddha teaching for forty years, and people still get angry, and Jesus teaching people to be humble and nobody is humble? But with a Delgado switchboard things are very simple. You can have your own switchboard. You can push the button and have any kind of pleasure that you want, any kind of hallucination, any kind of dream that you want.

But I suspect that these remote controls will not be given to people; they will be in the hands of the government. To me, this is more dangerous than nuclear weapons which can kill you, but at least you will die as a human being, with dignity. But it is worse than death that from the White House they make you happy. On Christmas day, a slightly bigger dose, and the whole country goes bananas! Everybody will think this must be the work of Jesus or his father or the Holy Ghost.

A madman is far better – at least nobody is in control of him. But he is also not in control of himself. The enlightened man is out of the mind but he has full control of his mind. He does not need a switchboard; just his awareness is enough. If you observe anything minutely, you will have a little experience of the enlightened man – not the full experience but a little taste, just a tongue-tip taste. If you observe your anger minutely, anger disappears. If you are feeling a sexual urge, watch it closely and soon it disappears.

If things evaporate just by your watching, what to say about the man who is continually above the mind, simply aware of the whole mind? Then all those ugly things that you would like to drop simply evaporate. And remember, they all have energy. Anger is energy; when anger evaporates, the energy which is left behind turns into compassion. It is the same energy. Through observation the anger has left – that was the mode, the form surrounding the energy – but the energy remains. Now, the energy of anger, without anger, is compassion. When sex disappears the tremendous energy of love is left behind. Each ugly thing in your mind, disappearing, leaves a great treasure behind.

The enlightened man has no need to drop anything and has no need to practice anything. All that is wrong drops of its own accord because it cannot stand up to his awareness, and all that is good evolves of its own accord because awareness is nourishment for it.

The madman can be helped very easily because he has tasted something out of the mind, but he needs to be shown the right door. In a better world our madhouses will not just be trying to make those people sane – that is meaningless. Our madhouses will be trying to help those people to use that opportunity to move through the right door. A madman going into a madhouse will come out enlightened –

not just the same old self again, miserable, suffering.

So, to me, madness has immense significance. It can become a way toward enlightenment. It should be used as a means. Yes, there is a tremendous difference between the two: the madman is only happy and does not know why, the enlightened man is blissful and knows perfectly well why. He cannot be cured because he is not sick, he is incurable.

My father used to tell me, "You are incurable."

I said, "You are right, because I am not sick. You are curable because you are sick."

He used to say I was incurable because he could not convince me about certain things he wanted me to do. For example, he wanted me to get married. Naturally, when I came back from the university he wanted me to get married. But he had no courage to say anything to me, or ask, "What about marriage?" because he knew already that it was going to become a great argument and there would be difficulty. He thought, "It is better not to hear 'No' directly from him, because once he says no then there is no way to change it into yes. So I will keep at least one possibility open: I have not asked him yet, I will let others ask first."

He asked one of his friends who was a Supreme Court advocate – and he asked him because it was known all over the country that this man had never been defeated in any case in his whole life, he had always been victorious. So my father gave him a challenge: "Here is a case – my boy: you have to convince him about marriage."

The advocate said, "That is a simple matter. I will come tomorrow."

My father said, "My friend is coming and he wants to meet you."

I said, "I know why he wants to meet me – let him come!"

My father said, "How do you know?"

I said, "Don't be worried. It is something to do with marriage."

That was the time he told me, "You are incurable. How did you manage to know?"

I said, "It is simple guesswork – no need to be a prophet. Why would you bring that idiot to me? You have never brought him before. I have just come from university, finished with university, and I knew from the very beginning that the first thing when I got back home would be the question of marriage. I have just arrived home and tomorrow he is coming. Let him come!"

The advocate came. He started arguing the way he must be arguing in the Supreme Court. I said, "Understand one thing first: if you convince me about marriage I will get married, I will be absolutely ready. Convinced, there is no problem. But if I convince you that it is wrong, then are you going to divorce your wife or not? This should be settled; otherwise it is an unbalanced case: only I am the loser. What is at stake? You put your wife, I am putting my life. You are not putting much more than me. I am putting my life – you put your wife."

He said, "Then I will have to think about it.

I said, "No, no need to think about it. Don't be such a coward. I leave it to you because I believe you are a just man, a fair man. I have always called you my uncle, and I trust you just as I trust my father. So I am not asking for a judge: I leave it to you to make the judgment about whether I am victorious or defeated. I will accept your judgment."

He said, "Still, wait. You are putting me into difficulties. You are making me the judge also; that is tricky because you are challenging my fairness. You are also saying, 'I have been calling you my uncle and I trust you,' so you are challenging my integrity. And the real thing is that I have never thought about marriage. It has never been a case in my life to convince somebody about marriage. Because you have put it that way, perhaps you are right – because my wife is such a pain in the neck!

"You may convince me; in fact, inside I am already convinced that if I had not got into this trouble it would have been far better. So there is a possibility you may bring my own inner conviction up. To be truthful with you, don't bother about marriage because it is really a trouble. Drop this thing completely. I will try to console your father, to get him to leave you alone."

My father said to him, "I told you before that you may have been victorious in all your cases but my son is incurable, he is simply impossible."

The advocate said, "You are right, because even before starting the argument I was defeated. We had not argued. In fact he managed to have me tell him, 'Don't get married.' He reminded me about my wife, and he knows everything about me and my wife, so I could not cheat him and could not lie in front of him. He knows everything. And he had said, 'I put my life on one side, you put your wife on the other side.' In fact I would have liked to lose the case, but my wife and my children and my whole family... It is too much. Forget about this boy – leave him alone."

If you can see the total aspect of anything, no problem arises. The problems arise because you see only one aspect and you don't see the other aspects. A bird's eye view is needed; and that is where the enlightened man is different from the madman. The madman has no vision, he has fallen into darkness; he is blind.

The enlightened man has risen into light and he has nothing but eyes, opening into all dimensions. He can see anything from all possible viewpoints simultaneously; hence, his answer is immediate. He has not to think about the answer: even before the question arises, the answer is there, because his vision is clear. He can see far and wide. His whole life is transparent. He has gone above the mechanical mind into a non-mechanical consciousness.

You can destroy the brain, then the mind will be finished, but you cannot destroy consciousness because it is not dependent on the brain or the brain system. You can destroy the body, you can destroy the brain, but if you have been able to free your consciousness from both, you know you are intact, untouched; not even a dent has been made on you.

Mansoor could laugh even on the cross. A man in the crowd asked, "Why are you laughing?"

He said, "I am laughing because they are crucifying somebody else, but they think it is me. I am just as much a watcher as you all are. You are watching al-Hillaj Mansoor being crucified; I am also watching – we are all watchers. But these people who are crucifying al-Hillaj Mansoor think they are crucifying *me*. That's why I am laughing – at how blind mankind is. They are killing somebody else, thinking that he is me."

An enlightened man can laugh even while dying. Even death is just a laughing matter because his experience proves that he is above time, above changes, above forms, that he is universal, that he is part of the whole continent of consciousness. Even death is just a coming back home.

The second question? My hands are not tired yet!

Osho,
Are the holy scriptures just useless? And are they holy or not?

The holy scriptures are not just useless, they are absolutely harmful. If they were just useless there would be no need to be concerned with them. They are positively harmful. They are preventing people from becoming religious because they make people knowledgeable, and people start thinking that knowledgeability is wisdom, is enlightenment. Because they know about great words, theological doctrines, dogmas, philosophies, naturally people think, "What else is there to know?" You have crammed the whole Bible or Gita or Koran; then what else is there? And by cramming the Koran, the Gita, or the Bible, you have not gained anything.

So the holy scriptures are not just useless. If they were useless there would be no harm: they could be preserved in libraries where many other useless books are preserved. I have read so many useless books – but *they* have to be preserved. They are only useless, they are not harmful. But I cannot say that holy scriptures should be preserved. They should be completely destroyed. As far as you are concerned, at least within you, you should make a bonfire of all the holy scriptures, because unless you burn all that nonsense you will never be able to know your innocence, you will never be able to know the beauty of your ignorance. Out of that innocent ignorance, knowing arises. It is not out of knowledge that knowing comes.

Knowledge hinders knowing because it pretends to be knowing. Ignorance is sincere, honest. It has no pretensions about it: it is simply ignorance. And because it is honest, true, sincere, it opens you, makes you available to know, makes you capable of seeing. Your eyes are no longer covered with knowledge, thick garbage. No, the holy scriptures are not just useless, they are positively harmful.

And you ask me: "Are they holy?" Yes, they are one hundred percent holy: fifty percent holy cow dung, fifty percent holy bullshit!

CHAPTER 7

The Beauty of the Human Soul

Osho,
Is it wrong to try to save somebody? Is it not part of compassion?

Compassion is a very delicate affair. It certainly has some place in making an effort to save others, but there are many conditions which have to be fulfilled first.

The first condition is that *you* are saved; otherwise, in the name of saving others you will be simply destroying them. And in the effort of saving others you will be missing the opportunity to save yourself. Only a person who has himself come home can be of any help to somebody. A blind man cannot help blind people. You must have your eyes opened, you must have seen light yourself before you start telling others what it is.

Compassion certainly includes the idea of saving others, but not against their will. If somebody does not want to be saved, you are not to force him; you do not have to save him at the point of a sword. That is not saving. That simply shows that in the name of saving you are trying to dominate people.

In Raipur there is an old, very ancient pond. Because of its ancientness it is called *boodha talub* – old, aged, pond, and it belongs to the part of Raipur which is the most ancient. That part of Raipur is called *boodha pada* – the ancient part, very old; *boodha* means old man. The pond is certainly very beautiful in its oldness; all the old stone steps are covered with thick moss.

I used to go there just to sit because nobody goes there. The pond has become dirty – thick moss floats on the water and the water is almost green. The pond has not been cleaned for years, so nobody goes there. And there are other ponds in other places, so there is no need; the water is not used any more. Because it was such a silent place I used to go there every evening to sit and see the sunset.

One day when I was sitting there a man suddenly fell into the pond and started shouting, "Help! Help!" I had not seen him when he came by, or how he slipped. Anybody could have slipped; those steps were so slippery with moss. I jumped in to help him and somehow I pulled him out. He was very angry.

He said to me, "Why did you do that?"

I said, "This is strange! You were asking for help."

He said, "Yes, I was asking for help because I became so afraid, but really I wanted to commit suicide – and you prevented me. I would not have shouted if I had any idea that somebody else was present. Nobody comes here. What are you doing here?"

I said, "This is strange. When you started shouting, 'Help! Help!' I thought you were drowning. I have unnecessarily become wet in this muddy pond and now you are angry."

He said, "Yes, I am certainly angry because that shout was just out of fear. I was not meaning to be saved."

So do you know what I did? I simply pushed him back in. What else to do? Again he started shouting, "Help! Help!"

And I said, "Now I am not going to help. I have helped twice: the first time by getting you out; the second, by pushing you back in. Now do whatsoever you want."

He said, "What kind of man are you?" And he was drowning – coming up and going down, and crying, "Help!"

I said, "Not against your will.

He said, "I am saying *help*" – but I simply sat there.

I said, "Try yourself." He was not far away from the bank because I had just pulled him out, he was just close, so it was perfectly clear that he would manage. And he did. He got a little water inside him but he came out and said, "You are a strange man."

I said, "I am a strange man? *You* are a strange man! First I saved you; you were angry. Then I helped you by throwing you back in; you were angry again, and started crying out for help."

He said, "Yes, when I get into water I become afraid of death, but really I want to commit suicide."

I said, "Then come at some other time because at this time I am always here, and if you start shouting, 'Help!' then it looks very strange not to help. But I cannot help you against your will."

Compassion cannot allow you even to do good to the other person who is not ready for it. Compassion gives total freedom, respect and dignity to the other person; all these people who have been trying to save others are just a by-product of Christianity and its conditioning.

In Buddhism there is no place for saving anybody. Buddha says, "I can show you the way, but you will have to walk. I cannot walk for you. If you don't want to walk, who am I to force you? At the most I can say I have walked the path, and I can describe the beauties of the path, but I cannot force you in any way. That will not be compassion, it will be cruelty. If it is your pleasure to go some other way, then all my blessings are with you. Even if you are going to hell, my blessings are with you."

Mahavira has taken a very clear stand: "Nobody has ever been saved by anybody else. It is not possible by its very nature because if somebody can save you, then somebody can unsave you also. Then your being saved is not something in your possession, it is given by somebody. It is just as somebody can give you money and somebody else can steal it – you are not the master of it. And at least your self-realization, your enlightenment, must be something of which you are the master, which nobody can deprive you of."

It is simple logic: if somebody can give it to you, then somebody can deprive you of it; there is no problem in it. If you can be forced to be enlightened, you can be forced to be unenlightened. Mahavira is very clear, and I agree with him, that at least one ultimate thing should be left to the individual. Enlightenment is the ultimate experience; it should not be borrowed, given, purchased, forced, otherwise it won't be the real thing.

It is Christian stupidity that has spread the idea; no other religion before Christianity had ever thought of saving somebody. If you know the way, you know the joys of the way, you can sing the song, you can dance the dance. If somebody feels like moving with you, being a fellow traveler, not a follower, then he is welcome. But there is no enforcement and you are not obliging him.

These are the beautiful points which have arisen in the Eastern consciousness over thousands of years. Even if you show the way, you give the details of the path and you give the discipline; you don't make the other person feel obliged to you. You are not doing it for him, it is just your own experience which wants to be shared. He is obliging you by hearing you, by giving you a chance to share your experience. He is helping you to be unburdened of the fragrance that you are carrying – and you want to be unburdened, you have to be thankful to the person – the question of saving does not arise.

But after Christianity it became an almost universal phenomenon. After Christianity came Mohammedanism, and of course they went to the very logical end: either you have to be ready to be saved or be ready to die. They don't give you any other choice, because they believe that if you go on living unsaved you may commit sins and you will suffer in hell. By killing you they are at least taking away all the opportunities of falling into hell.

To be killed by a savior is almost to be saved. That's what Mohammedans have been saying, that if you kill somebody in order to save him, he is saved; God will look after it. He is saved and you are accumulating more virtue in saving so many people. Mohammedans have killed millions of people in the East, and the strange thing is that they believed they were doing the right thing. Whenever somebody does a wrong thing believing that it is right, then it is more dangerous. You cannot persuade him otherwise, he does not give you a chance to be persuaded. In India I tried in every possible way to approach Mohammedan scholars, but they are unapproachable. They don't want to discuss any religious matter with somebody who is not a Mohammedan.

They have a word of condemnation for the person who is not a Mohammedan. Just as Christians call him a heretic, Mohammedans call him *kafir* – which is even worse than heretic. *Kafir* comes from a word, *kufr*; *kufr* means sin, a sinner. *Kafir* means a sinner: anybody who is not a Mohammedan is a sinner. There are no other categories, only two categories. Either you are a Mohammedan, then you are a saint: just by being a Mohammedan you are a saint, you are saved, because you believe in one God, one prophet – Mohammed – and one holy book, the Koran. Believing these three things is enough for you to be a saint. And those who are not Mohammedans are all *kafirs*, sinners.

It is a strange fact that India has the greatest population of Mohammedans – even today, after Pakistan was divided from India. Before the division, certainly India was the biggest Mohammedan country in the world. With Pakistan, it was hoped that now Mohammedans were going to have their own country. They got a great portion of the country, according to their population, but not all the Mohammedans moved to Pakistan. All the Hindus in Pakistan were killed, so Pakistan is purely a Mohammedan country. But the Mohammedans who did not move to Pakistan and who remain in India are still more in number than in any other country in the world, Pakistan included.

India, although a Hindu country, has the biggest number of Mohammedans. Still it is impossible to communicate, they will not. I have tried my best, but if you are not a Mohammedan then how can you understand? There is no question of any dialogue: you are a *kafir*.

I had a professor as my colleague in the university, who loved me very much. He was a Mohammedan. Jabalpur is one of the big centers of Mohammedans and it has great scholars. One very famous scholar, Burhanuddin, was there. He was old, and famous as a scholar of Mohammedanism all over India and outside India too. I asked Farid, "Find some way for me to have a dialogue with him."

He said, "It is really difficult – unless you can pretend to be a Mohammedan."

I said, "That too is very difficult, because then you have to teach me a few basic things of Mohammedanism – their prayer and what they do. Moreover Burhanuddin knows me – we have spoken many times from the same platform – so it will be very difficult for me to act. I can try, there is no harm. At the most we may get caught and we can laugh at the whole thing."

He said, "You can laugh, but my position will be very bad. They will kill me: 'You are a Mohammedan and you are supporting a *kafir*, and deceiving one of your great masters.'" But he was willing to do it. He started teaching me the language, Urdu. It was difficult to learn because it is just absolutely the opposite of any language that is born of Sanskrit. An Urdu book starts from the back and the sentence starts from the right corner and goes toward the left.

It is so difficult to get adjusted: it is just upside down, the whole thing. You have to open the book from the end; that is the beginning. And then the sentence starts from the right and moves toward the left. Because of the way the Urdu language is written, a perfect way has not yet been found to print it or type it. The way it is written is not scientific at all; most of it has to be guessed. So those who are accustomed to read it can read it because they can guess what it will be. But for somebody who is learning, it is very difficult to guess.

I tried for six months. I learned enough so that I could deceive somebody into thinking that I was not very educated, but a little bit. I learned their prayers, Farid managed to get a wig for me and cut my beard like the Mohammedans cut theirs. Their beards are so strange that even to think of it again now my stomach starts churning. But I went through it; they cut my mustache off completely and left just my beard.

I said, "My God. If you had told me before then I would not have wasted these six months!" In a way they were right, because I know that a mustache is such a difficult thing – particularly a mustache like mine which is not trimmed but is wild. I don't allow Mukta to trim it. It is difficult even to drink tea or to drink fruit juice because half of it will remain on the mustache. So Mohammedans have found a way: they cut off the mustache, they shave the mustache, and they keep the beard. But that looks so ugly.

But I said, "Okay, we will do it. Now, for a few days I will not leave my house. Just give me a wig and let me see Burhanuddin." It certainly changed my face completely when Farid cut my beard like the Mohammedans' – very thin along the jaw line and just a little bit of beard on the chin – like Lenin's, a little less. Without a mustache and with a wig I looked different.

We went there, but the old man detected something about my eyes. He said, "I have seen those eyes somewhere."

I said, "Farid, where could Maulana" – Maulana means master; he was known as Maulana Burhanuddin – "have seen me? I have never been to this city."

Farid was trembling, he was having a nervous breakdown: we had never thought about the eyes. That old man continued to look, and he said, "I suspect something."

I said, "Farid, he suspects something." Farid just fell at his feet and he said, "There is no need to suspect – you know this man. Forgive me, I was just trying to help him because he wanted to have a dialogue with you."

But he said, "First tell me who he is because as far as I can remember, I have known the man and I have seen him many times. You have just cut off his mustache."

I said, 'Now it is better, Farid, that you tell the whole thing, that not only have you cut off my mustache..." I took off the wig and I said, "Look at the wig."

The moment I was without the wig, Burhanuddin immediately recognized me, and he said, "*You*!"

I said, "What else to do? You know me perfectly but you will not have a personal talk with me. Do you think that just being a Mohammedan is enough to be a saint? What sin have I committed?

"Certainly I am not a Mohammedan, but Mohammed himself was not a Mohammedan when he was born. Was he a *kafir*, a sinner? And can you tell me who converted Mohammed to Islam? He was never converted. Just as Jesus remained a Jew, Mohammed remained a pagan all his life; Mohammedanism is something that started after his death. So if Mohammed, a *kafir*, can become the messenger of God, can't I discuss the message?"

Burhanuddin said, "This is what I was afraid of. This is why we don't encourage any dialogue between Mohammedans and non-Mohammedans."

I said, "That simply shows your weakness. What is the fear? I am opening myself to you, to be saved by you. Save me – and if you cannot save me then let me try to save you."

But he simply turned toward Farid and said, "Take him away – I don't want to talk any more. And you have to come to see me tomorrow."

Farid was punished, beaten. I could not believe it: he was a professor at the university, a well-known scholar who was a guide to many research students working on Mohammedanism, on Urdu literature, the Koran. Burhanuddin had a few hooligans there who gave Farid a good beating. He showed me his body; all over his body were signatures of the Mohammedan attitude.

He said, "I told you before, that if something went wrong... They have only beaten me because I am a well-known person – if I were somebody else they would have killed me."

The stupidity has moved from Christianity to Mohammedanism. But except for these two religions no religion believes that you can save anybody, and in fact the other religions know more about compassion than those two religions. This idea of being a savior is simply illogical. Try to understand it.

You have been living for many lives; you have been doing things on your own. Now it is your responsibility to undo all that. How can I undo it? I have not done it, I have never been a partner with you in doing it. You have lived an absolutely free, individual life for many lives, and according to that you have grown and come to the stage where you are. This is not accidental, it is the growth of a long, long process. Now to undo that process you will have to take great responsibility on yourself. I can show you the way I have undone my process. Certainly, the same method will help you to undo your process – perhaps with a little modification here and there that you have to work out.

You can work it out with me, but it is going to be a dialogue, not dictation. I cannot dictate to you, "Do this," and give you a simple panacea so that you will be saved: "Believe in me and you are saved." Then not believing in me would be the only problem. Do you think that not believing in me is the only problem? If that is the only problem then certainly in believing in me the problem is solved, you are saved. But that is not the problem. In your believing in me, your anger will still remain anger, your greed will still remain greed, your jealousy will still remain jealousy.

Believing in me or Jesus or Mohammed is not going to change anything. Do you think people who believe in Jesus are different in any way from people who don't believe in Jesus, who believe in Mohammed, who believe in somebody else? No, they are not different. Deep down they are the same people, with the same jealousy, with the same arrogance, the same egoism, the same violence. Everything is the same, all the garbage is the same. Believing changes nothing at all, so how can you be saved? The whole idea is idiotic.

Mahavira and Buddha are far more sophisticated than Jesus and Mohammed. One of my arguments with Jaina monks began with this same question. Mahavira says: "Nobody can save anybody except himself. Everybody has to save himself." Buddha says: "Be a light unto yourself." That was his last message before he died.

When Buddha was dying his closest disciple, Ananda, started

crying. There were thousands of disciples there, at least ten thousand disciples. They were all ready to burst into tears, but they were holding back their tears somehow because Buddha would not like it: "At least while he is going beyond our reach let him go feeling that his disciples have followed his message."

But Ananda could not contain himself. It was difficult for everybody, but for Ananda it was more difficult because for at least sixty years he had been like a shadow to Buddha, serving him in every possible way without asking anything in return. It was just a sheer joy to serve him and to sit silently while he was talking to others, answering others. Ananda would never interrupt. It is very difficult to find such a devoted person.

He was Buddha's elder brother, his cousin-brother; he was older than Buddha. Before he was initiated into sannyas Ananda had asked Buddha three things. He said, "After being initiated I will be your disciple; whatsoever you say there is no question, I have to do it, and I will do it. But right now I am still your elder brother, so as an elder brother promise me three things and then initiate me, because after that I will never be able to ask anything." He asked three things, but he never used a single promise.

One was: "You will not say to me, 'Ananda, go somewhere else to spread the word.' I am going to remain with you to serve you. You have to promise me." The second was: "Even if in the middle of the night I bring somebody who needs your help, you cannot refuse them. Anybody I bring to you, you have to help; whether you are tired after the whole day's work or not doesn't matter. If I bring somebody to you, you have to help him, you cannot refuse." And the third was: "If I ask a question, you cannot tell me, as you tell others, 'Be silent for two years, three years, meditate, and then I will answer.' No, you will have to answer immediately." As his younger brother, Buddha promised Ananda that these three things would be granted to him.

But Ananda was a rare man, otherwise Buddha would have hesitated to accept these conditions, because initiation cannot be given in a conditional way. He could have simply said, "If you put conditions on me then initiation is not possible" – because many other times other people had come with conditions and he had refused them; but to Ananda he gave the promise. That is unprecedented in the whole history of initiation. But I can understand why he did it;

he knew Ananda from his childhood – he was not a man to take advantage. Buddha knew that Ananda would never use those promises – he could be given them.

Ananda never used them. He never asked a single question, he never brought a single person, and of course, Buddha never told him to go away. If Buddha had said to, he would have gone – he would not have even mentioned the promise – but Buddha never asked him.

This man could not contain himself: sixty years was so long to be together. He had been just like a shadow – and now he was left alone. Tears came to his eyes. Buddha opened his eyes to look, to have a last look at his disciples. Seeing tears in Ananda's eyes he said, "Ananda, be a light unto yourself. I was not your light and I was not your savior. My death makes no difference. In fact, now you will have to understand what I have been telling you for sixty years: don't remain in any illusion just because you are serving me and you are being with me devotedly. It is very difficult to find such a devotion – still it is not going to save you."

You have to go through a transformation and that, only you can do. It is such an inner work that even the master cannot reach there. Except you, nobody can reach there. And this is the beauty of the human soul, that it is absolutely unavailable to anybody. Your center is so protected by existence that nobody can even touch it.

The question of saving somebody does not arise. Yes, the man of compassion tries his best to explain to you the way, to explain to you how it has happened to him. But that is simply sharing his story with you. Perhaps out of that story you can get some hints for yourself, but that is up to you.

In the twenty-five centuries since Mahavira and Buddha, Buddhism has completely disappeared from India because Buddhist monks could not compromise with Hinduism in any way. And I think that it is perfectly right: there is no need to compromise with anybody. Rather than compromising they preferred either to be killed, burned, or to leave the country. So a very strange thing happened: Buddhism was born in India, Buddha was born in India, and yet in India there are no Buddhists. There was a time when the whole of India was afire with Buddhism. Either they had to die or they had to compromise, but not a single Buddhist is known to have been converted, it is impossible. If you have understood something how can somebody else convert you?

They left the country and spread all over Asia, so the whole of Asia turned to Buddhism. Except for India the whole continent is Buddhist. Buddhists from all over Asia come to India to pay homage to the place where Buddha became enlightened. The temple that was made as a memorial for Buddha's enlightenment has a brahmin priest because Buddhists disappeared from India so totally that even to find a priest was impossible. For the memorial temple of Buddha's enlightenment there was no Buddhist available. And a brahmin – Buddha's whole revolution is against brahminism.

Brahmins are professional priests. You can tell them anything, you pay for it, and they will be the priest – it doesn't matter. And to them it really does not matter because Hinduism has thirty-three million gods. When you can worship thirty-three million gods, one or two more makes no difference. And they are not getting involved in your religion: they just worship purely as professionals.

I have talked with the brahmin priest who is worshipping in Buddha's temple, just as a heritage. For centuries his family has been worshipping there; they are almost the owners of the place. I asked him, "Are you influenced in any way by Buddha?"

He said, "The question does not arise – we are professional priests. Somebody is a professional doctor, somebody is a professional engineer, that does not mean that becomes his religion. My religion is Hinduism and I go to the Hindu temple to worship for myself. This is simply a paid job. I am being paid, and I go on receiving many gifts because people come from all the Buddhist countries – Sri Lanka, Japan, Vietnam, Indonesia, China, Korea, Taiwan, the whole of Asia. So many gifts go on coming to me, it is a really profitable job, but I am a brahmin and I am against Buddhism."

Buddhists disappeared because they did not compromise, and Jainism remained a small stream because it did compromise. It was one of the questions of debate for me all over India when meeting Jaina monks or meeting them on a stage in some conference. They would all say, "Mahavira was born to redeem the whole of mankind from sin."

I said, "This is absolutely wrong – you are just putting Mahavira's name in place of Jesus Christ. It is a Christian influence, it is not at all in tune with Mahavira. He was not born to redeem the whole world, and if he was, the proof is that the world is not redeemed. Nor has Jesus' crucifixion redeemed the world. Nobody has been able to redeem the world – it is nobody's business to. If you can redeem yourself, that is more than enough. And if you can spread a little bit of light and fragrance around you, you are fortunate and blessed."

Saving somebody is really a thankless job – you know, the way I saved the man in that ancient pond in Raipur. He was shouting, "Help! Help!" but he could not believe it when I pushed him back. When he came out he said, "The first time it was okay because I was shouting, 'Help! Help!' but I was just standing there and you pushed me!"

I said, "I was simply undoing what I had done because it was wrong, against your will. If you want to commit suicide all my blessings are with you. If just a little push is needed, I am not so miserly that I won't give it to you."

When I was a student, it happened that I had a friend who was in love with a Bengali girl. He was not a Bengali, but he was really a fanatic lover. He almost transformed himself into a Bengali; he even started speaking Hindi the way Bengalis speak. It was impossible to detect that he was not a Bengali because he was speaking Bengali very perfectly. That can be understood, but he also started speaking Hindi – which was his mother tongue – the way Bengalis speak it, and Bengalis destroy it!

He learned that too just to influence that girl and her parents, to show that although he was not a born Bengali, he was almost a Bengali. He started dressing himself the Bengali way and he started carrying an umbrella, which Bengalis always do – I don't know why. If it is raining it is okay, if it is hot it is okay; but no matter whether it is raining or not, hot or not, cold or not, an umbrella is always with them. It is a multipurpose thing: to drive dogs away, to beat somebody or to fight with somebody. It has many purposes and is always handy. It has just become part of the Bengali personality – so he started carrying an umbrella.

I said, "Thakur" – he was by caste a Thakur.

He said, "You are my friend, but don't call me Thakur, call me Thakoor. The way Bengalis say it, the *u* in Thakur becomes *o*: Thakoor – otherwise our friendship is finished."

I said, "I am not a Bengali and it looks so foolish to call you Thakoor, I will be unnecessarily wasting my breath. Thakur is perfectly good."

But the family refused him, because Bengalis are very arrogant in that matter. They are just like French people in Europe. They think their language is the best and their culture is the best. Even if a Frenchman understands English he won't speak it, he will speak in French. He cannot fall down so low and just speak English. Bengalis do the same: they can speak Hindi but they won't.

I have visited Kolkata hundreds of times but only Hindi-speaking people would come to listen to me. Even in Kolkata – which is the capital for Bengalis – not a single Bengali would turn up for a meeting. I had a few friends who would come to see me, and I asked them, "Why don't you come to the meetings?

They said, "Unless you start speaking in Bengali, no Bengali is going to come."

You will be surprised that in Kolkata they call everybody who is outside Bengal an Indian. They are Bengalis, and everybody, except them, is an Indian. That was strange to know. For the first time I came to know in Bengal that I am Indian and they are Bengalis.

So the family refused Thakur. They said, "You may speak Bengali, you may even speak Hindi the way Bengalis speak, you may carry an umbrella; you have managed everything well..." The boy started eating fish and rice, because that is the most important food for Bengalis – rice and fish. He would not eat any other sweets than Bengali sweets. He was really a Majnu, a Farhad, a Romeo – that kind of person. But the family refused him, they said, "We won't accept you." But he was not going to take no from them. He closed himself in his room and his family all tried to persuade him to open the door.

He said, "I am not going to open the door. I am going to die in this room unless you go and persuade that family. Either I have to marry their daughter or I am going to die."

Now the family said, "How can we persuade them? Those people don't even consider themselves Indians. You have become almost a Bengali."

"If they have refused you," the father said, "they will not even talk to me because that's far below them. Bengalis have culture, they have great poets and great scientists and everything great. They won't listen to me."

Still, he went – what else to do? Thakur was his only son, and he was being so foolish that he wouldn't open the door. The father went.

He was a well-known doctor, but the family said, "We are sorry, but we cannot give our daughter to an Indian family. You will not be able to give her the comforts, the food, the culture, that she is accustomed to, so it is not going to happen. Just persuade your son."

The trouble was that the girl was not interested, otherwise I would have managed something. I told the boy, "It is not a problem of being a Bengali or a non-Bengali. I would have managed something if the girl was interested in you, but she is not interested at all; otherwise you could have eloped. I would have managed it."

I had done it two or three times in my life. I had even arranged for my own brother to elope with a girl, because my younger brother fell in love with the daughter of the landlord of the house where I used to live.

My landlord was furious, but I said, "Don't be worried; I will persuade my brother when he comes next." – because he was studying in the engineering college, so he came whenever he had time; the engineering college was almost ten miles away from the place – "Whenever he comes I will explain things to him. Don't be worried."

Meanwhile I asked his daughter, "What do you want? If you are really willing then tomorrow you can both escape – I will arrange everything. He is madly in love with you but the question is, are you in love with him?"

She said, "I am more madly in love with him than he is with me."

So I said, "Then it is perfect." I arranged a magistrate, but he was not willing to do the marriage in Jabalpur because the legal procedure is that a month's notice has to be posted on the court board: "Such and such persons are going to be married. If anybody has any objection..."

But a month is a long time; if her father came to know... I said, "Do one thing. Post it tonight and back-date it a month. Who will prove that it was not there for a month? On your notice board there are hundreds of notices. Just paste it in a corner. It should be there – back-dated."

He said, "You don't know law or anything."

I said, "You *have* to do it. It is not a question of law, it is a question of love. You *have* to do it! I have never asked anything of you – and I am not asking for myself. But my young brother and this girl will both suffer their whole lives. They will suffer anyway but let them suffer together! If they want that then it is my duty to help – just help too."

He said okay. In the night he placed a back-dated notice on the board, but he was very afraid that even just in the morning something might go wrong – the court did not open till then. He said, "What I will do is this: I will go to a village nearby where I go occasionally for tours as a magistrate. So send your brother and the girl there – nobody will be able to prevent them."

So he went thirty or forty miles away and stayed in a guest-house. I drove my brother and his girlfriend there and got them married; the magistrate signed and sealed everything. But his fear was right, because a clerk from his court found that back-dated note. The clerk knew the girl's father, so he immediately phoned and said, "Do you know your girl is going to be married? Today is the last day to register any objections, and the magistrate is not here, he has gone on tour."

The father came running from his shop. I was missing and the girl was missing. They went around the whole town; their whole family was searching to find where we had gone. By the evening we returned. I went to Delhi; I said to my brother, "I am not coming home for a few days. Go to our father's house in the village, don't go to the girl's father. Go to our father's house; I will phone our father and tell him, 'I have got one of your sons married and I am sending him and his wife to you, so receive them well at the station.'"

My father said, "You are just a trouble, because you have already done it without asking me. Now I can't do anything about it – I will go to the station and receive them."

I said, "Give them a good reception because the girl's father is not going to give a reception. I will not be there because I don't want to be seen with them; he is my landlord and he will throw me out and make me leave the house."

After three days I came back. The landlord looked at me and he said, "Where have you been?"

I said, "I went to New Delhi."

He said, "Yes, I see you must have gone, but what happened to my daughter?"

I said, "I don't know. What happened to your daughter? I am not your daughter's guardian."

So he said, "You don't know anything?"

I said, "No, I don't."

He said, "They got married!"

I said, "This is news to me. Who married them?" Then I persuaded him: "If they have got married then why make an unnecessary fuss about it? Give them a good reception. They are already married – you cannot do anything. Legally she is adult, he is adult; you cannot do anything legally. And you have showed me the one month's notice: what were you doing for one month? *Now*, when they have married, you think about it? Be a little cool. This will be unnecessarily a scandal for your family. Why make it a scandal? Give them a good reception and say it is with your wishes that they have married."

He said, "It seems right; there is no point in doing otherwise."

So I arranged it; I arranged for my father to give them a good reception, and I organized things with the landlord, then I phoned my father: "Now you can bring the marriage procession to Jabalpur: her father is willing to give a good reception."

So I told Thakur, "I have arranged marriages – there is no problem – but the girl simply hates you, it is not just that she does not love you. Even if she were not in love I would have persuaded her, talked to her; at least she could feel compassion for you – because he had been trying to become a Bengali for six years continually, and he had become one. "But the girl simply hates you; she says it is impossible!"

He would not open the door and he was threatening, "If you do anything I have poison inside." He did have poison because he had got it from his father's dispensary. "I will drink it if you force me or if you try to break down the doors."

The father said to me, "Now do something."

I went to the door. I said, "Listen, Thakoor."

He said, "So it is you?" – because he understood, nobody else would call him Thakoor.

I said, "Yes, it is I."

He said, "I want to commit suicide."

I said, "I will arrange it – just come out with me. Here it will be difficult: even if you take the poison you are not going to die immediately. Your father is a doctor; the door can be broken down and you can be saved from the poison. It is not such a great thing.

I found out from your father that that poison can kill, but it will take at least eighteen to twenty-four hours for a man to die. Meanwhile the poison can be got out, or an antidote can be given. So you see it is simply foolish. Just come with me; my car is waiting outside, just come with me."

He came out and I took him home. I said, "The best place to die is by the marble rocks. It is one of the most beautiful places in the world." For two continuous miles the Narmada flows between two mountains of white marble. On the full-moon night it is an absolute dreamland: you can't believe that things can be so beautiful. So I said to him, "This is good; although it is not full-moon night it is very close. In just two days time it will be full moon. If you can wait for two days, good; otherwise still it is good light. You are going to die so what does it matter whether it is a full-moon night or a no-moon night?

"I will drive you early in the morning – because that is the best time. In the night there are people and you may be saved, because when the moon is there many people go for picnics or for boating, so it is full. But in the morning there is nobody. It is a night place. In the day there is no beauty – if you see it in the day you will not believe it is the same place that you saw in the night; a million-fold difference."

I had actually requested the governor, who was my friend, "Close this place during the day. Nobody should be allowed to enter to see the marble rocks then because it destroys the beauty of the marble rocks. It should be open only when the moon is there, just for a few nights."

He agreed but he said, "There is no law like that, and the Narmada is a holy river for Hindus: it will cause trouble if we prevent people. They will say they are going to take a bath – and this is a religious thing, so don't get me into trouble."

I told Thakur, "Five o'clock will be the right time, so I am fixing the alarm for four o'clock. It takes an hour to get from here to the marble rocks." So in my room, on a table between our beds, I put the clock. Thakur was tossing and turning; I said, "What is the matter? You don't feel like sleeping? This is the last night. Have a good sleep. You will never be able to sleep again, so just sleep."

He said, "Are you my friend?"

I said, "Yes, certainly, Thakur, I am your friend."

He said, "You are so interested in my suicide and you are making every arrangement: I wonder whether you are my friend or my enemy."

I said, "I am just your friend. You want to die – I am ready to help. If you want to live, I am ready to help. A friend is really known when a crucial moment comes and this is such a moment. If you are going to die at least I can help you." I brought the car to the porch, and I said, "In the morning somebody may get up late, so it is better if I go to the gas station to fill it up now; in the morning, at four o'clock, it may be difficult. We may not find the petrol pump owner, and a problem may arise, so I am making every arrangement."

The more arrangements I made, the more he became afraid of suicide. At four o'clock when the alarm went off he immediately put his hand on the clock. I caught his hand and said, "This is not good, because then we will be late."

He said, "But I am feeling too sleepy."

I said, "You can sleep in the car – don't be worried. And it only takes a few seconds, you just have to jump; if you cannot jump I can push you. Nobody can come out alive from the waterfall in the marble rocks; nobody ever has. Many people have committed suicide there; it is a special place. During examination times there are constables on duty twenty-four hours a day, because nobody can come out alive.

"The waterfall is big and it falls onto rocks; so when you take a jump the waterfall takes you down deep, perhaps a hundred feet or a hundred and fifty feet down, and then there are rocks all around. You may get hit on the rocks – nobody who has jumped there has ever come back alive." So I said, "Don't be worried: it is sure, guaranteed; there is no problem. Just have a good sleep in the car now."

He sat in the car very reluctantly. On the way he said, "Are you really going to the marble rocks?"

I said, "We decided on it."

He said, "Just take me to my home. I don't want to get married to that girl. To hell with that girl! I became a Bengali for her, and now I am going to commit suicide?"

I said, "This is strange – you wasted my whole night and all the arrangements I have made. Don't change your mind; keep to your word."

He said, "You are saying that! It is my life and you are preparing for my death."

I said, "If you want I can leave you at your house, but remember, never mention suicide again."

He said, "That I understand. I will certainly not mention suicide to you, nobody should mention it to you: you are dangerous."

I said, "I am simply helpful."

He is still alive. He got married to another girl and he has children. The last time I went to Jabalpur in '69, he said, "If I had followed you and committed suicide it would have been better."

I said, "I am still ready. You should not mention it to me because if you still want to, there is no problem."

He said, "No, I don't mean it. I am simply saying that getting married and having children and a job is worse than death."

I said, "If it is worse, I am still ready to help you."

There are people who are living a life which is worse than death, but they are not courageous enough even to commit suicide. And for transformation more courage is needed than for suicide. For suicide, only a few moments of courage are needed. You have to keep hold of yourself just for a few moments and then take a jump or shoot yourself. It is just a question of moments. Any coward can be brave enough for a single moment.

But transformation is a lifelong process – it is not a question of saving yourself for a few moments.

This is the reason people got interested in religions like Christianity, because Christianity sells the idea so cheap. You do not have to anything, no transformation – the word *transformation* does not even appear in the whole of the Bible – no meditation. The word is not Christian or Jewish. All that you need to do is to believe in the messiah and go to church every Sunday. They can talk about anything, because who listens to the boring preachers there? And because they are boring they cannot conceive that there is a possibility of listening to somebody with deep intimacy and love.

I saw on television a panel of three priests: a rabbi and two Christians. They discussed many things about me and about my commune – all rumors. There was nothing true in it. One thing they discussed was: "Osho has started speaking and he will be speaking every day now. Won't people get bored?"

Of course that is the experience of three priests. They don't speak every day for three hours continually. They speak only once a week, and not for three hours; otherwise people would kill them. All three priests were concerned that my people will get bored. They don't know me, they don't know my people.

I have been speaking for thirty years continually, and I have not seen a single person sitting in front of me, bored. It is impossible because whatever I am saying is not borrowed. I am opening my heart before you, and you are getting bored? That is impossible. I reveal myself to you, and you get bored? That is impossible. But what those three priests were saying had a certain relevance in their experience and so they all agreed that people would get bored.

The rabbi even suggested, "We should also start something like this, approaching people – because we have dropped talking about truth." They don't do that anymore because there is no need. Nobody wants to hear, nobody is interested in their God. Even they are not interested.

I have heard...

Three rabbis were discussing whose synagogue was the most modern. One said, "In my synagogue women are even allowed to sit side by side with men. Even girlfriends and boyfriends, those who are not married to each other, are allowed to sit together – even people sitting with others' wives, who I know are committing adultery. But my synagogue is ultra-modern and we move with the times."

The second one said, "This is nothing, because in my synagogue there is no preaching, no prayer, but a beautiful dinner is served and everybody enjoys it more than the sermon. The real question is enjoyment. With a sermon people get bored. You mention the Torah, you mention the Talmud, and they start thinking, How to escape from here? But just because of a delicious dinner everybody from the congregation comes."

The third one said, "This is nothing – *my* synagogue remains closed on Jewish holidays."

These people have nothing to do with truth, nothing to do with transformation, nothing to do with your personality: they are simply part of a business. These are firms of long, traditional standing. They are all doing business. The question is whose customer are you? That's what they mean by saving: "Why are you being saved by somebody else? We can save you in a less costly way, more cheaply, in a more ultra-modern way. We can even keep the synagogues closed on Jewish holidays. What more do you want?" They are offering you everything – just be saved by them.

That reminds me again of Natthu Kaka. I was a regular visitor to his salon. I had no beard at that time – I was a child – and no mustache, so there was no fear, but I had to use a scarf because I had long hair, and if Natthu Kaka was in the mood he might start cutting it. Once he had cut your hair you could not do anything. And he was such a nice man, he would say, "Why be worried? – you need not pay." It was a problem every day that he had shaved somebody without asking him, and the man was angry.

Particularly in India, people shave if they become sannyasins; that means they are dying in a ritualistic way. When a person dies he is shaved; it is just symbolic. Just as a person is shaved when he dies, in the same way when somebody becomes a traditional sannyasin he is shaved. Or if your father dies, traditionally all the sons will be shaved; but now they have found a more liberal way – only the eldest son has to be shaved. So to shave somebody's complete head without asking him... And Natthu Kaka was really a craftsman: with just one hand half of your skull was shaved clean; now there was no way except to let him shave your whole head, because with it only half shaven you would look more of an idiot than with it totally shaven.

So it was a question of a fight every day, and I enjoyed the scene. Natthu Kaka's shop was just in front of my father's shop so whenever there was something happening I would immediately go there. But I kept my scarf in Natthu Kaka's place because sometimes I might come by and just see some great thing happening – somebody ready to hit Natthu Kaka, and him saying, "You are getting unnecessarily upset. I am an old man, an opium addict. I don't know whom I am shaving and what is happening – it is all mixed up. Somehow you got into my hands, and it is just an old habit to shave people, so I did it."

So I used to keep my scarf there: the first thing I would do is put on my scarf. One day he shaved a man who was a kind of political leader. Of course the man was very angry and he said, "You have to be punished for this. I am going to the police, I am going to the court."

I was there. I said, "There is no need to be angry, and even by going to the police and to the court your hair will not be replaced.

This poor man is not even asking money from you. As far as your hair is concerned..." The man was educated, and I used to have discussions with him. So I told him, "You remember the Zen haiku: 'Sitting silently, doing nothing and the grass grows by itself'? Why be so worried? Just change *grass* and put *hair*."

That day an idea came to me. I made a small board and put it in Natthu Kaka's shop. Natthu Kaka is dead but perhaps in his shop there will still be the board on which I wrote the haiku, with a note: "If Natthu Kaka shaves somebody, don't get angry with him; he is just an old savior. And if he has shaved you, please meditate on this haiku: 'Sitting silently, doing nothing, the hair grows by itself.' The hair will grow – don't be worried."

Perhaps that board is still there, or perhaps the shop is finished, because his sons were not interested in doing business with him. They were trying to find employment because, they said, "With this old man we will lose business because we are not opium addicts. People forgive him because everybody comes running from all the shops around here saying, 'Don't be angry – he is a nice fellow.'"

When I last went to my village – that was in '70 – he was still alive but very old. I went to see him and he said, "Since you have left for your studies, nobody comes regularly the way you used to come, and there is nobody to help this old opium addict. I go on doing my thing – I can't help it." He would sometimes catch hold of children and shave them, and then their fathers would come and say, "What have you done?" And his only answer was, "I don't ask for any money, can't I even practice? Where am I supposed to practice? No customers are coming and I am sitting without doing anything."

In 1970 he told me, "You are the only person who can help me" – because in my childhood there was no legal prohibition on opium or any drugs; everything was available in the market. Only the person who was selling needed a license that cost five rupees per year; the people who were purchasing were not required to have any license or anything. But in 1970 when I went there, things had changed. All drugs were prohibited and the old addicts, like Natthu Kaka, were given licenses so that they could get a little quantity every day. He was very angry.

He said, "Only you can help, because I know how many people are opium addicts in the whole country. If you lead us, and if all the opium addicts become united, we can overturn this government."

I said, "Great, Natthu! You want me to become the leader of the opium addicts?"

He said, "I don't know anybody who would be as understanding as you."

I said, "The idea is good, but to collect all the opium addicts and to persuade them to make a party and overturn the government is a very difficult job. I would have to do everything alone. Your opium addicts would create trouble rather than be any help! Just drop this political act – this is not for opium addicts."

He said, "Think about it, because you go around the country: you can just tell all the opium addicts that this is simply unjust. I have lived my whole life with opium and I have not harmed anybody – except that once in a while I shave people, but I don't take any money. I have not done any crime; in fact I don't have any energy to do any crime, I am just enjoying my opium. My opium has made me so simple and so innocent that people come and milk my cow and I go on seeing what they are doing, but only later on I remember that it was my cow, that they were milking my cow and they have taken the milk.

"I have not committed any crime; on the contrary people have been committing crimes against me. They take soap from my shop, they take mirrors from my shop – and I am sitting there! But I enjoy my own world. So I don't see what the point is in prohibiting opium. You can prohibit any other drug – I am not concerned – but opium simply makes a man a gentleman."

I said, "It is true, Natthu Kaka, but it will be very difficult. I will try." And I actually told Indira Gandhi the whole story.

She laughed and said, "He is, in a way, right, that opium addicts don't create any trouble." Opium simply makes them hallucinate, and opium is a drug which makes you very happy, it never makes you depressed; all other drugs have that possibility. Sometimes if your mood is depressed and you take LSD, it will depress you more; if your mood is happy and you take LSD, it will raise your happiness. It depends on your mood: the drug only exaggerates your mood. Opium does not work that way. It simply relaxes you and helps you to hallucinate beautiful things, nice things. It never gives you any nightmares, because this Natthu Kaka and his friends – I have talked to all of them – never had any nightmares with opium.

So Indira told me, "What he is saying is right, but to collect the opium addicts will be difficult for you, and to overturn the government with their support will be really a revolution if it becomes possible."

This idea of saving is deeply insulting and humiliating to people. The moment you say, "I would like to save you," you are reducing that person to a subhuman being: you are a savior and he is just to be saved. It is ugly, it is just sick. It is not compassion. Compassion shares, and if somebody is available and open he absorbs it. But the credit never goes to you; you cannot claim, "I have saved you." The person saves himself: that's the only way, there is no other way.

Osho,
I have heard you say that you are not here to inspire anybody. However, the fact is that I come away from your recent talks totally afire and ignited by whatever it is that happens between you and us. Please comment.

Yes, I am not here to inspire, but you are here to be inspired. These are two different things. If you get inspired the credit goes to you. It is not me who is inspiring you, it is you who are open to me. If you bring your candle close to me and it becomes lighted, is it my flame that is responsible or is it you coming closer to me, bringing your unlighted candle? I don't move a single inch toward your candle, because that I consider a trespass.

I open myself completely to you and I make my candle available to you; you can bring your candle. It is just as when a thirsty man comes to the well: if he drinks and his thirst is quenched all credit goes to him. In fact the well feels grateful, thankful to him because as more water is taken out of the well, fresh water goes on flowing in. If people stop drinking from a well and drawing water from it, the water dies; its inner sources become closed. Soon the well becomes poisonous.

If a man of enlightenment remains closed – which is impossible, I am just saying it for argument's sake – if a man of enlightenment remains closed he will destroy his enlightenment. But it is impossible. Enlightenment becomes enlightenment only because he opens up. And he goes on opening – there is no end to his opening.

All that he is, is only a presence. That's why I say I don't do anything. I am just here for you to do something. You can come close to me. That's what happens when I am talking to you: unaware, you start moving closer to me. Your physical bodies remain where they are – and leave them there! – but you start moving toward me. Perhaps you will understand what I am saying: when somebody starts moving toward me, I can see – the body is left behind and the person has come very close to me. It is in that moment you feel afire, ignited. But the whole credit always goes to you.

I am not the savior, and I do not want ever to be known by that ugly word, *savior*. I am just a presence. You can save yourself. You can burn your candles from my fire and my fire will not lose anything. Yes, you will gain eternity, you will gain ultimate bliss.

CHAPTER 8

Is It Boredom, or Aloneness?

Osho,
What is boredom? Are you never bored with life?

It is one of the most significant questions to be asked because it is only man's privilege to be bored. No other animal has the capacity. Why has man the capacity to be bored? It is a by-product of intelligence. Nothing is wrong in it. Only idiots are not bored – or the enlightened ones, but they are few and far between. The major part of humanity, between these two poles of idiots and the enlightened ones, feels more or less bored.

Boredom means that you are intelligent enough to see that life is meaningless, that it is just futile to go on living: nothing comes out of it. Life is an effort to write your signature on water – not even on sand, because on sand it may remain for a while before the wind comes and destroys it. It is writing on water, and it disappears as it appears – immediately, instantly – and nothing is left behind, not even smoke.

How many millions of people have lived on the earth? What have they left behind? They were also people like you. They were doing everything that you are doing, thinking all kinds of thoughts, dreams, ideals. And they made every effort to be creative, to be fulfilled, to be contented. But what is left? Whether they had been or not makes no difference. If there had been not a single human being before us it would not make any difference. What difference are you going to make? And if you cannot make any difference then your life is uncreative.

Creativity means making a difference by your being here, not leaving the earth exactly the same as you had found it: your imprints will always remain there. You may be gone, but what you have created will go on influencing generations after generations.

Every man who has ever lived has thought about his life: what does it signify? Is it just vegetating? No animal is bored because no animal is bothered about meaning, no animal is concerned about creativity. A buffalo chewing grass is as contented as any Gautam the Buddha. She is not aware of her contentment – that is the difference. But she is perfectly contented: no tomorrow, no yesterday, no problems. Just watch a buffalo chewing grass and you can see the difference between man and animals.

A man may be sitting on a golden throne, or he may be a beggar – it does not make any difference – but both are immensely concerned about why they are here, for what? Is it just accidental, or is there some destiny to it? This question remains unanswered, hence the boredom. You cannot find contentment, blissfulness or meaning in anything. You see every day passing by and you know that death is coming closer, closer, closer, and life is not yielding anything. Your hands are empty.

Strangely, when a child is born he is born with closed hands, as if he is bringing something into life. When a man dies, he dies with open hands – all is lost. There is nothing to hold in his fist, there is no need for a fist. No man has ever died with closed fists, and no child has ever been born with open fists. It is significant. Physiologically it has different meanings. The child is not yet capable, not strong enough to open his hands. Physiologically they are not actually fists, it is because the child simply cannot open his hands. That is the physiological explanation, that he cannot open his hands yet. He needs a little strength, then he can open his hands.

And the dying man – his whole body becomes relaxed. Death is the ultimate relaxant. For the whole of his life he was tense; now life is leaving the body. The body was not tense, it was the life in it – the intelligence, the mind – that was making it tense. Now, the fist is a tense state of the hands. When life leaves the body, even if you are making a fist, it is bound to happen that your fist will open up, because now there is no more energy to keep the fist closed. The child had no energy to open it up, the old man has no more energy to keep it closed. It needs strength to keep it closed – that is a physiological explanation. But the metaphor is beautiful, and I am mentioning it as a metaphor.

Every child is born with the idea that there is going to be something great. Every child comes with hope, ambition, desire, and a confidence that all this is going to materialize; that his dreams are not going to remain dreams, they will become realities. To me, that is the metaphor of his closed fist. He is coming with a treasure, with a secret. He is not coming without a message – he is coming with a message to be fulfilled. He is coming with a destiny.

Hence children are not bored. They may cry, they may weep, they may laugh, they may smile, but you cannot find bored babies. They have not yet felt that life is not what it is supposed to be. They have not experienced life as made of the same stuff as dreams. It needs a little growth, a little experience. And the more intelligent a child is, the sooner he becomes bored. The stupid ones take a little longer, obviously, because to see the meaninglessness of life you need a very sharp intelligence.

You ask me, do I ever feel bored? Not now, but I don't think any one of you has felt as much boredom as I felt for the first twenty-one years of my life. Perhaps I finished the quota – there is a limit to everything!

My parents were puzzled. I never participated in any games. If I make a joke of football today, it is not new; I have been making jokes of all games as long as I can remember. I have never participated in any game, in any play. My teachers were concerned, my parents were concerned: "What kind of a child are you? And what do you go on doing? Go out and play."

I said to them, "Every parent is telling his children to come in and study – and you all go on forcing me to go out and play. Who is strange? Am I strange or are you strange? I don't see any point in playing, I don't see any outcome in it. It is just wasting time. Those who have time can waste it. I don't have much time."

From the day my maternal grandfather died, death became a constant companion to me. I was only seven years old when he died. He died on my lap. My maternal grandfather and my maternal grandmother used to live in a faraway village and I used to live with them. They had no other child than my mother. My mother was very young when I was born, but she had the whole responsibility of her husband's family because my father's mother died when I was only two years old. My father's brothers and sisters were too small, too young; my mother was also very young, but she had to take care of the whole family. So my maternal grandfather and grandmother decided that it would be better if I lived with them. I could have more freedom and they could take more care of me. My mother would be a little less burdened, so that she could take care of her husband's family now she was the oldest – although she was just a young girl.

The village was not very far away, only sixteen miles, but there was no road, no train. When my grandfather fell sick and the only physician in the village said, "It is beyond me – take him immediately to hospital," we took him in a bullock cart because there was no other way. Those sixteen miles looked like thousands of miles because he was dying.

I could see his pulse was slowing down, he was becoming unable to open his eyes; he started breathing in a very strange way, he stopped speaking. I saw death coming closer and closer. He was in my lap because my grandmother was in so much misery and suffering that she was constantly crying.

I told her, "You should think of me! I am only a child – now I am to take care of the dying man and to take care of you. And you had brought me here to take care of! This seems strange. At least don't cry, because if you cry then how can I stop myself from crying? I am not crying just so you can stop." But she was not in her senses. I was continuously watching in every possible way to see whether the man was still alive or gone, and I saw him slowly, slowly, slowly drowning. By the time we reached my father's place he was dead.

After that, death became a constant companion to me. That day I also died, because one thing became certain, that whether you live seven years or seventy years – he was seventy years old – what does it matter, you have to die.

My grandfather was a rare man. I could not conceive him telling a lie, breaking a promise, even judging somebody as bad.

I remember one night... In the village there was no police station, no police, nothing. My grandfather was the richest man in the village, and I used to sleep with him in his bed. One night a thief entered the house. My grandfather saw him cross the fencing and enter, and he started telling me a story. The thief had entered the house and was sitting in the corner – my grandfather started telling me a story and it seemed the thief also became interested in what he was saying.

My grandfather had the habit of continually chewing pan, the betel leaf. His bag was always with him, a very beautiful bag, and he was continually making his pan. This night he began to chew the pan and spit on the thief who was sitting in the corner! The thief could not escape, because he would be caught and he could not say, "You are destroying all my clothes."

Finally it was too much and the thief said, "Nana – because I used to call my grandfather nana; *nana* means maternal grandfather, and because of me the old man had become nana to the whole village; everybody started calling him nana. So the thief said, "Nana, it is too much. I am enjoying your story but I cannot enjoy your pan. Please stop! You will spoil my all my clothes."

My grandfather said, "Tomorrow you can come and take new clothes from me – because I have been deliberately spitting on you. It is not good of me, I should not have done it."

"But," the man said, "I am a thief, and you know I had come to steal."

My grandfather said, "It is your business whether you are a thief or not, but tomorrow come and take new clothes" – because my grandfather had a shop, a multi-purpose shop. In small villages there are only multi-purpose shops; in the one shop you get clothes, sweets, shoes, umbrellas, medicines – everything is available. There was no other shop; he had the only shop for everything the village needed.

The next day the thief came and I told him, "You seem to have some nerve! You have come with your whole shirt and dhoti spoiled with the red of the pan."

He said, "What else to do? I am a poor man, I cannot afford other clothes. Nana has promised me – and he is a man of his word."

I said, "Are you certain? He can collect the neighborhood and have you caught because you entered with the intention of stealing. You have admitted it, otherwise what are you doing here? He has left all these marks on you as proof."

He said, "Don't create doubt in me. I know your nana: even if

I had stolen – I have not stolen anything because I had no chance – he would never tell anybody." And he went in and got new clothes. I told my nana, "This seems to be going a little too far. Don't let him be caught, okay, don't judge him as a thief – but you are rewarding him."

He said, "No, I am not rewarding him. I spoiled his clothes; I am simply replacing what I have spoiled. And he has not stolen. Intentions are just intentions. Even if he had stolen, what is wrong in it? In this whole village everybody is poor, only I am rich; so if they take something away, it belongs to them. From where have I got all my riches? – from these poor people. They work for me: they work in my farm, they work in my garden. Everything that I have... I don't produce anything – I don't go to work in the field, to cut the crop or anything; these people do it. So if once in a while somebody steals, they are stealing their own things; I am not concerned in it.

He told me, "Don't think about that man as a thief. That is not your business. And we enjoyed it, it was such great entertainment."

I said, "That is true, we both enjoyed seeing him."

The thief went on slipping into the corner, but the further into the corner he went, the more he was caught. He wanted to escape from the juice of the betel leaf, but he could not get out because that corner was just close to my grandfather's bed. It was dark there, so in the beginning he thought that it was just accidental; but then he started slipping away and the spit started following him into the corner. Then finally he thought, "It is not accidental; that old man is spitting like a good shot. And the story he is telling is just to make me aware that he is awake: it will not be easy to steal anything." So finally he had to declare himself. He said, "I am here, and suffering. Now stop and let me go!"

My grandfather was such a good man and always nice and helpful to everybody; whoever came to him, he helped. He would give money to people. If they had come for a loan, and they wanted to put something down as mortgage, he never accepted it. He said, "I don't know – tomorrow I may die, then who will give you this mortgage back? Take the money. If you can manage to give it back, good. If you cannot manage, there is nothing to be worried about – I have enough."

He never took those people's signatures as proof that they had taken money. I told him, "You should have their signatures as proof that they have been lent money."

He said, "It is not a loan, it is their money. They may think it is a loan, but I am not thinking of it as a loan. So if they return it, good; if they don't return it, there is no loss because I was never expecting them to. They are so poor – how are they going to return it?"

Such a good man, a beautiful man, simply died. What was the meaning of his life? That became a tortuous question to me – what was the meaning? What had he attained? For seventy years he lived the life of a good man, but what was the point of it all? It simply ended. Not even a trace was left behind. His death made me immensely serious.

I was serious even before his death. By the age of four I started thinking of problems that people somehow manage to go on postponing to the very end. I don't believe in postponing. I started asking questions to my maternal grandfather and he would say, "These questions! You have your whole life – there is no hurry – and you are too young."

I said, "I have seen young boys dying in the village: they had not asked these questions, they have died without finding the answer. Can you guarantee me that I will not die tomorrow or the day after tomorrow? Can you give me a guarantee that I will die only after I have found the answer?"

He said, "I cannot guarantee that because death is not in my hands, nor is life in my hands."

"Then," I said, "you should not suggest any postponement to me. I want the answer now. If you know, then say that you know and give me the answer. If you don't know, then don't feel awkward in accepting your ignorance."

Soon he realized that with me there was no alternative. Either you had to say yes... But it was not easy: then you had to go into deeper details about it – and you could not deceive me. He started accepting his ignorance, that he didn't know.

I said, "You are very old, soon you will die. What have you been doing your whole life? At the moment of death you will have only ignorance in your hands and nothing else. And these are vital questions – I am not asking you any trivia.

"You go to the temple. I ask you why you go to the temple – have you found anything in the temple? You have been going your whole life, and you try to persuade me to come along with you." The temple was made by him.

One day he accepted that the truth was because he had made

the temple: "If even I don't go there, then who is going to go there? But before you I accept that it is futile. I have been going there my whole life and I have not gained anything."

Then I said, "Try something else. Don't die with the question – die with the answer." But he died with the question.

The last time he spoke to me, almost ten hours before he died, he opened his eyes and he said, "You were right: postponing is not right. I am dying with all the questions with me. So remember, whatever I was suggesting to you was wrong. You were right, don't postpone. If a question arises, try to find the answer as quickly as possible."

There are a thousand and one questions that every child asks you. And just because you are such a coward that you cannot accept your ignorance, you go on giving him bogus answers. He asks you, "Who created the world?" and you answer him, without knowing anything about God, "God created the world" – without even feeling ashamed, with no change on your face.

You answer as if you know, but you don't know; you are deceiving. And you are deceiving not only the child, you are also deceiving yourself. It works both ways. If you succeed in deceiving the child, you have succeeded in deceiving yourself into thinking that perhaps you know. Telling people again and again that God created the world, you will start believing in your own lie. Then certainly you will not feel so bored. Lies are very interesting because they are your inventions. The search for truth goes through much boredom: it is not an entertainment.

Somebody has asked the question: "Why are people so disinterested in the discovery of truth?" There is not far to go to seek the answer. Even to raise the question about truth means you have to become serious. It means you are leaving the world of entertainment behind, of circuses, movies, carnivals, football matches. You are leaving that world which keeps people occupied, and you are moving in the opposite direction to entertainment: that is boredom.

Why are people engaged in all these entertainments? Simply to avoid being bored. Just watch yourself left alone for one day in the house. You start doing bizarre things. You will turn the radio on, then put it off, then turn the TV on – not that you are really interested, but what else to do? When you are just left alone, boredom starts descending on you. You will start phoning friends, "Would you like to come to my place, or I can come to your place, or we can meet in

Zorba the Buddha." He is bored, you are bored. It is interesting that two bored people start entertaining each other. As far as I can see, this is absolutely against arithmetic.

I don't know much arithmetic. From the very beginning in my school I heard about these three *R*'s. "The whole of education consists of three *R*'s," one of my teachers said: "Reading, writing, 'rithmetic."

I said, "Whom are you trying to befool? 'rithmetic! Just to manage to make it the three *R*'s you are changing arithmetic into 'rithmetic." I told him, "Education consists only of two *R*'s: reading and writing. Arithmetic I don't take into account."

I have never been at ease with that 'rithmetic, but this much I can understand: two bored persons meeting will make the boredom double. That's what happens in marriages all around the world. Everybody knows both were alone and were feeling bored. They started entertaining each other, and immediately they fell into the fallacy that in their being together life would be interesting, there would be some juice in it. But that is possible only when you meet the girl or the boy on the sea beach, waiting twenty-three hours for one hour. Stolen kisses are sweet, otherwise how can kisses be sweet? It is stealing that makes them sweet.

I don't see that kisses can be sweet, particularly French kisses. If French kisses were sweet, every Frenchman would be suffering from diabetes – so much sugar! But there is no sugar at all so diabetic people can kiss without any fear. But stolen, there is the sweetness that you are creating a small world of your own.

But meeting once in a while, you are both prepared, you are both ready. You have taken a shower, she has taken a shower, and for at least three hours she has been before the mirror and used all kinds of perfumes and deodorants, and lip-stuff and whatnot. And then you meet for a few minutes or an hour. Of course you both are far away; only your personalities, the masks meet. She has come with painted smiles and you have come with painted smiles.

The strangest thing is that you know that you are not what you are pretending to be, she knows she is not what she is pretending to be – but both believe that the other is exactly what the other is pretending to be. This is something unbelievable. Then naturally they want to live together: if one hour is so sweet, if one hour is so miraculous that all boredom disappears, they start imagining how beautiful it will be to be together twenty-four hours a day. The fallacy has continued all through history, and I don't see any possibility that it is going to stop even in the future. If it stops it will be very significant, meaningful and it will give you a chance to understand boredom.

By understanding boredom, you can go beyond it. By avoiding it, you remain trapped in it. Marriage is a way to avoid it, just as there are so many other ways. But when you are together twenty-four hours a day, how long can you pretend? Pretension needs tremendous effort and energy. One day, two days, three days and the honeymoon is over: your mask starts slipping. You don't even care anymore if it slips and falls down, because the girl's mask is also slipping.

I have heard...

A man married a woman and they went on their honeymoon. The man said, "Before we go to bed, it is my old habit to put the light off. It is such a deep-rooted habit that I cannot go to bed unless I put the light off."

The woman said, "This is strange! You can go to bed, I am coming from the bathroom and I will put the light off."

He said, "Then I will wait outside the bed."

But the woman insisted, "This is my habit. I will go into the bathroom and come out only if you have gone to bed."

The man said, "This is strange: from the very beginning there is a conflict of habits." Then he said, "Now there is no point... The truth is that I don't have real legs, so I cannot undress in the light."

The woman said, "Then it is okay – because I don't have breasts. You can undress in the light, I can undress in the light. I was afraid that you may discover that I don't have any breasts."

The man said, "My God! I was afraid that you would discover that my legs are false."

But the marriage is already on the rocks. The honeymoon has not even started – the light is still on! Every honeymoon, more or less, in different ways, ends in the same way. Once you have known the woman, her physiology, her topography, once she has known you – your great lovemaking, huffing and puffing and perspiring and stinking – now you know you are going to bore each other as much as when you were alone. Before, at least you were alone and bored; now you are bored and somebody else is also there to bore you.

Then husband and wife go on living "happily ever after." That's how every story ends, how every film ends: "After that they lived happily ever after." After that, they did not live at all! They simply died. Every day they died more and more. But man's stupidity is such that he won't see the exact problem. You will think, "This woman failed me," "This man failed me." "Perhaps we are not meant for each other" – as if there is some woman who is meant for you or some man who is meant for you. Forgive me, there is no woman, just nobody is meant for you. You are born alone and you have to accept your aloneness. The sooner you do the better.

But aloneness is boredom because there is no entertainment, nothing interesting. Yes, for twenty-one years I was bored to death. Not only was I bored, I was boring everybody whom I could catch hold of. My father would immediately start looking in his books... I would see that he was sitting in the shop, not looking in the books, and as I entered he would start looking. Once I asked, "Why are you trying to look busy without business? I have seen you – you were just sitting. There is no customer, and you were not looking in the books. Why did you start looking in there?"

He said, "Can't I even allow myself to be engaged in something to avoid you? Go somewhere else! You must be bringing some problems. I have my own troubles – take care of your own problems."

My teachers would not allow me to raise my hand because – I don't know how it happens in other countries, but in India if you want to ask a question you have to raise your hand. My practice was that before the teacher entered the class my hand was up. He would not even be seated and my hand would be up. He would say, "This is something! At least let me sit down. Is there some emergency?"

I would say, "Everything is an emergency. Why should I waste time? When you start teaching, you force me to keep my hand down because you are teaching and I should not disturb you." Teachers would immediately start writing on the board so they could keep their backs toward me, but I was not so easily put off. Just the other day we were talking about Bible-bashing: I was book-bashing. I would go on hitting the book till they had to turn around.

I would say, "You cannot escape this way. My hand is up and I have a question" – and I had all kinds of questions. My teacher would say, "This question does not belong to my subject."

I would say, "It is not a question of subject. Life cannot be divided into subjects. Your school curriculum may be divided, but life is undivided. When I go in the history class I am the same person, when I go in the geography class I am the same person: I go into every class with the same problems. So I don't bother what subject you are teaching, I am concerned with my question. And my question is not only my question, it is yours too – that's what is freaking you out."

They were simple questions like, "What is the meaning of your life? Why are you living?"

Now, those teachers would say, "Do you want that we should commit suicide?"

I would say, "I have no objection, but before you commit suicide you will have to tell me why you are committing suicide. What are you going to gain out of it? You will have to answer that question. So suicide is not going to help, the question will remain the same: why are you living? Why are you dying? And if you can't answer such a simple question such as why you are living, then what else is there?

"You try to teach me history about Alexander the Great, and you don't know anything about yourself, even about your life. You want to teach me about religion, about Krishna and Rama – and you don't know anything about the living principle in you, from where you got it. Are you aware of the source, and where you are going?"

Once you are skeptical then everything can become the object of immensely important questions. And when you are surrounded by questions and no answer is coming from anywhere, you feel betrayed by existence, betrayed by your parents, betrayed by your teachers, betrayed by your priest – because there is no answer and yet you go on living: committing suicide is a crime.

It is a strange world. Just the other day, a news cutting was brought to me: a man died near the White House in Washington. Hungry, cold, frozen, he was found just by the wall of the White House. When they found the dead body in the morning, they searched him and it was found that he was a Second World War veteran. Can you believe this? They gave him all the respect that is given to a war veteran. Alive, he was hungry, with no clothes to cover him from the cold: nobody cared. Dead, with great respect, with all military respect, he was given the salute. What kind of world are we living in? A living person has no means to live, and a dead person is given great honor.

In the same way, it is so funny that all over the world suicide is one of the greatest crimes. Strange: you don't help people to find the meaning of their lives, and you force them to live – because to drop out of living, to just return the ticket and say, "I want to get out of this train of life, I am no longer interested," is to commit a crime.

It becomes even funnier. If you are caught committing suicide, then you will be sentenced to death! We are living with such intelligent people all around – the great law-makers, constitution makers. That's exactly what this man was going to do – die. Now, what is the need of all this hullabaloo? – catching hold of him, then for months keeping him in prison, and a court trial with the advocates fighting each other like cats and dogs, the great magistrate sitting seriously deciding. And the man is sentenced to death. When the poor man was doing it himself without any expense to the government, to the nation, to anybody, that was a crime!

Why is suicide a crime? From a very early age I have been thinking why suicide is a crime. It is a crime because it gives the idea to everybody else that life is not worth living: "That man did well." You are not courageous enough, you are cowardly: you cannot commit suicide. How to hide this cowardliness? Of course! – you can make a law that he has committed a crime, and this kind of crime has to be prevented; otherwise many more people will start committing it.

They are really trying to repress in everybody's mind the idea of dropping out of life. It is a well-known, well-established fact that anybody with a little intelligence thinks at least one time in his life – certainly that is the minimum – of committing suicide. Why? – because life seems to be just boredom. Marriage has failed. Religion has failed. Politics leads nowhere. You can have all the money in the world, still you are as poor as you were before.

Boredom is something very fundamental. It is part of not accepting your aloneness. It is part of not being able to enjoy your aloneness. You have been taught by the society to escape, to go on running, not to look back, but boredom follows you like a shadow. Boredom is your shadow.

Where are you going to escape to? You can't escape from it. Perhaps for a few moments you can drown it in alcohol, but the next morning it will come back, worse than it was before. Then you call it a hangover. You suffer the hangover; still again you are going to drink, knowing perfectly well that the hangover is coming. But at least for a few hours you are absent. Drunkards are not bored. You can go into any pub and see the drunkards. They are utterly happy and enjoying, shouting, screaming and beating people, doing all kinds of things but they are radiant. You will not see them miserable, sitting in a corner philosophically like Rodin's statue of *The Thinker*, with the hand under the chin, half-closed eyes.

The very posture of Rodin's statue *The Thinker* shows sadness, it has exactly caught the mood of boredom. He is so bored, he has no energy even to open his eyes and look around. Inside, questions upon questions are standing in a row, an endless row.

When one marriage fails, people start getting divorces and searching for another woman. I have heard about one Californiac – yes, I use the word *Californiac* because you can find that kind of people only in California; whoever gave the name California to this part of the world must have in mind the idea of Californiac – one Californiac married eight times, nothing surprising in America...

In India, of course, wives go on praying to find the same husband in the next life. I have always felt so sorry for the poor husband: if these prayers are heard...! Every year there is a particular day in India: the married woman fasts, that is purification, and after fasting she prays that she should get the same husband life after life. I feel sorry for the poor husband, because if those prayers are heard what is going to happen to him? And I feel very strange about the women: are they aware of what they are asking? You want this dodo life after life? One life is not enough? But it is just tradition. In fact every day the wives are a pain in the neck of the dodos – and the same dodo goes on doing the same to them.

Everybody in this instance follows Jesus Christ: "Do unto others whatever you want to be done to you by them." The husband is doing to the wife what he must want done to him; the wife is doing what she must want to be done to her. All are Christians in that way; particularly married couples are all Christians – whatever religion they belong to.

This man married eight times, and each time he found that somehow he ended up with the same type of woman. He must have been a slightly alert man. He watched, and thought, "This is strange." But this is not strange, it is simple psychology. You fall in love with a woman. You have certain ideas about beauty, form, aesthetics; and that woman fits into your formula of who is going to be the right wife for you – as if right wives exist or right husbands exist! All are wrong, because the whole institution of marriage is idiotic. So there is no right husband, no right wife – unless somebody like me manages the marriage of two people.

For example, I know one couple who would have been the right couple: Morarji Desai, ex-prime minister of India, and Mother Teresa. I can say with absolute certainty that if they were married they would be the most perfect couple in the whole of history. But it is very difficult to find such a couple. It took fifty years for me to discover this one couple.

Because you choose a woman, you forget that you have a certain formula unconsciously working. Why do you suddenly choose a particular woman? – there are so many women in the world. It is because this woman fits with your idea of a right wife. Now, you divorce after three months because although you found that her nose fits with the formula, her hair color fits with the formula, her body fits with the formula, she is not only a combination of hair, eyes, nose; these are nothing. She is an individual, hidden from you completely. So you have only seen the outer side of the woman, and you don't know her inner depths, where she really is. And she has only seen your outer form.

It is just like seeing a fence, and deciding this is the right house: you have only seen the fence around the house, not even the walls of the house – what to say about the inner chambers? What if there are scorpions or snakes, witches and devils? One never knows what is there, just the fence fits. But you can't live outside the fence. You get married just to go inside the house, and when you enter each other's house it is terrible because you have chosen each other out of boredom, not out of joy.

You have chosen not to share something but to get something. The woman has also chosen to get something because she is empty. Now two beggars are choosing each other thinking that the other is an emperor. Once you come closer, dreams are broken. You can divorce the woman, but how are you going to choose another woman? – You will choose again by the old formula that you know, that is fixed in your unconscious; perhaps you are not aware of it. The old formula will find the same kind of woman again, you cannot find anybody else. It is almost like marrying the same woman. And that's what happened, that's why I was going to tell the story.

The Californiac married eight women. When he married the eighth woman, after two days he found that he had married her once before. It took two days for him to discover it. They were all similar types but this one looked like an exact replica. And the woman was not yet aware that it was the same man; only when he told her did she become aware. He said, "My God! What have we done? Let's be together for two or three months and then divorce."

Wherever divorce has come as a fashion you are bound to find that you will always choose the same type. And the woman, on the other side, is going to choose the same type of man. You are perhaps not doing anything different than the Hindu wife. You are going into the unnecessary trouble of changing the wife, and the husband, and the house, and the job, and going through the courts. Hindus have discovered long before that it is pointless: you will again chose the same woman, she will again chose the same husband, so why not decide once forever, "We are going to be eternal companions, torturing each other, what is the point of changing? At least we will become accustomed of each other's torture, perhaps we may start loving each other's torture."

One just needs a little practice and one starts loving any kind of thing – and practice for lives together. I think Hindus have some insight into it: why practice again with another? It is better to have the old companion you know perfectly well, she knows you perfectly well. There is no need to start everything from *ABC*, you can start from *XYZ*. There is no need for a honeymoon. You know there is nothing like honeymoon in India. What is the point, because this woman has been your wife for many lives before and she is going to be your wife many more lives, so why waste time? Why waste money?

I have heard...

A very miserly Christian was going to a hill station. In the train somebody sitting by his side asked, "Where are you going?"

He said, "I am going on my honeymoon."

The man said, "But I don't see your wife."

He said, "She will be going next year because two persons going together is too expensive. So this time I am going, next year she will be going."

I think that too is insightful, at least they will not destroy their honeymoon.

People are doing all kinds of things for the simple reason that they can forget themselves – because the moment they remember themselves there is boredom. And the whole society, all the cultures teach you to escape quickly from yourself, the further away the better.

I was also bored but I did one thing differently, and that was that I decided I was going to live with the boredom; I was not going to escape because escape was not going to help. You will be surprised how I lived my boredom. My family, my friends started thinking that I had gone mad because I would not participate in any entertainment, I would not go for any picnic. I would lie down on the floor and look at the ceiling for hours together, just to be as bored as possible. Now you don't know Indian ceilings: you can't find anything uglier. Just ugly beams covered with mud tiles full of dirt, spider webs, rats running on the beams, and I would simply lie down on the floor looking at this beautiful scene.

I had decided that whatever boredom was, I was determined to live with it. If this was how nature wanted me to be alone, okay, then let nature take its own course. But the strangest thing happened with my determination to live with boredom. One day it disappeared. I was there alone but no longer lonely. And since then it has not appeared again. Right now I have almost forgotten how it tastes. You have asked the question so I am trying to answer you, but my own experience has fallen so far away.

I have lost psychological track of all memories. Factually I can describe them but I cannot relive them. These two words will be helpful to understand: *factual* memory and *psychological* memory. You insulted me thirty years ago and I was angry: I can remember it factually that you insulted me and I was angry – this is factual memory. But to get into that anger again, to have that insult become a real thing again, not as a memory but as a living experience, is psychological memory. I have lost the psychological track of all memories. Factually, I can describe it, but I cannot relive it.

My life is absolutely alone. This is strange to say because I have lived thirty-five years of my life in crowds. But I am alone in the crowd. You are there, but I am alone. Even in the crowd I am not different in any way than when I am sitting in my room alone. My aloneness persists; it is incorruptible.

I live in just one room almost the whole day. My life is as much a routine as possible. I have meticulously arranged everything that creates boredom around myself: I have not allowed anything that may help me to escape from my aloneness. In the morning exactly at a certain time I get up. And do you know what I do first thing? Even Vivek does not know. The first thing is that I pinch myself to see whether I am still here or it is finished. Only after pinching myself and being certain do I push the button for Vivek to bring my tea. Because what is the point of pushing the button if I am not here? She will unnecessarily get up and prepare the tea and bring it – and that is not right.

So first I make certain that I am still here. Then I push the button for her to bring my tea. And what is my tea? No milk, no sugar, just hot water with tea leaves. But I enjoy it because it is the purest taste of tea. Sugar and milk destroy the purity of tea completely.

Everything is set up exactly the same every day. I have half an hour in my bathroom, then half an hour in my swimming pool. It must be the hottest swimming pool in the world: ninety-nine degrees Fahrenheit. It is just cooking yourself completely, twenty minutes in it and you are cooked well. And I don't have a small swimming pool, it is Olympic size. You know I am a man of very simple tastes – I am satisfied with the best of anything: satisfied simply, but with the best of anything.

Sheela was asking me, "What are you going to do with the Olympic size?"

I said, "The point is not what I am going to do with the Olympic size. The size has to be Olympic: I cannot step into a smaller size swimming pool."

Half an hour in that hot water, then back for half an hour under an ice-cold shower. You cannot have that ice-cold shower for more than two minutes. But after the ninety-nine-degree hot water it is a tremendously beautiful experience to be under ice-cold water. The change from hot to the opposite, to very cold, is again a deeper pinching. The first was on the body, this is on the soul. Then I am perfectly certain that I am here and going to prevail, at least for today.

Vivek brings my breakfast, which is really a great breakfast – just a glass of juice, the same. It would be the same for everybody else, but not for me because I don't compare. Yesterday is gone and tomorrow has not come yet – I don't compare it. Vivek was asking me today, "Are you really excited with the same food every day?" – because yesterday I said I was excited. She was asking, "Are you *really* excited?"

I said, "I am always excited with the same juice, the same food, because the problem arises only when you start comparing. When you start thinking that for ten years you have been having the same juice, then there arises the fear, 'What are you doing?'" But I am not bored. I have dropped comparison. I don't carry any psychological memory with me: I go on dropping it moment to moment, and then I can enjoy the same thing for the whole of eternity.

She must have been worried because of what I said. She must have talked with my personal physician, Devaraj, and said, "Should we change Osho's complete menu?"

I said, "No, I am not going to allow you to change it. I am so settled with it that a change may create some trouble." I am not bored with it. It is difficult to believe, but I have learned one thing: if you can enjoy your aloneness then you can enjoy anything. And if you cannot enjoy your aloneness, you cannot enjoy anything. That is an absolutely fundamental principle.

I had a friend who was a school inspector. One day he came to me very excited and said, "Just listen. Can you believe this?"

I said, "Just settle down – don't be so excited. What has happened? I have never seen you excited. You are always bored with the same routine: going again and again to the same schools, to the same classes and the same questions. What has happened? Something extraordinary?"

He said, "You will not believe it! I went to a school..." First I have to explain to you the story, otherwise you won't follow him.

Sita is Rama's wife. Her father had declared, "Whosoever breaks the bow of Shiva" – that Shiva himself had given to Sita's father as a gift – "my daughter will put a garland on his neck." That was called *swayamvar* in India: the girl choosing her husband by a certain device. This was the device, and the device was really difficult. Shiva's bow was so heavy that to break it by hand was almost impossible. It was difficult even to pick it up with your hands from the platform on which it was lying. Princes after princes, kings after kings came. Finally Rama came: he broke Shiva's bow and married Sita.

This story was given to the students of a class to prepare for the next day, and by accident that was the day that my friend happened to visit the school. When he entered the class, the teacher was just asking the students, "Tell me, who broke Shiva's bow?" A boy, very afraid and nervous, raised his hand. The teacher was surprised – this was the last boy he would have imagined would answer. He had never answered anything, but now he was raising his hand. The principal was there and the inspector of schools was there, so he said, "Okay," but he was afraid that the boy would mess up the whole thing.

The boy stood up and said, "Sir, I have not broken it. And moreover, yesterday I did not even come to school." Now, he had really messed up the whole thing. The teacher was boiling: what would the inspector think, what would the principal think?

But before he could say anything or do anything, the principal said, "As far as I'm concerned, this boy seems to be mischievous: I think he *has* broken it." The inspector was at a loss. What to do now? This was becoming absolutely mad! He went to the chairman of the school committee to tell him what was going on.

The chairman said, "Don't be worried. I will just tell the carpenter and he will fix it. Children are children and furniture gets broken – it is nothing to be worried about."

I said, "But you should have enjoyed it – it was such a beautiful experience! But you don't seem to have enjoyed it, you have become worried about it."

He said, "Worried? It is a great concern. What is going on? Even the headmaster says, 'I suspect that this is the culprit – his face shows it.' And the chairman said, 'Don't be worried, I will tell the carpenter and he will fix it. This is an everyday affair. These children are children.'"

My friend said, "This is not the whole story. When I came home I told my wife, and my wife said, 'Will you come to your senses or not? In our house so many things are broken, and nobody bothers. I have been telling you the chair is broken, the lamp is broken – and you are worrying about Shiva's bow? What business is it of yours?'

"So I have come to you, to tell you that this is the state of affairs," my friend said.

I said, "I think this is a very beautiful state of affairs – just go and enjoy it! Don't get worried about it. The beauty of the story could not have been as good if the boy simply answered factually that Rama broke the bow. What would there have been in that? But the boy was original."

He said, "My God, you say that the boy was original?"

I said, "I think everybody was original because they all managed to find some new idea. They were not repeating old things."

To repeat old things becomes boring. There are two ways to get out of it: don't repeat old things, which is impossible because life consists of small things. You will have to brush your teeth every day. How many original ways can you find? I don't see that you can find many. As far as my dentist is concerned there is only one right way. Wrong ways you can find, but the right way is only one. If you start getting bored with that, then every morning you will start bored. Enjoy it, don't compare. What is there to compare? If you don't compare, it is no longer repetition; if you compare, it is repetition.

You will have to take a shower – and it is going to be the same. You will put on your clothes and you will do your work – it is all going to be the same, more or less. If you try to do everything new in order to be creative you will simply go crazy.

This story of Shiva's bow reminds me of another, which happened in front of me in my own village. It was the same story. Rama's life is played all over India every year, and this part is in it: Ravana was a competitor of Rama, and he was a mighty man. He was also as much a devotee of Shiva as Sita's father, perhaps a greater devotee. So there was great fear that he might break the bow. Neither Sita's father wanted that because Ravana was a monstrous man with ten heads, nor did Sita. She was afraid that he might succeed – everybody was afraid – so a conspiracy was created.

The moment Ravana was to stand up and go toward the bow, a man would come running in and say, "Your kingdom is on fire." Sri Lanka was Ravana's kingdom, and the story is that his capital in Sri Lanka was all made of gold. Of course if his kingdom was on fire then he would drop the idea of breaking the bow. He already had many wives, and he was not particularly interested in Sita: the only thing was the challenge to break the bow. He was interested in breaking the bow: Sita or no Sita was not the problem, as Ravana had many beautiful wives. So he dropped the idea and rushed toward Sri Lanka. Meanwhile Rama broke the bow and married Sita. This is the story and then the story goes on.

What happened in my village when this scene came, and the man came running and said, "Ravana, your kingdom is on fire," was that the man playing Ravana said, "Let it be!"

Nearabout twenty thousand people, many of whom were asleep, just woke up! The whole crowd was awake: "What has happened?"

Ravana said, "Let it be – this time I'm going to break Shiva's bow. Every year the same, the same, the same: 'Your kingdom is on fire' – and nothing is on fire." And he broke the bow. It was nothing, it was just a bamboo bow. He simply broke it in many pieces and threw all the pieces away, and told the father of Sita, "Where is the girl? Bring her!"

It was a great shock, but really original. And he declared to the people, "Now go home because the story is finished" – because that was the point of the whole story. Rama gets married to Sita, then Ravana finds out that it was a conspiracy, that his kingdom was not on fire – it is just a trick to get him out of the way and to give time to Rama, so Ravana steals Sita just to take revenge. Then the whole story goes on: he steals Sita, then Rama fights and gets Sita back...

But he finished the whole story. He said, "It is finished. You can go home, and from tomorrow there will be no Ram Leela. For this year I have done it." Later on it was found that the problem was that he had had a quarrel with the man who was managing the show. After the show they all used to get sweets and fruits, which people were bringing to offer to Rama. All the actors used to get them, and the day before, this man had got a smaller proportion. He was angry and he said, "Today I want double."

The manager said, "No, nothing doing. If I give you double then everybody else will ask for double."

He said, "Then watch out! If something goes wrong I am not responsible."

The manager said, "What can go wrong?" He had never conceived that the man could do this.

I went backstage, and I really appreciated the man. I said, "You did something original. Every year somebody needs to do something original."

The manager said, "You are supporting him! We are going to give him to the police because he has destroyed the whole thing. Now from where are we going to start the story tomorrow? Tickets have been sold and people will ask for their money back if the story is finished. It was just the opening day! We are going to give him to the police."

I said, "No, that is not right – he is such an original person. Tomorrow find somebody else to play the role – just release him from the role – and start again from the very beginning."

But the manager said, "How can we do that? – because he has broken the bow."

I said, "Simple, just open the show tomorrow. Declare that the show will be on and that it will be the first show. When the curtain opens, Janaka, the father of Sita, will declare, 'Yesterday, through the mistake of my servants, the real bow of Shiva was left in the palace. The bow that was broken was just a bow which children play with. Today, the real bow is here and the show starts.'"

The manager said, "That's good – that will do."

So the next day the show started. People were laughing because again it was a bamboo bow and if somebody wanted to break it, he could. But that Ravana was taken out and there was somebody else playing the role. The story continued and the people fell asleep and snored.

In life you cannot be original every moment. But what can be done... Since the moment I started enjoying just being myself, all psychological memory started falling like dust every day. Everything is new, is original because it is not compared with the past. I see you: I never feel that you are the same people, not for a single moment, because twenty-four hours have passed and you have all grown twenty-four hours older. So much water has gone down the Ganges, it is no longer the same water. So much life has flowed through you, you are not the same person. Yes, the face is similar, but not exactly the same.

Gautam Buddha used to say, "Life is just like a flame. You light a candle in the evening, and the whole night the candle burns. You can see that the flame is almost the same, but it is not the same flame. The flame is continually becoming smoke and a new flame is coming out. The old is disappearing and the new is appearing, but the disappearance of the old and the appearance of the new is so quick that you cannot see the gap between the two. That's why you think it is the same flame. In the morning when you blow out the candle, never think that you are blowing out the same candle you had kindled in the evening. It is not. In these twelve hours the flame has been continually changing: it is a flux."

So is life, so is everything – continuously changing, moving. Nothing is the same, nothing can remain the same for two consecutive moments. Once you understand that... But that understanding has to be first experienced in your own life flame. When you see that your own life flame is a flux, a continuity of movement, a continuum, then everything around it is always new – similar, but new.

The moment you can feel your newness, and everything's newness around you, boredom disappears. Animals are not bored, idiots are not bored, because they don't have the intelligence to see. Enlightened people are not bored because they can see the totality of their own being – that it is a constant newness, that dust does not gather there, that the mirror remains clean and everything that reflects in your consciousness is always new.

The tree outside the house will not be the same in the morning. Please don't behave with the tree as if it is just the same. New leaves have come, old leaves have fallen; new flowers may have blossomed, old flowers may have disappeared. Change is the only permanent phenomenon in existence. Nothing else is permanent except change. So what is there to be bored about? But it has not to be just an intellectual understanding: it has to arise from your experience of being a flame. You are a flame which goes on changing. Every second something new is coming into the flame and something old is becoming smoke.

Once your aloneness becomes a constant newness then whatever you do is creative, is original, is new. And you cannot manage in any way to feel bored.

I have tried to feel bored one more time at least, to see how it was, but I have to confess I could not succeed. I have tried every way, but everything is so new – what can you do? From where to bring in something old? There is nothing old ever: all is new forever. But let this understanding arise from your innermost experience of aloneness.

CHAPTER 9

The Only Sin Is to Forget Your Being

Osho,
Could you say something to us about bliss?

I have been blissed out for almost thirty-three years. That is exactly the time Jesus lived on the earth. Shankara also lived only thirty-three years, Vivekananda too. For the whole length of the life of Jesus I have been blissed out. This seems to be the right time to ask me what bliss is. It is almost impossible to answer, but remember I am saying "almost."

The "almost" depends on two things. First: if you are available, open, relaxed, with no idea of what bliss is, just a pure inquiry without any prejudice, without any mind; if your heart is available without any conditions from your side – then perhaps the almost impossible can become possible.

Secondly – and this is an even more difficult thing. It is as if a person has been dead for thirty-three years. Logically you can ask him, "What is death? – you have been experiencing death for thirty-three years, how long will you take to define it?" The dead man cannot answer; he is not there.

I am also not here – I am a dead man. This is the nature of bliss:

as it enters you, you are no longer there. They cannot exist together. The coexistence of the ego and bliss is absolutely impossible; only one can exist. It is like darkness and light. You cannot manage some kind of coexistence between darkness and light.

In the East we have a story that darkness appeared before God with tears in her eyes and complained against the sun: "I have not done anything against your sun. I am not even acquainted with him, we have never met; still he goes on harassing me. Wherever I go, sooner or later he reaches me and I am constantly on the run. Now I am really tired, and I want you to do something about it. Why is he after me?"

God called the sun and asked him, "Why are you after darkness? What wrong has she done to you?"

The sun said, "Who is darkness? I have never met her. I would like to be introduced."

God looked around to where darkness had been standing but nobody was there. Since then God has been trying to arrange some kind of meeting, a round-table conference, some kind of mediation, negotiation. But although all the religions say that God is all-powerful, in this case he has failed. He has not been able to bring the light, the sun, in front of darkness; only one appears at a time. The reason is very simple: darkness has no existence of its own. It is only the absence of light. When the light is present, how can its absence also be there? That absence is possible only when light is absent. This case is going to remain eternally on file, undecided.

The story is really significant; it says something about you and bliss. The ego is nothing but the absence of blissfulness. The more egoistic a person is, the more in anguish, in suffering, in misery, in darkness he is. His life is nothing but hell. There is no other hell than to live in the ego. There is no other heaven than to come out of the ego.

In coming out of the ego you come out of suffering, misery, anguish – that whole company. And when there is no ego, what remains is blissfulness. I close my eyes, it is there. I open my eyes, it is there. I walk, it walks with me. I sleep, it sleeps with me: I am no longer separate from it.

There is a beautiful statement of one of the great masters, Kabir. He says, "O my beloved, seeking and searching, seeking and searching, I have lost myself. The drop has dropped into the ocean; now where am I going to find myself? I was just a drop." After he had written this in the early morning, his disciples, who used to gather then, asked him what he had been writing. Kabir said, "I have written something, but I am not quite satisfied."

Let me repeat his words, they have a beauty of their own: "*Herat, herat hey sakhi rahya Kabir herai; bund samani samund mey so kat heri jai.* O my beloved friend, a great difficulty has arisen. I was searching, searching, seeking and seeking, and in all this search I forgot to take care of myself. I am lost, lost just as when a dewdrop falls into the ocean. The dewdrop finds the ocean, but at the cost of losing itself."

"But I'm not satisfied," Kabir said. "so just wait. Something is still not right." And he changed it – just a little change, a little difference, but what a difference it makes! "*Herat, herat hey sakhi rahya Kabir herai; samund samana bund mey so kat hero jai.* O my beloved, seeking and searching, Kabir is lost. The ocean has fallen into the dewdrop, now where am I going to find my dewdrop?"

Both ways are true, but the second way is truer than true. It has come very close to the ultimate expression of bliss. It *is* a finding, but very risky – on the condition of losing your self.

Ordinarily, in the dictionaries you will find bliss defined as happiness, pleasure, joy. Linguistically they all appear to have a similar meaning; existentially it is not so. And you will have to understand the subtle nuances and differences; only then you may be able to catch some hold of the phenomenon called bliss. Remember, you cannot hold bliss in your fist. You can hold bliss only in your open hand. Bliss is just like a breeze: your fist will miss it. Your open hand may have a little dance with it, a little love affair with it.

Let us start from the lowest because that will be easier to understand, that's where man biologically is born. Pleasure is physical. A great Sufi poet, Omar Khayyam, has the right definition of pleasure. He was not defining pleasure, he was writing a beautiful poem but, unknowingly, he has come very close to defining pleasure. He says: A cold winter night, having a good dinner; sitting by the fireside on your coziest chair, with a book of poetry in your lap, and a beautiful woman dancing and singing with a musical instrument… The warmth, the beauty, the good, delicious food, and a great book of poetry in your lap; the music… You are alone together in the cold night and the warmth of the fire. This is pleasure.

Physically you are healthy. You enjoy your food. You enjoy your lover, your beloved. You enjoy friends, or music, or painting – all this is physical. Nothing is wrong in it; as far as my religion is concerned I am all for pleasure. Of course, I don't stop there, I only start from there. All the other, old religions are against pleasure; and that's where they have missed, because if you miss the first step, please don't hope that you will be able to reach the highest step. The first rung of the ladder is as essential as the last: they are both part of the same ladder. I have no condemnation of the first rung on the ladder because without it the whole ladder will disappear.

I am all for pleasure, but I would like you to be reminded that there are higher things than pleasure. Happiness is higher than pleasure. It is not physical, it is more psychological. You may be hungry, you may be cold, freezing, and suddenly a friend knocks on your door. You forget your hunger and your cold and you simply give him a hug. It is something higher than the body can give you; it is in your psychology. A friend whom you have not seen for a long time: you forget your body – a tremendous happiness arises in you.

Animals have only pleasure, and most human beings are still animals. Most of them don't know of happiness. There are people who have never loved. Remember, sex is pleasure, love is happiness. Don't get confused between the two. Love can exist without sex; sex can exist without love. They can exist together too but there is no necessity for them to exist together.

Sex is given by nature; it is an inbuilt program in your biology. Love is not an inbuilt program, that's why so many people go on missing it. It has to be evolved. You have to learn it, it is an art. You have to understand one thing, that nature and biology have no need of love: sex is enough for life to continue. Reproduction is the end of sex, and biology is interested only in reproduction.

Love is a luxury. It has no biological function. Unless you start learning something that goes beyond your body, which is not a need of the body – the body can exist without it – you will never be able to know what love is. Experience poetry, the depth of music, or the beauty of a sunrise or a sunset. No animal bothers about sunset or sunrise. You should not be deceived by the birds in the morning chattering all around. It is not a song of happiness to welcome the sun, no. It is just the overflowing energy after the whole night's peaceful, relaxed state.

You don't get up so rejuvenated because you don't sleep well. Your mind goes on thinking and dreaming and projecting; your mind goes on keeping your body tense. Just watch somebody's face while he is sleeping, and you will wonder what he is doing. Sometimes his face becomes very tense, sometimes tension lines appear on his forehead, sometimes he is gnashing his teeth, sometimes he starts making sounds. Perhaps he is saying something but in sleep it becomes gibberish; you cannot figure out what he is saying. But so much is going on.

Just the other morning Vivek showed me one of the white peacocks which always comes near my sitting room and sleeps on a treetop. That is his religious practice every night; it may be raining, it may be snowing – it doesn't matter. The place where he sits seems to be so risky that he could fall any moment but he is so relaxed, almost one with the tree. Now, after these ten hours, twelve hours of going almost to the very source of his life in sleep, it is no wonder if he starts dancing in the morning.

It has nothing to do with the sun or the flowers, it has something to do with his inner energy which is overflowing. The birds are chirping, chitchatting – it is simply aliveness. But remember, animals or birds cannot have a taste of happiness; that is man's prerogative.

One thing to be remembered: pleasure has its counterpart – pain; happiness has its counterpart – unhappiness. You cannot have one without having the other too; they are inseparable. If you have pleasure, be ready for pain in the same amount. It is not possible to have ninety percent pleasure and ten percent pain. Nature does not function that way. It is very fair; it is always fifty-fifty, equally balanced.

Have you ever thought about why religious people, monks, saints, sages start renouncing pleasure? You may not have wondered. They are not renouncing pleasure, they are renouncing pain. But without renouncing pleasure there is no way to renounce pain – that is the difficulty. If it were possible to save pleasure and renounce pain, I don't think any saint would be so idiotic as to renounce pleasure.

They have to renounce pleasure because they have known that if you welcome pleasure, just behind the pleasure there is pain. It is almost like a door: on one side is written "push," on the other side is written "pull." It is the same door. Of course, if on one side it says "push," then on the other side it has to say "pull." It is the same phenomenon: on one side it is pleasure – pull – and you want to pull it as much as possible; on the other side is pain, and you want to push it as far away as possible.

But once you have chosen pleasure – and of course nobody chooses pain, except a few masochists. But even a masochist, by choosing pain, has to choose pleasure. A masochist is one who tortures himself and enjoys it: he has chosen pain, he is torturing himself, but you can see in his eyes he is enjoying it. You cannot divide the two – they are not two, just two sides of the same energy. In the same way happiness is joined with unhappiness. Everybody wants to be happy, and you will find everybody unhappy. The more you want happiness, the more you are inviting unhappiness.

The American Constitution has a very stupid idea in it. It says that the pursuit of happiness is man's birthright. The people who were writing this constitution had no idea what they were writing. If the pursuit of happiness is the birthright of mankind, then what about unhappiness? Whose birthright is unhappiness? Those people were not at all aware that if you ask for happiness, you have asked for unhappiness at the same time; whether you know it or not does not matter.

A certain painting makes you happy, the meeting of a friend makes you happy, a certain song makes you feel happy. But how long can you remain with the friend? In the meeting there is the departure; in life there is death. How long can you be happy with a song? Soon you will start getting bored by it, you will become fed up with it.

You can see it happening in every synagogue, in every church, in every temple, in every mosque: people are almost asleep. A few old fellows are even snoring, because they have heard the sermon so many times; just the very repetition of it brings boredom, and boredom brings sleep. This is a psychological mechanism. That's why all the methods that are suggested to people who are suffering from sleeplessness are really nothing but methods to get bored.

They are told, "Count from one to a hundred, and then count backward: one hundred, ninety-nine, ninety-eight, ninety-seven, count backward. Then from one to a hundred, and then count back again." Naturally you will get bored within five minutes. A few con people have sold this method as if they are giving you something of religious value – for example, Maharishi Mahesh Yogi. What he calls

Transcendental Meditation is nothing but transcendental boredom.

If you repeat any name continually for ten or twenty minutes you are bound to fall asleep. Of course it is a little different from your ordinary sleep: it is hypnosis. Hypnosis is deliberate sleep, not natural but created by a certain strategy, a certain mechanism – repeating, "Ave Maria, Ave Maria, Ave Maria," and fast. You have to repeat it fast so there is no gap between two "Ave Marias"; otherwise, some thought may enter and disturb your whole procedure, so you have to go really fast.

That's why Maharishi Mahesh Yogi does not give his mantra, the secret, openly to everybody. No, it has to be given in private. The reason is that for a Christian it has to be Ave Maria, for a Hindu it has to be Rama or Krishna, for a Mohammedan it has to be something else, for a Jew something else. You cannot declare the mantra publicly because Ave Maria will not appeal to a Hindu, he will not be ready to waste ten minutes on Ave Maria.

To a Christian, "Rama, Rama" does not make much sense – except for a few hippies. Everything makes sense for a few days and then it turns out to be nonsense. Hippies are constantly on the move. They are permanent seekers. They are not interested in finding, just moving, being on the move. Krishna is not meaningful to a Jew. A certain meaning, a certain conditioning from your childhood is needed to help you; otherwise the word which you are repeating will remain only on the surface of your mind. It won't get to your unconscious, and it is the unconscious which brings hypnosis.

Maharishi Mahesh Yogi was visiting Jabalpur when I was a professor there. I sent one of my students to take initiation from him, and I said, "Tell him that you are an atheist, that you don't believe in God, because I want to see what mantra he gives to you." Generally no atheist will go: in his whole life Mahesh Yogi would not have come across an atheist asking for a mantra. This boy was a very serious type, and I told him, "Remain very serious and follow the whole procedure. Whatsoever money is demanded, give it. You have to take flowers and a piece of silk cloth to offer."

So he went prepared. He touched Maharishi's feet – inside of course saying, "Go to hell, you son-of-a-bitch," but on the surface staying very serious. And when he touched Mahesh Yogi's feet, and put down the flowers and the silken piece of cloth, with folded hands he asked, "Please initiate me."

Mahesh Yogi said, "Okay. You seem to be really a seeker. What is your religion?"

The student said, "That is the difficulty. I am an atheist, I don't believe in God."

Maharishi Mahesh Yogi said, "This is the first time I have come across an atheist. I am at a loss as to what mantra to give you, because for an atheist all mantras are useless."

You cannot give him the name of Jesus: he does not believe in God, how can he believe in God's son? You cannot give him the name of Krishna: he does not believe in God, how can he believe in the incarnation of God?

Mahesh Yogi said to him, "Please come back tomorrow."

The boy came to me and he said that this had happened: "Mahesh Yogi thought for a few minutes and he said to come tomorrow."

I said, "He deceived you. Rush right now, ask for your money back, your flowers, your everything, because he is leaving tonight." So he rushed back.

The people outside Mahesh Yogi's camp tried to prevent him, saying, "This is not the time for initiation.

He said, "I don't care. I have not come for initiation; I have come to take back my things that I left here this morning." He was a strong young man, so he forced his way in and entered Mahesh Yogi's room.

Mahesh Yogi looked at him and said, "But I told you to come tomorrow."

The student said, "And tonight you are leaving. Your luggage is packed. Whom am I going to see tomorrow? Now please give me my money back. Where is my handkerchief and where are my flowers?" Mahesh Yogi had to find the student's money and things, and give them back to him.

These people are exploiting the whole world. What they are giving is just a simple method of hypnosis, autohypnosis. Anything will do; it has nothing to do with God's name. Any nonsense-sound will do. Just repeat it fast and get bored, and a certain sleep – for which a different name has been used, *hypnosis*, because there are no dreams in it – will descend on you. That's why after you wake up from transcendental boredom you will feel very fresh. But that's how everybody feels after hypnosis, exactly the same, because there are no dreams, no disturbance: you have tired the mind so much.

In India it is a known fact that if you say to a child, "Sit down in the corner and don't disturb me, we are doing something important," he is not going to sit down. In India the usual method is to tell the child, "Go and do twelve rounds of the house." After the twelfth round he is bound to sit down at least for half an hour and not bother anybody.

The same is the case with the mind. If you just sit and try to be silent you will find more thoughts are coming to you than ever, because they never usually find you so available. They are always standing in a queue waiting for their number to come up, and you are so late with your appointments that a few thoughts may be left standing there for years. But thoughts are stubborn, they can wait. For years they can wait: someday they will sneak in. So when you are sitting in meditation, prayer, contemplation, you are giving an opportunity to all the thoughts, desires, dreams which had not been able to attract your attention before.

Now you are available, so immediately there is a rush hour in the mind. Suddenly so many things start appearing out of nowhere. But if you are repeating a certain word, a certain name, then you don't give thoughts any chance. And if you are repeating words so fast that between two words there is no gap, then you give a chance for the mind to be bored with the same thing. This boredom brings a different quality of sleep – hypnosis, which is very refreshing, healthy. Nothing is wrong with it; all that is wrong is using it to cheat people and exploit people by giving them hypnosis as something spiritual. It is nothing spiritual.

Mind is capable of experiencing happiness, but the more dimensions of happiness are open to you, the more dimensions of unhappiness are also open to you. It is not something to be surprised about that people like Jean-Paul Sartre feel more anguish than so-called ordinary human beings. Sartre certainly is a genius. His mind had more dimensions open to happiness; obviously he had opened the door to unhappiness too.

One thing to remember about the relationship between happiness and time: happiness is so beautiful, so juicy, so groovy, that you feel time is passing very fast. The watch, the clock, have no idea that you are happy or unhappy – they are moving at the usual speed, but when you are happy you feel time fleeing fast because you would like to have as much of it as possible. You would like it to remain forever. You are clinging to it. You fear that it is going to slip out of your hands. In all this, the time has passed and suddenly you see that that great moment is no longer there.

So when happiness is there, it is momentary; when unhappiness is there you don't want it, it is an uninvited guest. You want to throw it back, but you are incapable of throwing it away. Time will seem to be moving slower, as if all the watches are conspiring against you. When you are happy they move fast; when you are unhappy they suddenly become lazy, lousy. No, they are not doing anything to you.

Albert Einstein was asked again and again, "What is your theory of relativity?" Now, his theory of relativity is a very complex phenomenon. He cannot just answer. You will have to go through a long process of education in higher mathematics and neo-physics, then you may be able to understand it a little bit. It is said that there were only twelve persons alive in Albert Einstein's time who understood his theory of relativity.

But he was bound to be asked. People had heard of the theory of relativity, and if Einstein happened to be somewhere, everybody would ask about it – so he had found an answer. The answer was that if you are sitting with your beloved – one situation – or you are sitting on a hotplate, burning hot, red-hot – another situation – will you feel time passing with the same speed? Obviously to the man sitting on a red-hot plate, a minute will look like a century; and being with his beloved, even a century will look like a moment. Einstein said, "This is what my theory of relativity is. More than that you will not be able to understand, but this is enough to get the idea." Time is relative to your mind, so much so that it can be said that time and mind are almost one phenomenon.

Now I can talk about bliss. Bliss has no counterpart to it. That is the first thing to understand. Pleasure has pain, happiness has unhappiness, but bliss has nothing as a counterpart; it is an organic whole. Gautam the Buddha used to say, "If you taste the ocean from anywhere, it is salty." So is the case with bliss: you can taste it from any corner, from any space, from any direction, it is just blissfulness. There is nothing opposite to it. Bliss is the only experience in life which has no polar opposite to it. That's why, once you are blissful, you cannot fall back. There is no way to be unblissful again. I have tried but nothing succeeds.

In Japan they have the statue of Bodhidharma – in Japanese his name has changed to Daruma. There is a doll called a Daruma doll, which was made according to a statement of Bodhidharma's. He said, "Whatever you do, you cannot put me upside down; I will always be upside up, downside down."

This statement gave an idea to a toymaker to make a doll. It is heavy at the bottom, so you can throw the doll any way and it always returns to sit in the lotus posture. You can push it, throw it, hit it, do whatever you can do, but it represents Bodhidharma – it always settles in a lotus posture.

So is the case with bliss: whatever you do to it, whatever happens around you, it is absolutely the same, unchanging. Bliss has some quality of pleasure in it, it has some quality of happiness in it, but it is much more. And the plus is that you feel absolutely fulfilled, contented, with no desire, no expectation. This very moment you are where everybody wants to be, and there is a tremendous feeling that more than this is not possible. There is no way for more than this to be possible – just as there can be nothing bigger than the sky; it is unbounded. It is inconceivable to the mind because the mind can only conceive of limited things. Here you can feel how limited the mind is. It cannot even conceive something unlimited.

The sky is there, without boundaries. You cannot come to a point where you can say, "Here is the boundary." Just think about it. How can you say, "Here is the boundary?" because a boundary means that something must be *beyond* the boundary. Two things are needed, absolutely needed, to make a boundary. If there is nothing beyond, then nothing is making a boundary: then there is no boundary, you will have to go into nothing. But you can never come to a point where you will find a board: "Here ends the universe." It ends nowhere, it begins nowhere. The same is the experience of bliss.

Bliss is within you, without you. Bliss is in life, it is in death. It is when you are healthy, it is when you are sick; it is when you are young, it is when you are old. Nothing makes any difference to it. It is simply transcendental to all that exists in the universe. And because it is universal, everywhere – within you, within me – howsoever difficult it may be to explain it, to experience it is not as difficult. Let me repeat my statement because that may look a little crazy: to explain bliss is more difficult than to experience it.

How can you explain what beauty is? What do you think hundreds of poets, philosophers, thinkers, and painters have been trying to do in these thousands of years? They have been trying to find the definition of beauty. They have created many beautiful things, but beauty remains undefined.

One man this century did a really arduous job. His name is G. E. Moore – one of the great philosophers of this century. He devoted his whole life to a single question: "What is good?" He was a moral thinker, and morality is impossible if you cannot even define what is good. Then how can you say what is bad? How can you say what is right and what is wrong, and how can you say what is sin and what is virtue? The basic thing has to be first tackled, and this is: "What is good?"

G. E. Moore has written his whole life's experience in a big volume. The name of the book is *Principia Ethica*. He had given the name before he started the book; otherwise, I don't think he would have given it that name, *Principia Ethica*. He was thinking he was going to find the basic principle of ethics, but after his whole life's research work, where he ends is really sad. He ends the book with the statement: "Good is indefinable."

You go through his book, which is very arduous, complicated, with arguments for and against – he has covered the whole history of moral philosophy, but finally he says, "Excuse me, good is indefinable, because good is a simple quality like yellow. If somebody asks you to define yellow, what can you do? I was simply stupid to have wasted my time."

What is yellow? You will say "Yellow is yellow," but that is not a definition – yet you know what yellow is, don't you? I know what bliss is, but please don't ask me what it is. If you cannot answer what yellow is – such a mundane and third-rate question – then it is difficult to define what beauty is, what good is. Perhaps a man like Michelangelo may create a statue, and tell you, "See, feel, touch it – this is beauty." Although you may not necessarily be satisfied, Michelangelo can at least create something objective.

A Picasso may create a painting; a Rabindranath Tagore may write a poem and say, "Somewhere here in this poem, between the words, between the lines, there is beauty. Just try to find it – just dive into it." They can at least give you something objective. It may not be sufficient to define it – it is not, and they know it – but at least working in their dimension gives them an opportunity to create something.

But my world is subjective. I cannot paint, I cannot write poetry, I cannot make a song, I cannot create or compose music about bliss. There is no way because bliss is a subjective experience, it is not a thing. You cannot observe it; it cannot be placed in front of you as an object. But there has been only one way, and that is to be in close proximity to a person who has experienced it.

That's what the meaning of the whole phenomenon of master and disciplehood is. The master has bliss, the disciple has bliss, but the master knows that he has bliss and the disciple does not know that he has it. As far as having bliss is concerned, there is no difference. The difference is only that the master's eyes are open and the disciple's eyes are closed.

Being in close proximity to the master, in some unexpected movement you may have a taste of it, just like a breeze passing through you and the feel of the coolness; or suddenly a fragrance passing by you that you cannot catch hold of. By the time you try to catch hold of it, it is already gone. Fragrances are not to be caught in your fist.

This is the whole function of my commune, to answer this question: "What is bliss." I am inviting you to be here, to be with me because there is only one possibility: that just by your being here, a synchronicity may happen. It has happened before, it can happen again. And you have to remember, there is no other way for it to happen. It happens only in this way.

Let me try to explain to you something about synchronicity, because that is the fundamental law of bliss. Have you ever experienced that you are sad, miserable, then a few friends come and they are gossiping, talking – and only later on do you remember, "My God, what happened to my misery and my suffering?" You got completely lost in gossiping and forgot about your misery. Those people were laughing and enjoying and joking, and something of their energy started to trigger something in you.

In Indian classical music it is an ancient, established fact that you can place a sitar – an Indian musical instrument – in one corner of an empty room, and on the other side, just facing the sitar, let a master sitarist play. You will be surprised: if the master is really a maestro, the other sitar sitting in the corner starts vibrating with the same tune. This is synchronicity. An invisible vibe of the music that is being played by the master slowly starts moving in the room. It is just like when you throw a stone into a silent lake, and ripples arise and go on spreading to the farther and farther shores.

In the same way every note of the master is creating a ripple in the air around him, and those ripples are going farther away. When passing the other sitar they will strike its strings. But the master has to be a very refined sitarist, because the strings on the other sitar need a very delicate touch – then they start slowly vibrating. Great masters have played it, showed it, exhibited it.

The Mogul Emperor of India, Akbar, was very interested when he heard about this, and he had one of the greatest musicians, Tansen, in his court, so he asked Tansen about it. Tansen said, "I am a great musician, but this is beyond me. My master can do it."

Akbar said, "Is there somebody who can play better than you?" – because so many musicians had come to try to defeat Tansen. It was a constant thing to want to become a member of the group Akbar had created, called "The Nine Jewels": nine masterminds, one for each dimension of life. Tansen was one of them.

Tansen said, "Yes, there is only one man, my master."

Akbar said, "I would like to invite him. We will give him the greatest welcome ever given to anybody, but I would like to listen to him."

Tansen said, "That's why I have never mentioned his name to you. I sing, I play music because I am full of desires, expectations. You have given me so much, but the desires are unending: I still go on playing because I want to get something. My master has got it. He plays because he has got something that he has to play and spread. I play because I want to get something. I am a beggar, he is a master. He will not come to the court; only beggars like me can come to court.

"For what will he come? If you are interested you will have to go to him – the thirsty go to the well. That's why I have never mentioned his name, because mentioning his name will mean you will ask me to call him; and then it will look discourteous, unmannerly, to refuse you. But I am helpless.

"He is an old beggar in the eyes of the world. He lives just near your palace, not far away, by the side of the Yamuna River. He has a small hut there – you will have to go to him. And you cannot just demand of him, 'Play!' When he is playing you can listen – hiding, because seeing us he may stop just to welcome us, to receive us. But every day at three o'clock in the morning he plays, so we have to go and hide outside the hut. You can take my sitar there, outside the hut, and watch."

Tansen and Akbar went, took the sitar there and sat outside waiting for the time. Exactly at three o'clock Tansen's master started playing. His name was Haridas. Perhaps India has never produced any other musician of his quality. The moment he started playing, the sitar outside started vibrating with exactly the same tune.

In Indian classical music there are ragas: particular music to be played at particular times of the day, throughout the twenty-four hours. For the morning there is one raga, for the evening there is another. They have worked for thousands of years to find what tune will fit for each period of time, so that the raga can be absorbed by it. Indian classical music is not like jazz music. No Eastern musician will accept jazz as music at all: "This is simply a crazy crowd jumping about." Of course they are making sound, but just to make sounds is not to make music. They have found that each period of time is vulnerable to a certain music.

At three o'clock, early in the morning, Akbar saw with his own eyes the other sitar vibrating, replying, as if the master were playing on both – as if some invisible fingers had reached out to the sitar waiting outside. For the first time Akbar started weeping. Tears came into his eyes, just out of joy.

They went home slowly. They remained silent all the way, but when Akbar was entering his palace, and Tansen was taking leave to go to his house, Akbar said, "Tansen, I used to think that nobody could play better than you, but I am sorry to say that you are nowhere near your master. Why are you wasting your time in my court? You should be with your master. If even a dead musical instrument is receptive to that man's music, what is impossible between you and him? Miracles are possible. Just forget this court, forget me. And he is an old man; be with him, just sit by his side and let his energy flow in you, let his music make you afire."

This is the law of synchronicity. The disciple is joined with the master by the law of synchronicity. A disciple is not a disciple unless the law of synchronicity starts functioning, unless something invisible transpires between you and the master.

The master is full of bliss, he is showering all that he has – because in the world of bliss the more you give, the more you have.

Ordinary economics is not applicable there. In ordinary economics, the more you give, the less you have. Something of a higher economics, totally different and opposite, functions: the more you give, the more you have. The master is showering.

Whether you get drenched with it or not is up to you, because you may be holding an umbrella. Your umbrella may get drenched, but umbrellas don't feel bliss. You will remain dry, and you will go on asking, "What is the definition of bliss? What is bliss?" Just close your umbrellas, put them aside. Better be utterly nude so nothing prevents – I mean spiritually be nude – so there is no barrier. When there is no barrier you will discover there has always been a bridge underneath the barrier.

I can help you to experience bliss, and when I can help you to experience it, why bother about the definition? Even if I define bliss, it won't make any sense to you. I can define it, but the definition will be simply words: "Bliss is ecstasy." But then you will ask, "What is ecstasy?" And that will lead to an infinite regression. I will go on saying *A* is *B*, *B* is *C*, *C* is *D*, and the whole round: *Z* is *A*, and *A* is *B*... No, a definition is not going to help at all.

The world of religion is not the world of definitions. The world of religion is the world of experiences. That's the difference between a teacher and a master: a teacher gives you definitions, explains the scriptures to you. The master allows you to go with him into the unknown. He does not give you definitions, scriptures: he gives you a push. He throws you into the bottomless abyss of existence. All my words are just pushes. They have nothing to do with answering your questions.

I want you to experience, and bliss is such an experience that it makes you dumb. You know it, you feel it, you are it, but you cannot say what it is. It is indefinable verbally, but existentially it is transferable. Yes, I can give it to you. My hands are not empty, they are full of it but you have to be empty to receive it.

I remember the famous story about Nan-in:

A university professor of philosophy went to see Nan-in, a great master. The professor was full of questions, all the way from his university to the hill where Nan-in used to live in a temple. He was just brooding and brooding. There were so many questions, what to ask? The professor had heard so much about Nan-in, and one rarely meets such a man. He went in.

The first thing Nan-in said to him was, "Please come in, but leave the crowd outside."

The professor looked all around; there was nobody. Crowd? – he was alone. Nan-in said, "Don't look here and there, look within: the crowd is there. It has been there all the way."

The professor was almost shocked. But a professor, after all, is a professor. He said, "You are right. It is a crowd, but I am a professor; I deal with this crowd. This is my profession, so excuse me, I cannot leave the crowd outside. It is going to be with me, but it will sit here silently. Don't take any notice of it."

Nan-in said, "But you are tired and you are perspiring. Sit, cool down and meanwhile I will prepare a cup of tea for you." Nan-in prepared a cup of tea, brought it in, gave the empty cup and saucer to the professor, and poured the tea from his kettle into the cup. The professor was watching: the cup was getting fuller and fuller and fuller. It was absolutely full and Nan-in was still pouring tea.

The tea started running out of the cup into the saucer. The professor tried hard to be patient because he had said the crowd would sit silently, but the crowd was there and it was saying, "This man is just nuts! Is this the way?" And the Japanese are very particular about tea; it is part of their culture and etiquette – this is never done. But Nan-in went on pouring. When the saucer was also full and the tea was just going to spill over the professor's clothes, the professor said, "Wait! What are you doing? The cup is full. It cannot hold a single drop more."

Nan-in said, "You have understood rightly. Can you give me a little space in you? Can you have just a drop of me in you? You are overfull, just like this cup and saucer. But you are a sensible man; you understood that by pouring in more tea, it will simply spill. But have you observed how much tea is spilling from your skull? My whole hut is becoming wet. When you come here next time, bring an empty cup; then I am willing to share whatsoever I have. But you are so full that it is useless: I cannot get into you from anywhere. I am looking from all sides – you are overcrowded. There is no space, not a single inch."

This is what the art of being a disciple is: becoming an empty cup and allowing the master, so that he can pour all that is within him. The master is not going to become poorer because he shared his bliss with you. It is a treasure that goes on growing. But it is one of the most difficult things in the world to allow and welcome bliss within you, because before that, you have to be ready. You have to clean yourself and nothing less than emptiness will be accepted as cleanliness.

In the West they say, "Cleanliness is next to godliness." There is no God so there is no question about that. But I say, "Cleanliness is just next to emptiness." In fact, cleanliness is another name for inner emptiness. Throw out all the rotten furniture and rags. And what kind of things you have collected!

I used to live with a man who was very rich, but very miserly also, *so* miserly. He was alone – no children, no wife. He never married for the simple reason that it was too expensive. He said, "I have seen all my friends: once they got married they lost all that they had. A woman is too expensive, I cannot afford one. And one thing follows another: a woman comes, then children come, and they will destroy everything that I have been collecting."

He really was a collector. One day I was going for a morning walk and he asked, "Can I come with you?"

I said, "You can come with me but what will you do? There is no earning in the morning walk." He always only did things which were economically useful. I said, "There is no economic use of a morning walk. You will be wasting your time – do something else."

He said, "No. It's just that you go every day and you look so happy, and when you come back you look so happy. I thought perhaps there is something in it, so for just one day..."

I said, "Okay, you can come. Perhaps you can find something." And he found something. What did he find? – the handle of a bicycle! Somebody had thrown it on the side of the road. He immediately picked it up. I said, "What are you doing?"

He said, "You don't know: I have two wheels which I collected this way. One day you will see with your own eyes the whole bicycle."

And he actually managed it one day. It took years for him, but one day he showed me. He said, "Come on, I have to show you something." Yes, there was a bicycle – with no tires, no tube, just two wheels, crooked: no chain, no mudguards and no seat. The handlebars were there, and he had found one carrier.

He said, "Nothing much is missing, the cycle is almost complete.

I just have to get a seat, tire and tube, and a chain, and I will have a brand-new cycle."

I said, "This is better than brand-new, this is unique!"

In his house such things were all over the place. It was difficult to walk into his house without stumbling into something unique, antique, which he had not purchased but simply collected. He had at least ten houses, and he was collecting so much rent, but he was living the life of the poorest man. He used to walk everywhere – he was waiting for the cycle to be ready.

I said, "In this life, perhaps in the next life... And I hope you manage to be born again in the same house, because you are leaving so many things here." According to Hinduism, when you are attached to so many things your soul is pulled back to the place you are attached to.

He said, "No, in *this* life. I am not a pessimist. You seem to be a pessimist – I am optimistic, hopeful."

In 1969 I visited his house for the last time. He had added a few more things to the bicycle. I said, "How much is missing?"

He said, "Very little, just a tire and a tube; but it is very difficult to find a tire and tube."

I said, "Do one thing: at least purchase a tire and a tube. You have managed to find everything else."

He said, "That is too expensive, particularly nowadays; prices have gone up. I will find them; if I could find the rest... I am an optimist."

I said, "Good, be an optimist and collect them."

He wouldn't even allow *me* to throw out anything. I had to throw things out when he was not in the house; otherwise he would immediately grab them and say, "Don't throw that out – one never knows what utility it may have. Right now I am not clear what it will do, but it may fit somewhere, in something."

You can laugh about this man, you can feel sad for him, but this is the situation of every man as far as the mind is concerned. What have you collected? It is all garbage, simply crap. And when I say throw it away, empty your mind, I am not telling you to throw out your diamonds and your rubies and your emeralds, no. You don't have any of those precious stones. You have only rotten rubbish: words, all borrowed, and not a single word representing your authentic experience about anything.

What do you know about love? What do you know about beauty? What do you know about goodness? What do you know about grace, gratitude? What do you know about yourself, who you are? Nothing! And you know everything about the whole world, the whole geography of the world, the whole history of the world. All kinds of idiots in history are all there: Genghis Khan, Tamerlane, Nadirshah, Alexander the Great, Napoleon Bonaparte, Ivan the Terrible...

I was not a student of history. It was my practice in the university that I never attended my own subjects, because I knew them far better than the people who were teaching, and the library was available. So I used to attend other people's classes. The professor of history was so involved in it that you could ask him any absurd question and there was immediately an answer.

You could ask, "How old was Socrates when he got married?" Now is that a question that somebody can answer immediately? But he was that type of man. You could ask such a question as, "At what place, by whom, on what date, was the first bullet shot? – and immediately, the answer! He was a computer.

When I entered his class one day, he said, "I have told you again and again that this is not your subject, but you go on insisting on coming."

I said, "This is not your subject either."

He said, "What do you mean? I am head of the department of history, and this is not my subject?"

I said, "No, this is not your subject. Answer a single question: 'Who are you?' What does it matter when Socrates got married? Monday, Sunday, Tuesday – any day will do. In seven days, on one day he must have got married. And what did he get out of that marriage? A woman called Xanthippe who was just like her name – really difficult." I don't know how to pronounce it. It does not look Greek – "Xanthippe" – it looks like something from far away, some eastern Fiji island. Xanthippe? And she tortured him his whole life.

I said, "You are worrying about when he got married. I am worried why he got married at all! This is not my subject, this is not your subject either. My subject is your subject."

He said, "What is your subject?"

I said, "My own subjectivity is my subject. History can be an object but it can never be a subject. There is only one subject, your subjectivity. And unless you know it, all your knowing is bullshit."

Don't ask me, "What is bliss?" Ask me, "How can I be a participant in it?" Ask the right question. I have given you the right answer. I don't care whether your question is right or wrong – I always give the right answer. You were asking about a definition; that is verbal. Bliss is existential.

Bliss is a taste, a feel, and so overwhelming and so intense that once you have got it you cannot believe how you have been missing it all along: "I cannot figure it out because it is simply there. It was always there; how did I manage to miss it for so many lives?" Once you get it, this is the problem that arises: how have you been missing it? Bliss is just sitting at the very center of your being, ready to be remembered.

Bliss has not to be found, but only to be remembered. This word, *remember* is quite significant. *Remember* simply means to make it a part of your being again. *Remember* does not mean to recall; no, it simply means making something a part of your being again. It is there, it is just that you have completely forgotten it. Remember where you have forgotten it, where you have put it. So in the sense of remembering, the word is beautiful. In the sense of re-membering – making it again an essential part of you – it is again significant.

In the same reference I would like you to understand the original word for *sin*. The root from where it comes means forgetfulness. This is just strange: *sin* means forgetfulness. Then the whole of religion has only one meaning: remembering. There is only one sin – to forget your being. And there is only one virtue – to remember it.

The moment you know who you are, instantly, immediately, all the bliss of the whole existence is yours. You are so full of bliss that you can bless everybody, the whole existence, without ever exhausting it.

CHAPTER 10

I Don't Want My Truth to Be Your Theory

Osho,
Is the theory of reincarnation not true?

I do not deal in theories. I am a simple man, not a theoretician. A theoretician is a great thinker: he knows nothing about reality, but he goes on creating theories about it. He goes around and around his whole life. That's the actual meaning of the word *about*. A theory is always about and about. And the truth, the reality, is just at the center, it is never around. But the theoretician is skilled in beating around the bush.

The moment you ask me, "Is the theory of reincarnation not true?" your question says many things to me. First: you want my support for your belief. Belief is always in need of support. Truth is never in need of any support: it is enough unto itself. Truth needs no evidence, no witnesses. Even if the whole world is against the man of truth, he will not care at all – because truth is not something that depends on the number of people who support it. A single man may be right, and the whole world may be wrong. Truth is not something political that you have to vote for.

Your question is indicative that you believe in the theory of reincarnation. Belief is always shaky, afraid, because deep down you are aware that you don't know: it may be right, it may not be. You would like somebody in whom you have some kind of trust to support your theory, your belief. Your question comes from that space. You love me, you trust me. If I can say to you, "Yes, it is true," then it is as if a blood transfusion is given to somebody who has lost too much blood: your theory, your belief starts appearing stronger, more stable. *You* don't know but at least somebody who knows is supporting it, and you trust that somebody. He cannot lie.

I don't want you to trust me in that way. Give your love to me but don't trust me. The moment you start trusting somebody else, you stop inquiring on your own. And I would not like you to stop your own individual inquiry. Loving is perfectly good because you are sharing something, but in the name of trust you are really deceiving yourself. This is how man has been deceived and exploited for thousands of years. I want to destroy that whole strategy at its very roots. Trust only your own experience. It does not matter whether I say yes or no, it is irrelevant. What matters is whether you have experienced it or not. That is going to be decisive, that is going to transform your life.

There are three religions – Judaism, Christianity, Mohammedanism – which have taken a negative stand on the theory of reincarnation. They say it is not true. This is a negative belief. Remember that belief can be either negative or positive, but it does not change its nature. This is a negative belief. These three religions are under the influence of a negative belief: there is no reincarnation.

Parallel to these three, there are three religions – Hinduism, Buddhism, Jainism – which have taken a positive attitude. They say yes, reincarnation is a reality. But that is also a belief, a positive belief.

My approach is a third one which has not been tried up to now, and which I say is the right approach. I say to you: accept the theory as hypothetical, saying neither yes nor saying no. Accepting it as hypothetical means, "I am ready to inquire into it with no prejudice, positive or negative. I am ready to go into it without any preconceived idea, to see what the truth is."

Religions have not used the word *hypothesis* at all. Either you are a believer or you are a non-believer. The non-believer is also a believer, only negatively. They are not qualitatively different, they are the same type of people. And when you take a negative belief or a positive belief your mind has already decided. Before knowing, before experiencing, you have already decided what the truth is. This I call insincere, dishonest. And once you accept something negatively or positively, the mind has the capacity to create a hallucination of your belief.

You can see it. In Mohammedans, in Christians, in Jews, you will not find children being born who remember their past lives. But in Hinduism, Jainism, Buddhism almost every day, somewhere, some child is found who remembers his past lives. People have tried to see whether the remembrance has any facts behind it or if it is just imagination, and so many cases have been found in which the facts were clearly in support of it.

For example, I myself was deeply involved with such a case. A girl born in Katni – a small city eighty miles away from Jabalpur – remembered that she had been the wife of a certain man who lived in Jabalpur and who owned a garage: his name, his age, where his house was, and where his garage was. Now, this man, Ramakant Parekh was his name, lived just four or five houses away from me. That's how I became involved in the whole thing.

One day he came running to me. He said, "A phone call has come from Katni that a girl remembers that she was my wife. My wife has certainly died, and the dates coincide exactly with the date the girl was born. She was born in the evening, and my wife had died in the morning. She remembers my name, she remembers my job, my house, my work. What do you think? What should I do?"

I said, "Just come along with me. We will go to Katni. It is not far away, it is just a two-hour drive, and it is better to go without announcing ourselves. You are not to say that you are Ramakant Parekh. I will say I am Ramakant Parekh, and that I own the garage."

I said to them, "I am Ramakant Parekh," and immediately the girl recognized me as her husband. Then I told the parents, "Don't try to take advantage of a belief in Hinduism. I am not Ramakant Parekh. I don't own any garage, I don't have any wife, so the question of her death does not arise. *This* man is Ramakant Parekh. His wife has died, and you must have known when. Please tell me the exact truth, otherwise I am going to the police, and you will be in trouble because your daughter recognized me. She knows nothing about who Ramakant Parekh is. It is not even certain that *this* is Ramakant Parekh. Only I am saying so. So don't think that you can change your mind in the police station and say that this man is Ramakant Parekh. Tell me exactly what you were trying to do."

Her father became very afraid and told the whole story of how he had prepared the girl. One of his friends had suggested this name, and the date, because he knew Ramakant Parekh. He was going to bring a photo of Ramakant Parekh, and then they were going to Jabalpur with the girl, with the media people, so she could recognize the house: "My friend was going to give us all the information because he knows everything about Ramakant Parekh – his wife, his house, his garage. The girl was to go inside the house and find things that she used to keep, then she was going to go and find the garage, and show the car that she used to love.

"Please forgive me," he said. "We were just creating a business." In India, once a reincarnation is established, then the girl becomes almost a goddess, and people start worshipping her, bringing money, and bringing sweets and fruits: it is a great business. He was a brahmin, and the thing would be managed perfectly well.

If this man, Ramakant, had not come to a wrong man like me, he would have been perfectly befooled. Once the girl had seen the picture, then she would have found the man in a crowd of hundreds of people. And behind the whole thing was a friend of Ramakant's. I asked, "What was he going to gain?"

The man said, "Half-half, fifty-fifty."

In India it happens almost every day, in one place, in another place, that there is a child who remembers. Immediately you have a business without any investment or publicity. And no Hindu, no Buddhist, no Jaina is going to really inquire into it because they are afraid their theory may prove wrong. They are ready to support it.

You will be surprised that when I exposed it and gave a statement to the newspapers that this was all a bogus thing, the brahmins and the Jainas approached me, their leaders, who knew me perfectly well, approached me. They said, "You should not have done that. What does it matter if that poor brahmin gets a little money out of this? That is not important. The important thing is our theory, our philosophy. Just to expose a single case of fraud does not mean that the theory is wrong."

I said, "Yes, it does not mean that, so why are you worried? You can still believe in your theory, and if I find anybody else, I am going to expose him too. Hundreds of people can be exposed and still it does not destroy the theory. Perhaps all these people are frauds; it does not mean that reincarnation is wrong. But why have you come to me if it does not mean that reincarnation is wrong? I am not saying it is wrong. All that I have said was that this man was trying to exploit the superstition, the belief of the whole country." Now you cannot do that in a Mohammedan country. You cannot even think of it.

One young boy – perhaps Vivek was there – was brought to Woodlands where I used to live in Mumbai. He was no more than nine years old, and he was giving sermons on the Shrimad Bhagavadgita, the Upanishads. I was giving talks on Mahavira in Patkar Hall in Mumbai. The father of the boy and the boy himself had come to listen to me. Listening to me, the father thought that if he brought the boy to me, and if I gave him some support, then his boy could be a celebrity in Mumbai too.

Naturally the boy was an instant success everywhere, because you cannot expect that a nine-year old boy can even understand the Gita, or the Upanishads, and he was quoting from them in pure Sanskrit, commenting on them. So he was introduced to me there after the meeting, and I told them to come to my place.

I told the father, "In a way you have come to the wrong person. I can see you have destroyed this small boy's whole mind. This is nothing but a deep experiment in hypnotism. You have been hypnotizing the boy and repeating the *shlokas*. In a hypnotic state the age does not matter: whatsoever is repeated by the hypnotist is simply recorded, it is not a question of memorizing it. So you have been repeating all these sutras, all these commentaries to this boy when he is under hypnosis. Nothing is new in them" – because when they came I told the boy to sit on the sofa and start one of his sermons.

He asked, "Which one? The one-hour, the thirty-minute one or the ten-minute one?"

I said, "The ten-minute one."

He immediately sat in a lotus posture – he looked beautiful, a very nice child – and he started a ten-minute sermon. I listened to him, and I told his father, "Not a single word is original. It has all been written before. You have been repeating it to the boy while he has been in hypnotic sleep, and you have prepared him."

The boy was after all a boy, so when I asked him to start, he asked "Which one?" His father had prepared him because sometimes there was time only for ten minutes in a big conference, so he used the ten-minute sermon; the thirty-minute if they had more time, and if they had enough time, then the sixty-minute one.

I said to the boy, "Can you give me a sermon of only three minutes?"

He said, "Three minutes? But I don't know a three-minute sermon. I know only three sermons: ten minutes, thirty minutes, and sixty minutes. I don't know any other." He repeated in a beautiful way – and Upanishadic sutras, their meaning, commentaries coming from a nine-year-old child looked great.

But I told the father, "What you have done is good business. You are doing good business but you are destroying this child's intelligence. His whole life he will be a zombie. Withdraw all that you have forced into his mind. Hypnotize him and tell him to forget all that you have taught him."

The father was in shock. He said, "It is strange: how could you discover it so quickly? I have been traveling around the whole country. I earned thousands of rupees, and respect, and publicity everywhere. He has even been invited by the president of India, so he could listen to the boy's sermon in his own house. And when the president was listening, then all the MP's and the ministers and others were bound to be present. The president himself garlanded him and gave him a gold medal. You are shattering the whole thing."

I said, "I am shattering the whole thing because I am not concerned with your business, I am concerned with this child's whole life. He is an intelligent child, more intelligent than average. He has a great future, a destiny of his own. Do you want him just to go on doing ten-minute, thirty-minute and sixty-minute sermons? Do you remember what happens to such children?"

In India so many girls and boys are worshipped when they are small. Naturally, hearing such beautiful discourses from a nine-year-old child impresses people. But these children are not going to remain nine years old always. The same sermon when the child is thirty will look idiotic. Who is going to listen?

"Can you tell me where all these children disappear to? Every year you will hear somewhere some child expounding great theories. Then what happens when they grow up? Then nobody bothers about them because what they are saying is not a miracle for a thirty-year-old man to say. It may be a miracle for a six-year-old child, a five-year-old child. Your child will also go the same way.

"Remaining in a kind of zombie state for thirty years, repeating something which has been given in hypnosis is dangerous. It is keeping him addicted to a certain drug. If he has been in that drugged state for thirty years he will come out mediocre, stupid. And what do you want to prove through it? Reincarnation? That this is a proof of reincarnation?" A nine-year-old child is not capable of understanding or memorizing such long passages. So they say it is from his past life when he was a scholar, a great scholar, and that memory still persists, that memory is revived. This proves reincarnation, they say. So it is a double business: for his sermons he is earning money and he is earning for his reincarnation.

I said, "Go back home" – he was from Ujjain – "and get this child back to normal. Don't exploit your own child."

I knew he was not going to do it, although he said, "I will try."

I said, "I don't believe that you will try. You have so much invested in the whole thing." And he did not stop it. I went on inquiring from my friends in Ujjain: the show is going on. The child is taken to every fair and every religious conference. It continues, and he is earning a lot of money.

But you cannot do that in a Christian country, in a Jewish community, in a Mohammedan land, because they have accepted that this kind of thing is absolutely unreal.

As far as I am concerned, reincarnation is a reality. It is my own experience. But what is truth to me becomes theory to you; that is the difficulty. I don't want my truth to be your theory. I want it to be a truth for you also. That's why I said I don't deal in theories, in beliefs. My profession is truth.

That reminds me of Socrates, who for the first time used *profession* for truth. Otherwise, you don't use the word *profession* for truth…

When he was sentenced to death by the court they gave him a few alternatives because he was a man of such superior intelligence. Even those who were against him were not happy that he should be killed. He was the pride of Athens. Without Socrates, what would Athens be? They gave him some alternatives. They said, "If you stop speaking the truth, if you completely stop teaching people, you can be saved."

Socrates said, "That is impossible. It is my profession to speak the truth and to teach the truth. This is not an alternative. I would rather be dead than drop my profession. At least nobody will be able to say that Socrates was a coward: just to save his life he sold his truth."

They said, "Then the second alternative is that you leave Athens." In those days Greece was divided into city democracies, each city was an independent democracy. "So if you go beyond the boundaries of Athens, we have no problem. You can have your school anywhere. Your students can go there, and you can continue your profession."

Socrates said, "Do you want me to face another trial somewhere else? One is enough. If Athens, which is the pinnacle of Greek civilization, is not able to understand me and absorb me, who is going to understand me and absorb me? And what will Athens be without me? I will miss Athens, Athens will miss me. No, that is not going to be my way. I have made Athens what Athens is."

And he was really right. He had not made the buildings and the roads, but if Athens still lives in the memory of man, it is because of Socrates and his disciples. Plato was his disciple, Aristotle was Plato's disciple, and these three men are the very cream of the Athenian culture, civilization, genius. Plato and Aristotle don't come anywhere near Socrates; the master is really incomparable.

In the history of philosophy, Plato is more important because Plato is a great philosopher, and Socrates never wrote anything. This is something to be understood: the people who have known truth have chosen to speak rather than to write. All over the world – it cannot be just coincidence – in all the centuries, all over the world, they have chosen to speak. There is some fundamental significance in it. They all know the word cannot convey the truth, but the spoken word can at least have something alive in it.

The gesture of the master, the eyes of the master – *something* of the master is bound to be moving with the word, like an aroma, a fragrance which you cannot catch hold of, you cannot pinpoint. But the spoken word has a totally different dimension than the written word. The same word written is just a corpse of the same man who was alive.

The written word is like a corpse, and the spoken word is throbbing with life – at least for the moment when somebody is there to listen to it. Between the listener and the speaker, for a moment, there is an alive vibration. The word is not alone: the gesture, the eyes, the voice, the depth from where it is coming... Where will you find the depth on a flat piece of paper? Where will you find the eyes, the gestures, the sound in ink? It will just be dead. It will be the same word but the fire will not be in it. It will be a candle without flame. But the candle is not important; what is important is the live flame.

But historians have missed, for the simple reason that Plato's books are available, the evidence is there. Aristotle's books are there, the evidence is there. The spoken word was alive, lived and danced, and disappeared. Socrates is remembered only because Plato mentions him and records his dialogues. How much is Socrates in it and how much is Plato is difficult to say because there is no way to judge. Socrates has left nothing. But I know perfectly well because there have been other disciples of Socrates who also wrote notes, and all those notes are different.

Plato's are the most famous because he was really a great writer. The other disciples were simply taking notes, class notes. But I have looked into those class notes, and I can say with certainty that ninety percent in Plato is his imagination. He is imaginative and creative. Something of Socrates *is* there but it is very difficult to find where: it is too mixed with Plato – but Plato is important.

Socrates is almost mythological. There are many people who think that Socrates never existed, that he was just a character in Plato's dialogues. In the same way Gurdjieff used to say that Jesus never existed, he was only part of a drama which was played every year in Jerusalem.

It is difficult to prove that Jesus was really a historical person because except for the four gospels – which were written by his own disciples – there is no reference to Jesus in any Jewish literature, no reference in any contemporary scripture, on any stones, on buildings, nowhere at all in any Roman records. If a man was crucified, there must at least be a record that a man was crucified. And if you were going to crucify a man like Jesus, at least you owe him a record. But there is no record. And none of the poor four disciples is of the quality of Plato. Nor is Jesus of the quality of Socrates.

Socrates is a giant, a Himalayan giant. His every word is immensely meaningful. He said, "I am not going to leave Athens. Without me, what will Athens be? Kill me – that will make Athens immortal." Those idiots could not understand what he was saying.

He was speaking the truth: it *is* because Socrates was poisoned in Athens by Athenian people that Athens has become immortal.

I remembered him because he was the first man who used the word *profession* for truth: "I am not going to leave my profession." In fact, even if he had wanted to he could not have left it. It is not within the capacity of a man who has arrived to stop the process of spreading what he has attained.

I say that to me, reincarnation is a truth. But I am not telling you to believe in my experience, because it is not going to become your experience by believing, nor is it going to help you in any way to experience it. On the contrary it will be a hindrance for you to experience it. If you believe in what I say then there is no need to inquire.

Religious truth, subjective truth, is different from objective truth, scientific truth. Albert Einstein finds out a certain truth about physics. Now, everybody need not go through the whole inquiry again – that would be stupid. What Albert Einstein had to work on for years, you can do in hours. It depends on your intelligence; you may even get hold of it within minutes. There is no need for you to search.

Edison worked for three years to make the first electric bulb. Now, if everyone is going to work for three years to produce one electric bulb, it would be stupid. Bulbs are available in the market. Nobody ever thinks that there was a concentrated inquiry for three years. And Edison was working sixteen hours a day, eighteen hours a day, late in the night. I am reminded of the last night when he discovered it:

You can understand his ecstasy: three years of arduous work and finally the bulb was there. The light had come on. He could not believe it, he was sitting there, dazed. He had been working for three years, hoping that someday he was going to find the right clue. If that clue failed, he would try another: he went on trying, went on trying. His disciples got fed up and left him. Only his wife remained with him. She loved the poor man and she felt sorry for him. She used to suggest to him, "Stop this nonsense. You are capable of making so many things."

Edison discovered the greatest number of things in the whole history of man – he has one thousand discoveries to his name. His wife was saying, "Wasting your whole life doesn't seem rational. In three years you could have worked on many more things. Three years are just gone and you are becoming old: in three years you look as if you have aged thirty years." But she remained with him.

That last night, the night when he discovered it – he discovered it nearabout midnight – Edison was so dazed with his own discovery, in such ecstasy, that it was three o'clock in the morning when his wife shouted, "Will you put that light out" – she had no idea what light was there – "and come to bed?"

Then he realized it was three o' clock. He rushed to his wife and said, "First, come and see the light."

She said, "Put the light out!" She was thinking of the lamp that he used to work by.

Edison said, "It is not the lamp that I used to turn on and off. It is the light that I have been working on for three years – and you say to me, 'Put the light out'! Just for a moment come and see that it has happened."

You don't have to work for three years just to make a light bulb. You don't have to work for years to make a radio. No, in science it is objective truth. Once the principles of something are known, then anybody can make it in a very short period. In fact there is no need to make it, it is being manufactured.

But the subjective truth cannot be manufactured – although the priests have tried exactly that. What are their holy scriptures? – they have tried to manufacture truth. They have tried to put truth into words. They have tried to sell the holy books: "You have the Bible and what more did Jesus have? Just keep those four gospels close to your heart, and that's enough."

Jesus of course had them a little closer to his heart, behind his ribs; your Bible will be just in front of the ribs – but a difference of a few inches does not make much difference. Or if you are really a Jesus freak, you can have an operation and have the Bible sewed to your heart, your lungs, and declare yourself Jesus Christ. Because those are the words he had in his heart: now you have them. That's what thousands of Christian priests are doing around the world, these Bible-bashing Christians. One feels a little sorry for poor Jesus. And what are they doing to his Bible? Bashing! And why are they bashing it?

One of my vice-chancellors was a great law expert – Doctor Harisingh Gaur. He was a world authority. I don't think there has been another man again of his caliber and fame in the world of law. He had an office in Beijing, another in New Delhi, and another in London, and he was just continually moving from this office to that office. He was fighting cases in China, in India, in England, and in other countries. Wherever there was a case that was impossible to deal with, he was the man.

I used to attend his law classes although I was not a law student. But he loved me, and even waited for me. If sometimes I was late he would say to his students, "Just wait: one of my students is on the way. He will be coming because I can hear his wooden sandals. He is coming in just a few minutes."

His students were really angry; they said, "He is not even enrolled in the law department and you pay him more respect than you even bother to pay us."

He said, "You will not understand it – you just try to understand law. But that young man is trying something totally different, that you cannot understand. He is continually trying to find out if law is nothing but an extension of logic. And I am interested in his inquiry. I want to wait for him."

He used to say to his students, "When you have a case which is absolutely favorable – the facts are with you, the case is going to be won by you absolutely – then be very humble before the court, very polite, just suggestive. Bring out all the facts, but don't be aggressive. There is no need, the facts are enough.

"But when you have a case which you are not sure to win and you are hesitant – it is a fifty-fifty chance – then don't be humble, don't be meek. Bring as many law books as you can bring into the court, with quotations from laws and from other cases and other precedents. You don't have facts, so you have to create a great smoke of words, and laws, and precedents, and clauses, and amendments. You have to create so much legal jargon that the facts are completely hidden behind the cloud.

"But if you are one hundred percent certain that you are going to lose the case, because all the facts are against you, all the witnesses are against you – your client has been caught red-handed – then be aggressive, violent. Throw the law books, bash the books and beat the table. Be a nuisance, less than that won't do. You don't have any chance unless you are so violent and so aggressive, throwing the books and laws around and bashing them, that you create confusion. Perhaps that may help.

"Just confuse the court, and let the court know: if a man is so assertive and so violent and so certain, then there must be something in it, that he is so bravely facing them. So create the suspicion, the doubt, and take advantage of the doubt."

The Bible-bashing people are simply trying to be assertive, aggressive. Facts are not in their favor; facts are never in your favor when you believe in something. Only when you experience something is there no need to be so aggressive. Then you can talk with a sense of humor.

Then you need not throw out a rabbi because of a very healthy and hygienic clean joke. I could have understood it if the Catholics had expelled some bishop or cardinal or even the pope, but I don't understand the rabbis because they have the most beautiful jokes in the world. There is no comparison: they have the best sense of humor. But England is such a dump! Even Jewish rabbis have lost their sense of humor.

Just a few days ago a bishop was expelled. Perhaps the Jews are trying to compete – now a rabbi has to be expelled. Nobody wants to be behind anybody else: if you can do that, we can also do it. But that bishop was certainly responsible for saying something which is destructive to Christianity. I am not saying that he should be expelled, but what he said was certainly dangerous to Christianity. I would have supported him if I was the archbishop, and I would have told all other bishops to follow him.

He should not be expelled; he should be exalted, praised, because at least once in two thousand years, one bishop has spoken the truth – half the truth, not the full truth. But even to speak half the truth needs courage. This poor rabbi has done nothing at all! It is really a shame that a rabbi should be expelled for telling a joke. Jews have survived just because of their sense of humor. There was nothing else to support them. They lost their country, they lost everything; in every country they were persecuted, killed, murdered. But they have certainly proved that they have some mettle, that you cannot destroy them.

And what has been their power? As far as I can see their power has been their sense of humor. Even in the greatest misery they could joke and laugh. I can see, even in the gas chambers, before the switch was turned on, the Jews must have been joking. It was a beautiful scene, worth joking about. This Adolf Hitler was mad, but he did some really humorous things.

Before sending anybody to the gas chamber he used to shave them completely. Most of the rabbis had beards: they were shaved of all their hair. Strange. Why was he against hair? They were forced to be naked, and they were told that they were going to have a shower. The gas chamber was known as "the great shower." Of course, nobody returned from the great shower, so nobody could say what happened inside. But every day the people who went were told, "Now take a shower."

So, naked and completely shaved, thousands of Jews – including hundreds of rabbis – went inside. What do you think they would have been doing there? Before the switch was turned on and they all evaporated, they must have been joking and laughing. They could survive in a very antagonistic world for the simple reason that they never lost their sense of humor. Howsoever great the misery and the anguish, they were able to laugh.

This is the first case in the whole history of Judaism where a rabbi has been expelled for telling a joke which is not dirty at all. In fact no joke is dirty. The jokes which are called dirty, are called dirty because first you think sex is dirty. It is a corollary: because sex is dirty, any joke that has something to do with sex becomes dirty. Now, it is very strange: you are born out of sex, and you are not dirty. According to Christians, you are. You are born out of original sin. That is their way of saying utterly dirty, ultimately dirty. There is no way to clean you – even dry cleaning won't help.

Dry cleaning reminds me…

A man was washing his cat with soap. The cat was trying to run away, and he was forcing her to keep still. Somebody passing by, looked in and asked, "What are you doing? Such an old-fashioned fellow! This way the cat will make the whole house and all your clothes wet. These days you can get a dry cleaner."

He said, "That's a good idea. I'll use a dry cleaner."

Next day the passerby met him and said, "How are things going?"

He said, "Things are really bad – the cat died."

The man said, "The cat died? What happened?"

He said, "Nothing as far as the dry cleaning was concerned, but when I was drying the cat in the machine, it died." He had gone ultramodern – he had bought a dry-cleaner *and* a drying machine!

Once you have accepted that sex is dirty then there is no way to have anything clean in the world, because everything arises out of the same sexual energy. Then the birds calling their mates are dirty – expel them from existence. The peacocks dancing to attract the female – expel them, they are being really dirty fellows, and what a dirty trick to spread your tail so colorfully. The poor female is bound to be attracted to these really dirty fellows doing their tricks. If you expel sex from the world, life is expelled.

No joke is dirty. By expelling that rabbi, the council of rabbis in England has proved only one thing: that they are dirty old fellows. It shows their minds.

A psychoanalyst was checking a patient. He drew a line on the paper and asked, "Just look, concentrate on the line. What does it remind you of?"

He said, "Of a beautiful woman."

The psychiatrist said, "We are on the right track." He drew a triangle and again he said, "Now concentrate."

The patient said, "There is no need to concentrate – it reminds me of a very beautiful woman."

The psychiatrist said, "Strange." He drew a circle, and he asked, "Now...?"

The psychiatrist was shocked because the patient said, "Your mind is full of sex and nothing else – continually drawing naked women, this way, that way, this way. Can't you draw anything else?"

That fellow thinks that the psychiatrist's mind is so full of sex! These rabbis and their council must have been really sex-obsessed.

All these people have been telling you what is right, what is wrong, what is true, what is untrue; and you have believed them. This belief has brought the whole of humanity to this mess. My effort is to completely stop the process of believing. You are not to believe in me. If I say that this is the truth that I have experienced, all that you have to do is to take it as a hypothesis and try it.

There are ways to remember your past lives, simple methods to remember your past lives. There is no need to believe. We have the rebirthing process – just go a little deeper. When you have reached the point of birth, the same process has to be followed. You will come to the point of impregnation. Continue the same process and you will come to your death in the past life. Go on, and you will be surprised that all that has happened to you in millions of lives is still contained in the deep reservoirs of your memory. In your collective unconscious nothing has ever been missed out.

Even when you are not paying attention to something, your collective unconscious is collecting it. Now they call it subliminal memory, and they are using it in a few countries. In some countries it has been banned, but nobody knows when it is being used. Even if you ban it, it can be used: you go to see a movie, and in the movie they can use subliminal advertisements. Just in between, a dozen times during the film, the word *Coca-Cola* appears, but it comes and goes so fast that you can't see it with your eyes; you don't see it.

If you have seen a movie you will know how the film functions. All the pictures are still. For example, I raise my hand: in the film there will be hundreds of pictures – one position, another position, another position. Just raising this hand means hundreds of still pictures of different positions, and they are moving so fast that you don't see them as separate, static pictures. The pictures move so fast that you can see the hand moving, but not the still pictures of different postures of the hand.

If you wind the film slowly you will be able to see it. Just in the gap, in between two pictures of the hand moving – and they are moving so fast that you cannot see the gap – *Coca-Cola* is put, perhaps twelve times in the whole film. You will not be able to remember that you have seen it, but that day outside the movie house, sales of *Coca-Cola* will be doubled, trebled. There is an average for how much is sold every day, but on that day treble the number is sold. What happened? Your unconscious mind goes on collecting even those things which your eyes do not see, your ears do not hear, your body does not feel.

You will be surprised. If you are hypnotized and you are asked what happened on the first of January 1971, from the very early morning when you got up, to the end when you went to bed again, consciously you will say, "The first of January '71? – I don't remember." Who remembers the first of January '71, unless something very important happened: your mother died, your father died, you got divorced from your wife or something. Ordinarily, if it was a usual day you cannot remember it, but if you are put into hypnosis you can remember. And it is a very simple affair to put you into hypnosis.

You just have to be told to look at any shining thing hanging above your head, to relax your body, and to go on looking at it without blinking your eyes. The person who is hypnotizing you will go on saying, "You are falling asleep. Your eyes are becoming heavy, heavy, heavy, heavier, heavier." You will start to feel your lids becoming heavier, but you have to keep them open as long as you can. You are not to close them, he is telling you not to close them. You have been instructed to keep them open to the very last. So you are trying hard, and the eyes go on becoming heavier and heavier, and you start feeling that the body is becoming numb.

The hypnotist goes on saying, "Your whole body is numb. You cannot even move your hand if you want, you cannot move your leg if you want: your body has become almost a stone." And your eyes are just about to close. You make a last effort, just as a drowning man makes his last effort for help, and then drowns and is gone. You can see that now you cannot keep your eyes open, they are really heavy; stones are hanging from your eyelids.

This takes no more than three minutes; you fall asleep. But the difference between ordinary sleep and hypnosis is that in ordinary sleep you are oblivious of everything around you. In hypnosis, you are available to the hypnotist and oblivious of everything else. If somebody else says something, you won't listen. Even if he calls your name, you won't answer. But if the hypnotist even whispers something, you will hear it.

The hypnotist can tell you, "Please go back to 1971, the first of January. What happened in the morning, from when you got up?" You will start relating everything. It can be recorded: "When I got up, the first thing was that I was missing my shoes for the bathroom. In the bathroom I was holding the brush and it fell on the floor" – such things which have no significance. You will go into absolute detail about what you ate for breakfast, what you did after that, up to the time when you went to bed again.

You can be awakened by just the reverse process: "Now the time is over, and your body is becoming lighter, and your eyes are becoming less heavy, less heavy, less heavy, and now you can open your eyes." And you will not remember that you have related all the incidents of the first of January 1971. But if they are shown to you, you will recognize them: "Yes, this did happen, but how did you know about it?" You will not be aware that you yourself have given the whole thing.

Hypnosis is one of the great dimensions which have not yet been explored. There is nothing wrong in it, but all the religions have been against it. Religions are strange: they are against everything that can lead you to some truth. They have created the atmosphere all around the earth that hypnosis is something wrong. It is a condemnation if somebody says, "You are hypnotized." It is a humiliation: hypnotized? Me?

But you will be surprised that only very intelligent people can be hypnotized. Mediocre people are very difficult to hypnotize, and idiots, impossible. That is a simple criterion: if you try it on three people you can find who the idiot is. Now it is a scientifically established fact that idiots cannot be hypnotized, for these simple reasons: first, you tell them to look at the shiny object and they will look somewhere else, you tell them to keep their eyes open and they will keep them closed, you tell them to lie down and they will stand up. For an idiot everything is possible. Hypnosis is impossible because they don't have any intelligence to grasp the idea, and it all depends on them.

A wrong notion is rumored around the world, that it is the power of the hypnotist. Absolutely wrong: the hypnotist has no power. There is nothing like hypnotic power, that it is the hypnotist's power that makes you hypnotized. That is not at all true, scientifically. It is your intelligence cooperating with the directions given by the hypnotist, which can be given by a tape recorder. The hypnotist is not needed at all. You can't say, "This tape recorder has hypnotic power." The hypnotist is simply repeating certain suggestions. If you are cooperating with him intelligently the sleep will come to you.

But he said, "I like the people here. My friends are here, and everybody knows me. In a new place" – he was very nervous – "in a new place, new people..."

I said, "I will come with you. I will introduce you to everybody." No way. Then I said, "I'd better try hypnosis on you," because I had tried hypnosis on him before. He was a very intelligent person who always came first in all his examinations – he is now a professor.

I was continually experimenting on him – he was a good medium for hypnosis – and everything that I suggested, he did. He had even followed post-hypnotic suggestions, minute to minute. For example, once I had told him in hypnosis, "Tomorrow at exactly twelve o' clock when the clock tower" – the clock tower was very near to us – "strikes twelve, you will kiss your pillow." And I took him out of his hypnosis.

The next day, from eleven forty-five I was standing near his bed so he could not go to it. He had no idea what was going on, but he wanted to go there. I was standing there so he couldn't. Then I took his pillow and went out into the garden. He followed me, not knowing what was happening, and exactly when the clock struck twelve, he jumped, took the pillow, kissed it and became so ashamed that he ran away.

I said, "What are you doing?"

He said, "I myself don't know. I have never kissed my pillow – I tell you truly! Why should I kiss a pillow? But for a few moments I was not thinking of anything else but the pillow, I was worried. And why were you carrying my pillow into the garden? I have never seen you carrying my pillow. I feel so ashamed. I am sorry that I had to pull the pillow from you, and did such a stupid act, kissing the pillow."

I said, "It's nothing to be worried about. This was a post-hypnotic suggestion. You were simply following instructions. You were unable to prevent it, it was unconscious." You will be puzzled: when I tried hypnosis to persuade him to change his job – he was afraid, because I had been trying for two, three days to persuade him without hypnosis and he was reluctant. So he went into hypnosis, but the moment I said to him, "Change your job from the old office which is rotten," he just sat up immediately.

He said, "No!"

I said, "But you were in hypnosis."

He said, "I was, but this one thing kept coming to me, that you were going to say something to me about my job." Even in his hypnosis, he remembered that if his job was mentioned he would come out immediately.

So it is not the power of the hypnotist, it is the intelligence and the cooperation – because he was uncooperative on one point, but ninety-nine percent he listened to me, did whatever I said.

You can say, "Just sit down. A cow is standing there, milk the cow," and the person will sit there and start milking the cow which is not there. You can say anything and the person will do it – but there is no way against his will. So people who think you can be hypnotized against your will are absolutely wrong. It is not power in the hands of the hypnotist, it is your power. If you allow the hypnotist to suggest to you and you cooperate... If you resist, you cannot be hypnotized. So very great intelligence is needed, trust is needed. Only intelligent and trusting people can be hypnotized.

Hypnosis is one of the ignored, rejected dimensions of life. It can help you reveal all your past lives so quickly that there is no problem in it – you need not believe in them, first go into hypnosis. And in hypnosis you can be given a post-hypnotic suggestion that the hypnotist will not be needed. Instead, count from one to one hundred, and by the time you reach one hundred you will fall into hypnosis on your own.

Whatsoever you want to happen in your hypnosis, you have to remind yourself of, before you start counting from one to a hundred. You just say, "I want to go into my past life," and start counting from one to a hundred, and you will fall asleep. And the second thing that you have to say is, "After ten minutes or fifteen minutes I will come out again on my own" – because there is no hypnotist, you are doing it on your own. But a hypnotist is very helpful: he can easily break the ice, make the road, and give you the key. Anything will work: "Repeat your own name three times and you will be hypnotized."

So, my suggestion is, don't ask me whether the theory of reincarnation is true or not. To me it is true, to you it is not – not yet. Don't take any position, negative or positive. Just remain open to the hypothesis. Explore. If you can go into your own past lives, that's enough proof that everybody has a long, long past. And it gives another insight: if there are past lives, that means there are going to be future lives. This life is only just in the middle. Of course, to enter future lives is not possible because the future has not yet happened. But to enter the past is absolutely easy because it has already happened: the memory is there and the record is there. It is just that you have forgotten the way to the room where it is recorded.

Take it as a hypothesis. With me everything is a hypothesis. If you can trust me only this much, that you are ready to explore, inquire, that will do. I have no doctrines to teach you, but only methods for you to find out the truth by yourself. Any truth that is not found by you is not truth. Truth is truth only when *you* have found it. That is an essential quality of the truth, that it has been found by you, that it is authentically yours, that you can say on your own authority that it is so.

But don't become authoritative. Do you see the difference between the two words? I say on my own authority that reincarnation is true, but I am not authoritative. If I say that you have to believe it, that it is true, then I am authoritative. The authority is simply my experience. To be authoritative means I want to enforce it on you and make it a belief for you.

My religion has no doctrines, no tenets, no theories. It is a strange religion. No such thing has happened before, but that's the beauty of it. It leaves you totally free. If I can give you only freedom I have given you everything. If I can help you to be free from all the nonsense that others have tied around you, that is more than can be expected. Once you are free, then all dimensions are there, open. You can travel on your own. And to travel on your own is so beautiful.

Have you watched little children? When they start walking, if you want to hold their hands they are not willing. You are trying to be helpful, you are afraid the child may fall, but you don't understand the child's ecstasy. You are destroying his ecstasy by holding his hand. He would rather fall than not be on his own. And what is the harm if he falls once, twice, thrice? He will learn how not to fall. Simply watch so that he does not move into danger. Otherwise, if he is falling just on the plain ground and not into an abyss, there is no need to be worried. Let him learn, because it is better he falls and learns how not to fall. Then your watching will not be needed; then he can be left alone even by the side of an abyss.

In my childhood I used to have a strange very dangerous game, invented by myself. I would challenge the neighborhood children to walk on a plank of wood that was just lying there on the ground. Our new house was being built, and there were many planks of wood; this was a long, flat plank. I would tell the children to walk on it, and they would. There was no problem. I would say, "You can walk on it? Then I will put it across two balconies." Then I would say, "Now walk on it. It is the same plank: you walked on it when it was on the floor. There is no difference, except that now it is high above."

They would all say, "We cannot walk on it."

But I asked, "What is the difference? It is the same plank which you have walked along many times, and you did not fall." I would show them, I would walk on it. My mother used to run out when she saw me on the plank again. I would tell her with my finger, "Keep quiet, because if you say anything I may fall," so she would stand there not even breathing.

I would walk the plank and she would go crazy and scream and say, "What is this?"

I told my mother, "This is a game that I have invented, and this is the game I am going to play my whole life."

She said, "What! Your whole life?"

I said, "This is the game. Later on I may call it a different name, but this is the game." And I am still playing the same game. Awareness – that's all you need. On the ground you can walk very easily because you know there is no fear of falling. It is the same plank, the same size, the same breadth, but the fear has arisen that you can fall. But if you are alert you can walk on it; there is no problem.

Just be alert, then you can walk on any hypothesis and there is no danger of falling into belief. Remain alert. Use any hypothesis. You are bound to find some truth, and any truth is good because it is an aspect of the whole truth. From that you can move and find the whole truth.

Just catch the tail of the elephant. That is enough: you have found the elephant. It may take a little time to discover the rest – the elephant is big – but the whole problem is to catch hold of the right tail.

Belief is not the right thing, and I will not support any kind of belief, positive or negative. I support only hypotheses.

Osho,
You have said that one cannot pull the leg of a man of awareness.
Were you just pulling our legs?

Yes, that is true: one cannot pull the leg of a man of awareness. But the second part is a little complex, because the man of awareness will not want to pull your leg. He pulls your head up. That expression – pulling somebody's head up – is not in any language, but that is the work of the man of awareness.

In this life everybody is pulling everybody's legs to pull them down, so they can go up. The man of awareness is far above you. It is very difficult for him to reach your leg – and particularly in the Big Muddy Ranch. He will have to dive deep into the mud to find your leg. No man of awareness is going to do that.

But he will pull something; he will not leave you alone. He will pull your head up, and that's the only way when somebody is deep in the mud. This big, muddy ranch is really very representative of the whole world, because everybody is in mud, deep in the mud, going down and down. Even to find your head is so difficult, what to say about your leg – unless you are standing on your head! Then perhaps you will have to be pulled by your leg, but that is very rare. People don't do headstands in mud.

That kind of practice happens... I am reminded of a story:

It is sometime in the future when Morarji Desai dies: he was hoping to go to heaven of course, but the Devil welcomed him into hell. Morarji Desai said, "What! I am the ex-prime minister, Morarji Desai, don't you know?"

The Devil said, "We know you well. We have been waiting for you a long time, but you went on drinking your urine, and you stink so much that death went many times to take you away, but went away – just the stink was too much. But finally we had to force death, telling him, 'Now something has to be done. This man has lived too long.' You are a very great politician, leader, celebrity, so this much of a favor I can do: we have three sections in hell, you can choose."

Morarji Desai looked in the first one: people were being thrown into a fire. And although they were being thrown into a fire, they were burning but they were not dying. It was tremendously painful. They were being pulled out again and thrown back again. He said, "No, this is not the place."

The second one he saw was a little better than the first, but not for him. Strange, so many insects he had never seen before were passing through people's bodies, making holes, going in and coming out from another hole. Each man's body was nothing but holes because those insects went on coming in, going out, coming in, going out. Morarji Desai said, "No, this is not the place for me. I would like to see the third."

The third one he saw he felt at ease with, because it was not much trouble compared to those other two. Also he was a little bit accustomed to this place: it was full of shit and urine. Fifty percent he was acquainted with, fifty percent he would learn – what else to do, these were the three places. One thing was good, it was only up to the knees, and people were standing in it and drinking coffee.

Morarji Desai said, "This is perfectly good – this will do."

As he entered the Devil shouted, "Now the coffee break is over." So everybody threw his coffee back. "Now be in a headstand."

Then Morarji Desai understood that this was not at all so easy.

So only in that third kind of hell are people standing on their heads. In the world, people are deep in mud but still standing on their feet. The enlightened person pulls you up by your head. There is no expression like that because languages are not made by men of enlightenment. They are made by unconscious people, for unconscious people, for unconscious purposes.

No language exists in the world which is made by enlightened people, for enlightened people, for the purpose of enlightenment. That's the difficulty; that's why they all feel that truth cannot be expressed. There is no language which has been made by people who know the truth. In fact, there have never been so many people knowing truth that there was any need to create a language. It happens rarely, once in a while, that somebody is enlightened. Of what use is language? To whom is he going to speak the enlightened language?

But my problem is that I am trying to pull your head up, so on the way I go on making up my own phrases, creating my own language, my own words. If the message somehow reaches you, even a little bit of it, it will be enough – because even a little bit of fire is enough to put the whole jungle on fire. Your whole life can be aflame with just a little flame jumping into you.

About Osho

Osho defies categorization. His thousands of talks cover everything from the individual quest for meaning to the most urgent social and political issues facing society today. Osho's books are not written but are transcribed from audio and video recordings of his extemporaneous talks to international audiences. As he puts it, "So remember: whatever I am saying is not just for you... I am talking also for the future generations."

Osho has been described by *The Sunday Times* in London as one of the "1000 Makers of the 20th Century" and by American author Tom Robbins as "the most dangerous man since Jesus Christ." *Sunday Mid-Day* (India) has selected Osho as one of ten people – along with Gandhi, Nehru and Buddha – who have changed the destiny of India.

About his own work Osho has said that he is helping to create the conditions for the birth of a new kind of human being. He often characterizes this new human being as "Zorba the Buddha" – capable both of enjoying the earthy pleasures of a Zorba the Greek and the silent serenity of a Gautama the Buddha.

Running like a thread through all aspects of Osho's talks and meditations is a vision that encompasses both the timeless wisdom of all ages past and the highest potential of today's (and tomorrow's) science and technology.

Osho is known for his revolutionary contribution to the science of inner transformation, with an approach to meditation that acknowledges the accelerated pace of contemporary life. His unique OSHO Active Meditations are designed to first release the accumulated stresses of body and mind, so that it is then easier to take an experience of stillness and thought-free relaxation into daily life.

Two autobiographical works by the author are available:
Autobiography of a Spiritually Incorrect Mystic,
St Martins Press, New York (book and eBook)
Glimpses of a Golden Childhood,
OSHO Media International, Pune, India (book and eBook)

OSHO International Meditation Resort

Location

Located 100 miles southeast of Mumbai in the thriving modern city of Pune, India, the OSHO International Meditation Resort is a holiday destination with a difference. The Meditation Resort is spread over 28 acres of spectacular gardens in a beautiful tree-lined residential area.

Uniqueness

Each year the Meditation Resort welcomes thousands of people from more than 100 countries. The unique campus provides an opportunity for a direct personal experience of a new way of living – with more awareness, relaxation, celebration and creativity. A great variety of around-the-clock and around-the-year program options are available. Doing nothing and just relaxing is one of them!

All programs are based on the OSHO vision of "Zorba the Buddha" – a qualitatively new kind of human being who is able *both* to participate creatively in everyday life *and* to relax into silence and meditation.

THE DETAILS

OSHO Meditations

A full daily schedule of meditations for every type of person includes methods that are active and passive, traditional and revolutionary, and in particular the OSHO Active Meditations™. The meditations take place in what must be the world's largest meditation hall, the OSHO Auditorium.

OSHO Multiversity

Individual sessions, courses and workshops cover everything from creative arts to holistic health, personal transformation, relationship and life transition, work-as-meditation, esoteric sciences, and the "Zen" approach to sports and recreation. The secret of the OSHO Multiversity's success lies in the fact that all its programs are combined with meditation, supporting the understanding that as human beings we are far more than the sum of our parts.

OSHO Basho Spa
The luxurious Basho Spa provides for leisurely open-air swimming surrounded by trees and tropical green. The uniquely styled, spacious Jacuzzi, the saunas, gym, tennis courts...all these are enhanced by their stunningly beautiful setting.

Cuisine
A variety of different eating areas serve delicious Western, Asian and Indian vegetarian food – most of it organically grown especially for the Meditation Resort. Breads and cakes are baked in the resort's own bakery.

Night life
There are many evening events to choose from – dancing being at the top of the list! Other activities include full-moon meditations beneath the stars, variety shows, music performances and meditations for daily life.

Or you can just enjoy meeting people at the Plaza Café, or walking in the nighttime serenity of the gardens of this fairytale environment.

Facilities
You can buy all your basic necessities and toiletries in the Galleria. The Multimedia Gallery sells a large range of OSHO media products. There is also a bank, a travel agency and a Cyber Café on-campus. For those who enjoy shopping, Pune provides all the options, ranging from traditional and ethnic Indian products to all of the global brand-name stores.

Accommodation
You can choose to stay in the elegant rooms of the OSHO Guesthouse, or for longer stays opt for one of the OSHO Living-In program packages. Additionally there is a plentiful variety of nearby hotels and serviced apartments.

www.osho.com/meditationresort
www.osho.com/guesthouse
www.osho.com/livingin

more books and eBooks by OSHO media international

The God Conspiracy:
The Path from Superstition to Super Consciousness

Discover the Buddha: 53 Meditations to Meet the Buddha Within
Gold Nuggets: Messages from Existence

OSHO Classics
The Book of Wisdom: The Heart of Tibetan Buddhism.
The Mustard Seed: The Revolutionary Teachings of Jesus
Ancient Music in the Pines: In Zen, Mind Suddenly Stops
The Empty Boat: Encounters with Nothingness
A Bird on the Wing: Zen Anecdotes for Everyday Life
The Path of Yoga: Discovering the Essence and Origin of Yoga
And the Flowers Showered: The Freudian Couch and Zen
Nirvana: The Last Nightmare: Learning to Trust in Life
The Goose Is Out: Zen in Action
Absolute Tao: Subtle Is the Way to Love, Happiness and Truth

The Tantra Experience: Evolution through Love
Tantric Transformation: When Love Meets Meditation

Pillars of Consciousness (illustrated)
BUDDHA: His Life and Teachings and Impact on Humanity
ZEN: Its History and Teachings and Impact on Humanity
TANTRA: The Way of Acceptance
TAO: The State and the Art

Authentic Living

Danger: Truth at Work: The Courage to Accept the Unknowable
The Magic of Self-Respect: Awakening to Your Own Awareness
Born With a Question Mark in Your Heart

OSHO eBooks and "OSHO-Singles"

Emotions: Freedom from Anger, Jealousy and Fear
Meditation: The First and Last Freedom
What Is Meditation?
The Book of Secrets: 112 Meditations to Discover the Mystery Within

20 Difficult Things to Accomplish in This World
Compassion, Love and Sex
Hypnosis in the Service of Meditation
Why Is Communication So Difficult, Particularly between Lovers?
Bringing Up Children
Why Should I Grieve Now?: facing a loss and letting it go
Love and Hate: just two sides of the same coin

Next Time You Feel Angry...
Next Time You Feel Lonely...
Next Time You Feel Suicidal...

OSHO Media BLOG
http://oshomedia.blog.osho.com

For More Information

www.**OSHO**.com

a comprehensive multi-language website including a magazine, OSHO Books, OSHO Talks in audio and video formats, the OSHO Library text archive in English and Hindi and extensive information about OSHO Meditations. You will also find the program schedule of the OSHO Multiversity and information about the OSHO International Meditation Resort.

http://OSHO.com/AllAboutOSHO
http://OSHO.com/Resort
http://OSHO.com/Shop
http://www.youtube.com/OSHO
http://www.Twitter.com/OSHO
http://www.facebook.com/pages/OSHO.International

To contact OSHO International Foundation:
www.osho.com/oshointernational,
oshointernational@oshointernational.com